GOOGLE CLOUD CERTIFIED PROFESSIONAL CLOUD DEVOPS ENGINEER

MASTER THE EXAM: 10 PRACTICE TESTS, 500 RIGOROUS QUESTIONS, SOLID FOUNDATION TO EXAM, EXPERT EXPLANATIONS, GAIN WEALTH OF INSIGHTS AND ONE ULTIMATE GOAL

ANAND M
AMEENA PUBLICATIONS

DEDICATION

To the Visionaries in My Professional Odyssey

This book is dedicated to the mentors and leaders who guided me through triumph and adversity in my professional universe. Your guidance has illuminated the path to success and taught me to seize opportunities and surmount obstacles. Thank you for imparting the advice to those who taught me the value of strategic thinking and the significance of innovation to transform obstacles into stepping stones. Your visionary leadership has inspired my creativity and motivated me to forge new paths.

Thank you for sharing the best and worst of your experiences with me, kind and severe employers. As I present this book to the world, I am aware that you have been my inspiration. All of your roles as mentors, advisors, and even occasional adversaries have helped me become a better professional and storyteller.

This dedication is a tribute to your impact on my journey, a narrative woven with threads of gratitude, introspection, and profound gratitude for the lessons you've inscribed into my story.

With deep gratitude and enduring respect,
Anand M

FROM TECH TO LIFE SKILLS – MY EBOOKS COLLECTION

Dive into my rich collection of eBooks, curated meticulously across diverse and essential domains.

Pro Tips and Tricks Series: *Empower yourself with life-enhancing skills and professional essentials with our well-crafted guides.*

Hot IT Certifications and Tech Series: *Stay ahead in the tech game. Whether you're eyeing certifications in AWS, PMP, or prompt engineering, harnessing the power of ChatGPT with tools like Excel, PowerPoint, Word, and more!, we've got you covered!*

Essential Life Skills: *Embark on a journey within. From yoga to holistic well-being, Master the art of culinary, baking, and more delve deep and rediscover yourself.*

Stay Updated & Engaged
For an entire world of my knowledge, tips, and treasures, follow me on Amazon
https://www.amazon.com/author/anandm

Your Feedback Matters!
Your support, feedback, and ratings are the wind beneath my wings. It drives me to curate content that brings immense value to every aspect of life. Please take a moment to share your thoughts and rate the books. Together, let's keep the flame of knowledge burning bright!

★★★★⯪

Best Regards,

ANAND M

INTRODUCTION

Embark on your journey to mastering the Google Cloud Professional Cloud DevOps Engineer exam with this essential guide, *"GOOGLE CLOUD PROFESSIONAL CLOUD DEVOPS ENGINEER: MASTER THE EXAM."* This comprehensive resource is your ultimate companion, offering an exceptional array of 10 practice tests, encompassing 500 rigorously formulated questions, designed to challenge, refine, and elevate your understanding of Google Cloud's DevOps principles and practices.

In the ever-evolving landscape of cloud technology, a Google Cloud certification is not just an asset—it is a definitive marker of your expertise and proficiency. Achieving the status of a Google Cloud Certified Professional Cloud DevOps Engineer is a testament to your deep-seated knowledge and command over the critical aspects of DevOps within the Google Cloud ecosystem. This book is crafted for both seasoned Google Cloud professionals aiming to validate their expertise and newcomers embarking on their journey in cloud DevOps, providing a solid foundation in this pivotal field.

Every question in this guide has been meticulously structured and comes with expert explanations that unravel complex topics, offering insightful strategies and perspectives. The book guides you through the intricacies of Google Cloud's DevOps environment, ensuring your preparation is comprehensive and well-rounded.

In a digital world where cloud computing drives innovation and business efficiency, holding the esteemed Google Cloud Professional Cloud DevOps Engineer certification distinguishes your stature in the cloud computing domain. Whether you aim to excel as a Cloud DevOps Engineer, a Google Cloud Architect, or to enhance your skills in Google Cloud's DevOps solutions, this book lays the groundwork for your journey to expertise.

For those prepared to embark on this challenging yet rewarding path, here's what the Google Cloud Professional Cloud DevOps Engineer exam encompasses:

Duration: 120 minutes
Language Options: Primarily available in English
Exam Format: A blend of multiple-choice and multiple-answer questions, aimed at assessing both your practical skills and theoretical knowledge, in a proctored, Google-approved examination setting.
Pre-requisites: A fundamental understanding of Google Cloud principles and at least one year of hands-on experience in managing Google Cloud DevOps solutions.
Experience (Recommended): In-depth experience in developing, deploying, and maintaining solutions on Google Cloud.

Set forth on your quest to Google Cloud DevOps mastery with this guide as your all-encompassing navigator, illuminating your path to success in the Google Cloud Professional Cloud DevOps Engineer exam.

ADVANTAGES OF CERTIFICATION

Before delving into the intricacies of the Google Cloud Professional Cloud DevOps Engineer exam, it's crucial to understand the substantial benefits this esteemed certification provides. As you embark on your journey to attain the Google Cloud Professional Cloud DevOps Engineer credential, consider these persuasive advantages:

Elevated Professional Recognition: *In the dynamic and rapidly evolving realm of cloud computing, Google Cloud is a leading force. Earning the Google Cloud Professional Cloud DevOps Engineer certification places you in a select group of DevOps professionals. It validates your skills and expertise in one of the most sought-after areas of cloud technology, serving as an endorsement of your comprehensive understanding of Google Cloud's DevOps tools and best practices, and setting you apart in the industry.*

Career Advancement and Opportunities: *This certification signifies more than skill proficiency; it represents your commitment and depth of knowledge in cloud DevOps. It acts as a lever for professional growth, often opening doors to more challenging roles and higher-level positions in cloud computing and DevOps fields.*

Financial Benefits: *Specialized certifications are often linked to enhanced earning potential. The Google Cloud Professional Cloud DevOps Engineer certification is associated with increased salary prospects, reflecting a significant return on the investment of your time and effort.*

Competitive Edge in the Job Market: *In the competitive landscape of IT, cloud computing, and DevOps, this certification helps you stand out. It strategically positions you for roles that match your expertise and career aspirations, making you a sought-after candidate for premier positions.*

In-Depth Knowledge and Hands-On Experience: *Beyond theoretical understanding, this certification emphasizes practical skills in deploying, managing, and optimizing Google Cloud services. As a certified professional, you'll be adept at implementing efficient, reliable, and scalable DevOps solutions in Google Cloud, demonstrating a level of expertise that transcends basic knowledge.*

Networking and Community Involvement: *Achieving this certification connects you to a worldwide community of like-minded professionals. This network is a rich resource for collaboration, knowledge exchange, and discovering new career opportunities, adding significant value to your professional growth.*

In summary, the Google Cloud Professional Cloud DevOps Engineer certification is a transformative milestone in your career. It not only enhances your standing in the domain of cloud DevOps but also arms you with the skills, knowledge, and network to confidently navigate the ever-changing landscape of cloud computing and DevOps.

CONTENTS

PRACTICE TEST 1 - QUESTIONS ONLY

QUESTION 1

Your team is responsible for managing a large-scale e-commerce application on Google Cloud. You want to ensure high availability and disaster recovery for your application. Which combination of Google Cloud services and strategies should you consider for achieving these objectives, following Google's recommended DevOps practices?

A) Deploy the application across multiple Google Cloud regions, implement Google Cloud CDN for content delivery, and use Google Cloud Storage for data backup and recovery
 B) Set up Google Cloud Armor for DDoS protection, utilize Google Cloud Cost Management tools for cost optimization, and deploy Google Cloud Private Clusters for enhanced security
 C) Use Google Cloud Endpoints for API management, configure Google Kubernetes Engine (GKE) for container orchestration, and implement Google Cloud VPN for secure cross-cloud communication
 D) Implement Google Cloud Bigtable for high-throughput database requirements, leverage Google Cloud Pub/Sub for real-time event streaming, and configure Google Cloud IAM for access control
 E) Utilize Google Cloud Operations for monitoring, set up Google Cloud Memorystore for caching, and deploy Google Cloud Functions for serverless computing
 F) Deploy the application on a single Google Cloud region, utilize Google Cloud Identity and Access Management (IAM) for access control, and configure Google Cloud Pub/Sub for cross-cloud event streaming.

QUESTION 2

Your organization is implementing a CI/CD pipeline for a microservices-based application on Google Cloud. You want to ensure that each microservice is independently deployable, and changes to one microservice do not impact others. What CI/CD strategy should you follow to achieve this, adhering to Google's recommended DevOps practices?

A) Use a monolithic CI/CD pipeline that builds and deploys all microservices together for consistency.
 B) Implement a single CI/CD pipeline for all microservices with conditional deployment based on changes.
 C) Set up individual CI/CD pipelines for each microservice, allowing independent builds and deployments.
 D) Create separate development and production CI/CD pipelines for each microservice to isolate changes.

QUESTION 3

You are responsible for deploying a new version of a containerized web application on Google Kubernetes Engine (GKE). To ensure a smooth transition and minimize potential issues, you want to implement a blue-green deployment strategy. Which two Kubernetes concepts or techniques should you consider for this purpose? I. Utilize a Helm chart for managing application versions. 2. Create separate GKE clusters for blue and green environments. 3. Use Kubernetes Services for routing traffic between versions. 4. Implement a DaemonSet for deploying the new version.

A) 1 and 3
B) 2 and 4
C) 3 and 4
D) 1 and 2

QUESTION 4

Your organization is transitioning to a microservices architecture on Google Kubernetes Engine (GKE). You want to ensure effective communication and coordination among microservices. Which two Kubernetes features should you use to achieve this goal? I. Implement Kubernetes Services to enable DNS-based service discovery. 2. Utilize Ingress controllers to manage external access to microservices. 3. Set up Kubernetes ConfigMaps for sharing configuration data. 4. Deploy Kubernetes Network Policies to control network traffic between microservices.

A) 1 and 2
B) 2 and 3
C) 3 and 4
D) 1 and 4

QUESTION 5

In your role, you need to create a method for setting up new departments and core infrastructure in Google Cloud that is both scalable and dependable. What should you do?

A) Develop a script using the gcloud command-line tool to insert the required parameters from the submission. Archive the script in a version control system.
 B) Construct a Terraform configuration and store it in your version control system. Duplicate and execute the terraform apply instruction to generate the new department.
 C) Utilize the Terraform templates from the Cloud Foundation Toolkit. Implement the templates with the necessary parameters to establish the Google Cloud department and requisite infrastructure.
 D) Manually configure each department through the Google Cloud console.

QUESTION 6

After a major network disruption, in accordance with Site Reliability Engineering practices, what should be your first step when briefing key stakeholders?

A) Craft a comprehensive incident report for distribution among the stakeholders.
 B) Circulate the Incident Summary Document to every stakeholder immediately.
 C) Individually phone each stakeholder to detail the events that transpired.
 D) Instruct the network engineer at fault to compose a personal apology letter to every stakeholder.

QUESTION 7

Your organization is looking to enhance the efficiency of its media processing workflow in Google Cloud's Dataflow. What steps should you prioritize for optimization? (Choose two.)

A) Segment the automation procedures into finer-grained components.

B) Implement automatic progression confirmations transferring from the staging area to the production zone.

C) Run a script to facilitate the setup of the media processing workflow in Google Cloud Dataflow.

D) Set up an alert to inform the designated team to proceed with the next phase when human input is needed.

E) Increase the number of personnel to execute hands-on steps.

QUESTION 8

You are managing a cloud-based image processing application on a Regional GKE cluster. The application is designed to handle bursty image analysis workloads, which vary significantly throughout the week. Your goal is to maintain optimal performance during high-demand periods and minimize resource wastage during low-demand periods. How should you configure your GKE environment?

A) Implement a Horizontal Pod Autoscaler based on CPU utilization.

B) Use a Vertical Pod Autoscaler to adjust pod sizes automatically.

C) Set up a cron job to scale the number of pods according to a fixed schedule.

D) Configure node pool autoscaling based on memory and CPU metrics.

E) Manually adjust the pod count based on weekly usage patterns.

QUESTION 9

Your organization is set to launch a high-availability web application that will experience variable load, requiring autoscaling and multi-regional deployment in Google Cloud. The application is expected to handle large amounts of user data. What is the most critical initial step to take?

A) Configure the application to use the n2-highmem machine type for efficient memory usage.

B) Implement a regional Managed Instance Group with autoscaling based on CPU utilization.

C) Begin with a limited regional deployment to test load capacity before expanding to multiple regions.

D) Ensure the application's resource requirements do not exceed the allocated regional network and compute quotas.

E) Set up a detailed logging and monitoring system to track resource usage and performance in real-time.

QUESTION 10

Your organization's Cloud Run service needs to securely access an external document storage API that requires an OAuth 2.0 token. What is the best method to store and retrieve this token in a secure and efficient manner according to Google Cloud best practices?

A) Hard-code the OAuth 2.0 token in the service's source code and deploy it to Cloud Run.

B) Store the OAuth 2.0 token in an environment variable directly in the Cloud Run service.

C) Use Cloud Key Management Service (KMS) to encrypt the token and store the encrypted token in Firestore.

D) Save the OAuth 2.0 token in Secret Manager and access it in Cloud Run through environment variables.

E) Keep the token in a Google Cloud Storage bucket and access it from Cloud Run during runtime.

QUESTION 11

Your company's security team needs read-only access to the audit logs of a Cloud Storage bucket used for sensitive data storage. The access should align with Google Cloud's best practices and the principle of least privilege. How should you proceed?

A) Assign the roles/storage.objectViewer role to each member of the security team.
B) Assign the roles/storage.objectViewer role to a Google Group containing all security team members.
C) Grant the roles/storage.admin role to the security team for comprehensive access to the Cloud Storage bucket.
D) Assign the roles/logging.viewer role to a Google Group containing all security team members.
E) Create a custom role with specific permissions for audit log access and assign it to the security team.

QUESTION 12

You have a globally distributed application with GKE clusters running in the europe-west1 and northamerica-northeast1 regions. Your CI/CD pipeline generates container images that need to be deployed across these regions. What is the best approach for storing and distributing these images?

A) Push the images to Google Container Registry using a single global hostname like gcr.io.
B) Use separate Google Container Registry hostnames for each region, like eu.gcr.io for europe-west1 and us.gcr.io for northamerica-northeast1.
C) Store images in a third-party container registry service with data centers in both regions.
D) Deploy regional Google Cloud Storage buckets in each region for storing the container images.
E) Set up a custom replication mechanism to synchronize images between regional GCR repositories.

QUESTION 13

You have a workflow in Cloud Build that generates various configuration files, which are then stored in GCS. It's crucial to associate each file with the specific build ID from Cloud Build. What strategy should you use to ensure easy tracking of these files to their respective builds?

A) Include the Cloud Build ID in the filenames of the configuration files stored in GCS.
B) Use GCS object versioning, associating each file version with the corresponding Cloud Build ID.
C) Store the Cloud Build ID in the custom metadata of each GCS object.
D) Organize the configuration files in GCS buckets named after their respective Cloud Build IDs.
E) Create a Cloud SQL database to record the mapping of Cloud Build IDs to the URLs of the configuration files in GCS.

QUESTION 14

Your company's development team is deploying a new application across multiple Google Cloud projects. As part of the security strategy, you need a centralized system for monitoring and analyzing logs from all these projects. What approach should you use to streamline log management and security analysis?

A) Set up individual log sinks in each project to forward logs to respective Cloud Logging buckets.
B) Implement a centralized Cloud Monitoring dashboard to collect and display logs from all projects.
C) Create an aggregated log sink at the organization level, directing all logs to a single Pub/Sub topic for analysis.
D) Use Cloud Functions to collect logs from each project and store them in a BigQuery dataset for

analysis.

E) Configure an aggregated log sink for each project, sending logs to a dedicated Cloud Logging bucket for centralized analysis.

QUESTION 15

Your company is transitioning a multi-tier web application to Google Cloud and requires a deployment solution that allows for traffic routing based on URL paths, as well as the ability to conduct blue-green deployments. What deployment option should you choose to meet these requirements?

A) Migrate the application to App Engine Standard Environment, using services and versions to manage blue-green deployments and URL path routing.

B) Utilize Google Kubernetes Engine (GKE) with an Ingress controller for URL path-based routing and deploy new versions alongside old ones for blue-green deployment.

C) Host the application on Compute Engine VMs with a custom-configured NGINX reverse proxy for URL path routing and manual version management for blue-green deployments.

D) Deploy the application on Cloud Run, setting up different services for each URL path, and use traffic splitting for blue-green deployments.

E) Implement the application in Cloud Functions, creating separate functions for each URL path and manually switching between versions for blue-green deployments.

QUESTION 16

You're responsible for a mission-critical application running on a single Google Cloud Compute Engine instance. To improve reliability, you want to implement a solution that automatically replaces the instance if it fails while adhering to Site Reliability Engineering (SRE) practices. What should you do?

A) Notify the application development team about the instance failures so they can investigate and fix the underlying issues.

 B) Create a Load Balancer in front of the Compute Engine instance to distribute traffic and provide failover capabilities.

 C) Establish a Managed Instance Group with a single instance and configure health checks to monitor its status.

 D) Set up a Google Cloud Monitoring dashboard to manually track the instance's health and take action when necessary.

QUESTION 17

Your organization's data processing scripts are managed in Cloud Source Repositories. You want to establish an automated workflow that runs the latest script version on Google Compute Engine (GCE) instances upon each new commit, while keeping the setup straightforward. What should you do?

A) Deploy a custom service in App Engine to trigger Cloud Functions.

B) Use Cloud Pub/Sub to initiate a Cloud Build workflow.

C) Implement Cloud Pub/Sub to activate a custom orchestrator service hosted on Compute Engine.

D) Configure Cloud Scheduler to trigger a Cloud Build workflow.

QUESTION 18

Your team is responsible for managing a CI/CD pipeline for a large-scale application on Google Cloud. You want to ensure that deployments are automated, consistent, and can be rolled back easily in case of issues. What approach should you follow to achieve this?

A) Use manual deployment scripts to ensure control over the process.
 B) Implement a CI/CD pipeline with Google Cloud Build and Google Cloud Deployment Manager templates, enabling automated deployments and version control.
 C) Rely on ad-hoc manual deployments to minimize complexity and risk.
 D) Establish separate pipelines for different application components to achieve deployment isolation.

QUESTION 19

You need to create a service account key for a partner analytics platform, but you encounter an organization policy constraint error: 'iam.disableServiceAccountKeyCreation is enforced.' To ensure secure practices aligned with Google's recommendations, what should you do?

A) Temporarily relax the iam.disableServiceAccountKeyCreation policy constraint at the organization level, create the key, and then re-enforce the policy.
 B) Override the policy preventing service account key creation at the project level within the department and generate a key.
 C) Enable the default service account key and retrieve it for the partner analytics platform.
 D) Modify your project's IAM policy to disable the iam.disableServiceAccountKeyCreation constraint and proceed to create the necessary key.

QUESTION 20

Your organization employs Apache Maven on Google Cloud Compute Engine instances for software build automation. The task at hand is to introduce configuration management automation with Ansible while ensuring that the Ansible Maven instance possesses the necessary authorization to manage Google Cloud assets, following Google Cloud's best practices. What action should you take to achieve this?

A) Implement a Terraform module to enable Secret Manager to access credentials.
 B) Ensure the Maven Compute Engine instance is associated with a linked service account containing the required Identity and Access Management (1AM) roles.
 C) Integrate the gcloud auth application-default login command into the Maven build process prior to executing Ansible playbooks.
 D) Create a dedicated service account exclusively for the Ansible host, download the service account key, and set the GOOGLE_CREDENTIALS environment variable within the Maven environment.

QUESTION 21

Your cloud infrastructure experienced a prolonged outage that impacted multiple services. You are responsible for creating a post-incident report to prevent similar outages in the future. What should be included in the report?

A) A list of customer support tickets generated during the outage.
B) A summary of the financial losses incurred due to the outage.
C) A detailed timeline of events leading up to and during the outage.

D) Personal assessments of the skills and expertise of the technical team.
E) Identification of root causes and recommended actions to prevent future outages.

QUESTION 22

You are responsible for updating a machine learning model used for customer recommendations in your e-commerce platform. What should you do to minimize the impact on users during the model update?

A) Update the model without any prior notice to users to avoid raising concerns. Notify users after the update is complete.
B) Announce the update to users in advance, providing details about the changes, and roll out the new model gradually while monitoring its performance.
C) Update the model during peak usage hours to ensure that the most users are impacted. Notify users of the update afterward.
D) Deploy the new model and immediately retire the old one without any communication to users.

QUESTION 23

Your team is managing a multi-container application on Google Kubernetes Engine (GKE). You need to ensure that the containers within a pod share the same network namespace and can communicate with each other using localhost. What should you configure in the pod's YAML definition?

A) hostNetwork: true
B) podNetwork: same
C) networkMode: host
D) containerSharing: true

QUESTION 24

You are in charge of a network of Kubernetes clusters on Google Cloud for a technology startup, and security and compliance are of utmost importance. What actions should you take to meet these requirements effectively?

A) Deploy a single cluster for all applications and manually configure security settings.
B) Utilize unmanaged clusters without specific security configurations to minimize costs.
C) Implement Google Kubernetes Engine (GKE) Autopilot clusters for automated security and compliance management.
D) Use separate clusters for each application without implementing security controls.

QUESTION 25

As a cloud engineer, you are evaluating the response time of a cloud-based API service. Your goal is to ensure that the API response time remains below 200 ms. Which method would be the most accurate for calculating this SLI, in line with Google's best practices?

A) Calculate the average response time of the API.
B) Count the number of API requests responded to within 200 ms and divide this by the total number of API requests.
C) Determine the median and 80th percentile of the API response times.

D) Monitor the number of API timeouts and divide this by the total number of API requests.

E) Record the time taken for the API to become available each day and compute the weekly average.

QUESTION 26

Your organization utilizes cloud services for its e-commerce platform. The SRE and Application Development teams must collaborate for efficient operation. What is the best way to define their roles and responsibilities?

A) SRE team: System monitoring and troubleshooting; App Dev team: Code development and setting performance metrics.

B) Shared: System monitoring and SLI/SLO management; SRE team: Infrastructure maintenance; App Dev team: Feature development.

C) SRE team: Overall system maintenance and defining SLIs/SLOs; App Dev team: Code deployment and on-call support.

D) App Dev team: Entire system development and deployment; SRE team: On-call support and performance analysis.

E) Shared: Code review and deployment; SRE team: On-call duties and SLI/SLO management; App Dev team: New feature development.

QUESTION 27

Your team is managing a cloud-based API service and aims to set an SLO that ensures the API response is within 500 ms for 98% of the time each week. What is the appropriate metric and evaluation method to use?

A) Response time metric with a window-based method of evaluation.

B) Throughput metric with a window-based method of evaluation.

C) Error rate metric with a request-based method of evaluation.

D) Response time metric with a request-based method of evaluation.

E) Uptime metric with a window-based method of evaluation.

QUESTION 28

You oversee the cloud infrastructure for an online media streaming service. Your error budget analysis indicates underutilization. You wish to optimize the SLOs while maintaining user satisfaction and service quality. Which two actions should you consider?

A) Increase the frequency of new feature deployments to the service.

B) Add more SLIs related to user engagement and streaming quality.

C) Upgrade network infrastructure to improve overall service speed.

D) Adjust the SLOs to more accurately reflect the service's current reliability.

E) Implement more aggressive auto-scaling to reduce costs.

QUESTION 29

As part of a cloud infrastructure modernization project, you are tasked with ensuring all current and future App Engine instances in your Google Cloud project are properly monitored. How do you configure the environment to send detailed operation logs to Cloud Operations?

A) Enable detailed logging for each App Engine instance manually in the Cloud Console.
 B) Use an App Engine Admin API script to update logging configurations for all instances.
 C) Configure an organization-wide policy to automatically enable detailed logging for all App Engine applications.
 D) Include logging configuration commands in the App Engine app.yaml for each application.
 E) Rely on App Engine's default logging settings, assuming they meet the detailed logging requirements.

QUESTION 30

Your organization's application infrastructure spans across Google Cloud and several on-premises servers. You are tasked with setting up a system to monitor application response times and availability in both environments. Which approach aligns best with Google-recommended practices?

A) Develop a set of custom scripts for response time monitoring in each environment, then aggregate the results.
 B) Install the Cloud Monitoring agent on the on-premises servers and use built-in GCP tools for the cloud portion, unifying the data.
 C) Rely on external monitoring services for on-premises infrastructure, while using Cloud Monitoring for the cloud components.
 D) Configure Cloud Trace in Google Cloud and a similar tracing tool on-premises, integrating the data for analysis.
 E) Use third-party APM tools across both cloud and on-premises environments, sending all data to a centralized analytics service.

QUESTION 31

You are managing a Cloud Run service that relies on secrets stored in Secret Manager. The service deploys successfully, but during runtime, it fails to access the required secrets. The error message indicates insufficient permissions. To resolve this issue, what action should you take while following Google Cloud best practices?

A) Modify the Cloud Run service configuration to use environment variables instead of secrets.
B) Grant the Cloud Run service account the role of roles/secretmanager.secretAccessor on the relevant Secret Manager secret.
C) Create a new Cloud Run service with different permissions.
D) Disable secret access in the Cloud Run service configuration.

QUESTION 32

Your company is using WebSocket connections to interact with a public Cloud Run service accessible at https://api-financialxy.z.run.app. You need to enable your development team to validate new revisions of this service before making them generally available. How should you proceed?

A) Assign the roles/run.invoker role to the development team members who are testing the report-service. Use the https://api-financialxy.private.run.app URL for testing.
B) Invoke the curl -H "Authorization:Bearer $(gcloud auth print-identity-token)" command to authenticate. Use the https://api-financialxy.z.run.app URL for private testing.
C) Run the gcloud run deploy report-service --no-traffic --tag dev command. Use the https://dev-api-financialxy.z.run.app URL for testing.

D) Run the gcloud run services update-traffic report-service --to-revisions LATEST=100 command. Use the https://api-financialxy.z.run.app URL for testing.

QUESTION 33

You are responsible for configuring a new Google Cloud environment for a logistics company. The company has expressed concerns about potential security vulnerabilities associated with the use of JSON service account keys within Google Cloud. Your task is to devise a strategy that completely mitigates the risks associated with JSON service account key usage while keeping operational efforts to a minimum. What course of action should you take?

A) Assign specific IAM roles to dedicated teams for managing service account keys.
B) Customize predefined roles to eliminate permissions related to service account key management.
C) Impose organization-level constraints to prohibit service account key creation.
D) Implement guidelines to control service account key uploads.

QUESTION 34

Your organization operates a critical healthcare application on Google Kubernetes Engine (GKE). You need to ensure that access to sensitive data is tightly controlled, and only authorized personnel can interact with the application. What should you implement to meet this requirement effectively?

A) Deploy a Cloud Identity-Aware Proxy (Cloud IAP) in front of your GKE application to enforce identity-based access control.
B) Implement a custom OAuth2-based authentication solution for your GKE application to have fine-grained control over user access.
C) Use Google Cloud Armor to create a Web Application Firewall (WAF) for your GKE application to filter incoming traffic based on predefined rules.
D) Configure GKE Network Policies to restrict traffic to your application to specific IP ranges and ports.

QUESTION 35

Your healthcare organization is using Cloud Build to deploy a critical service and needs to handle sensitive information like API keys securely. What is the best approach to integrate these secrets with minimal disruption to your existing workflows?

A) Implement encryption and decryption logic within your application code to handle sensitive information securely.
B) Store API keys in environment variables and configure Cloud Build to access them directly.
C) Create a new Cloud Storage bucket and store sensitive information with object-level permissions configured for Cloud Build access.
D) Utilize Google Cloud's Secret Manager service to securely store and manage sensitive information, integrating them into your Cloud Build deployment script.

QUESTION 36

You are managing a cloud-based document management system on Google Cloud Platform (GCP). You've discovered that confidential document access logs are inadvertently being logged and are collected through Cloud Logging. These sensitive logs are marked with the label "AccessLogs." What action should you take to securely store these logs for compliance purposes and prevent their exposure through Cloud Logging?

A) Establish a custom log filter in Cloud Logging to identify the "AccessLogs" label, create a log sink directed to Cloud Storage, and then establish a log exclusion based on the "AccessLogs" filter.
B) Define a basic log filter in Cloud Logging to detect the "AccessLogs" label and configure a log sink directed at a Cloud Storage bucket to archive these entries.
C) Implement a Fluentd filter plugin with the Cloud Logging Agent to filter out log entries tagged with "AccessLogs," and route the filtered entries to a dedicated Cloud Storage bucket for secure storage.
D) Create a custom log sink in Cloud Logging to direct logs with the "AccessLogs" label to Cloud Storage while excluding them from regular Cloud Logging processing.

QUESTION 37

You are responsible for deploying a microservices-based e-commerce platform on Google Kubernetes Engine (GKE). Your goal is to enable a seamless rollback to the previous version in case of any problems with the update. Which deployment strategy should you choose?

A) Opt for canary releases, and perform continuous evaluations of the updated microservices.
B) Implement a red/black deployment method, and evaluate the new version upon deployment completion.
C) Choose rolling updates, and evaluate the new microservices after the deployment stage concludes.
D) Utilize a green/blue deployment approach, and assess the new microservices once the deployment process is finalized.

QUESTION 38

Your video processing service on Google Cloud encounters frequent, brief interruptions where instances become unresponsive but recover automatically within seconds. Alerts are triggered for each occurrence. To enhance service reliability while following Site Reliability Engineering (SRE) principles, what should you do?

A) Adjust the associated Service Level Objective (SLO) to account for these frequent restarts within the error budget.
B) Create comprehensive incident reports for every alert received to analyze the underlying causes.
C) Distribute alert notifications among team members located in different geographic regions.
D) Implement a system to escalate alerts to higher management for quick resolution.

QUESTION 39

Your organization utilizes multiple BigQuery datasets for different projects. Each project team has its own dataset. You need to streamline the process of calculating the costs associated with each team's BigQuery usage. How should you proceed?

A) Name each dataset according to the project team, export usage statistics to Cloud Storage, and analyze the costs using Dataflow pipelines.
B) Apply labels to each BigQuery dataset reflective of the project team, enable billing export to BigQuery, and perform cost analysis using SQL queries.
C) Embed project-specific metadata into each dataset, use Cloud Logging to export usage logs to

BigQuery, and analyze costs through metadata.
D) Manually review and compile cost data for each project team's BigQuery usage from the Google Cloud Console.
E) Create a bespoke application that aggregates usage data from BigQuery APIs based on project teams and computes costs, storing this in a Cloud SQL database.

QUESTION 40

Your organization's cloud-based image processing application, written in Python and using Cloud Functions and BigQuery, experiences random slowdowns during peak usage. You need a solution to identify inefficient code segments with minimal impact on performance. Which approach should you take?

A) Integrate Cloud Profiler and add the google-cloud-profiler library to your Python application.
B) Set up periodic triggers to run the py-spy utility on your application instances and analyze the output using BigQuery.
C) Implement a dedicated profiling service on a separate VM instance to gather performance data from your application.
D) Use Cloud Monitoring to track the execution time of Cloud Functions and BigQuery queries.

QUESTION 41

As the SRE lead for a large-scale web application hosted on Google Cloud, you notice your team is frequently interrupted by alerts for minor issues that resolve themselves. What strategy should you employ to manage alerts more effectively and reduce burnout?

A) Document each alert and its resolution in a detailed log.
B) Implement an on-call schedule that distributes alert responsibilities across the team.
C) Adjust the Service Level Objectives (SLOs) to account for these minor and self-resolving issues.
D) Suppress notifications for alerts that are transient and have minimal impact on the overall service.

QUESTION 42

In a complex project involving multi-environment deployments using Terraform for cloud infrastructure and Anthos for Kubernetes configuration, what is the most effective way to organize your source control repositories for infrastructure and application code?

A) Consolidate all Terraform and Anthos Config Management configurations into a single repository with distinct branches for each environment, and use separate repositories for each application service with a branching strategy based on features.
B) Create individual repositories for Terraform configurations for each environment, a central repository for Anthos Config Management with overlays for each environment, and a monolithic repository for all application services with feature-based branching.
C) Use a single repository for all Terraform configurations with folders for each environment, a shared repository for Anthos Config Management with environment-specific directories, and separate repositories for each application service with branches for development and production.
D) Maintain separate repositories for each environment's Terraform configurations and Anthos Config Management, and use a unified repository for all application services, with directory-based separation for features.

QUESTION 43

You are managing cloud infrastructure for a large retail company with several departments, each running multiple projects in Google Cloud. You need to create Cloud Monitoring dashboards for each department, ensuring they only display relevant project metrics. How should you configure these dashboards?

A) Assign each department's primary project as the scoped project for their respective dashboards.
B) Create a unique scoped project for each department and migrate their respective projects under these.
C) Use a centralized scoped project for all departments and filter metrics by project names within the dashboards.
D) Set up individual dashboards for each project within a department, and then group them under a department-specific dashboard.

QUESTION 44

Managing an e-commerce platform on App Engine, you notice delayed responses and high CPU usage during seasonal sales. The platform relies on Cloud SQL for transactions and Cloud Storage for image hosting. Anticipating future sales events, what action should you take to ensure smooth operation?

A) Configure App Engine for automatic scaling to manage varying loads efficiently.
B) Migrate the e-commerce platform to a Kubernetes Engine cluster for enhanced scalability.
C) Enable Cloud SQL's high availability configuration to improve database performance.
D) Upgrade Cloud Storage to a higher performance class to reduce image retrieval times.

QUESTION 45

In a cloud-hosted web application, you've identified that the single Compute Engine instance used for backend processing is often overwhelmed, leading to missed SLO targets. What steps can you take to enhance the processing efficiency and meet your SLI?

A) Reassess and adjust the SLO to better reflect the current performance of the Compute Engine instance.
B) Switch to a higher-capacity Compute Engine instance to increase the processing power available.
C) Distribute the processing load across a cluster of Compute Engine instances using a load balancer.
D) Deploy backup Compute Engine instances in other zones, activated when the primary instance is overloaded.

QUESTION 46

You are overseeing a financial application in Google Cloud that handles sensitive financial data. What measures should you take to ensure this data is securely managed and protected against unauthorized access?

A) Use hard-coded credentials in the application for direct access to sensitive data.
B) Integrate with an Identity and Access Management (IAM) provider for secure authentication and access control.
C) Regularly generate new credentials for the application through an automated script.
D) Store encryption keys in Cloud Key Management Service (KMS) and enable automatic key rotation.

QUESTION 47

In your GKE deployment, one of the microservices starts to show latency issues after running for extended periods. You are working on a long-term fix but need a temporary solution to minimize disruptions. What should be your approach to address this issue with minimal manual intervention?

A) Implement a TCP readiness probe in the microservice's Deployment configuration to detect and handle latency issues.
B) Configure a liveness probe for the microservice in question, which restarts the pod when it becomes unresponsive.
C) Set up a custom script that monitors the microservice and restarts its pods when they exhibit high latency.
D) Create a routine in your CI/CD pipeline that periodically restarts the microservice's pods as a precautionary measure.

QUESTION 48

Your organization has adopted a microservices architecture, and you're responsible for securing the containerized deployments. To address code vulnerabilities and outdated dependencies, what approach should you take?

A) Configure a web application firewall (WAF) to inspect incoming traffic to the microservices.
B) Implement manual code reviews for each microservice to identify vulnerabilities.
C) Leverage a container scanning tool integrated into your CI/CD pipeline to assess the container images for vulnerabilities.
D) Apply runtime application security protection (RASP) tools to monitor and protect the live microservices.
E) Enable automated container image updates in your CI/CD pipeline to keep dependencies current.

QUESTION 49

Your organization is transitioning to a DevOps culture, and your software application encountered intermittent performance issues recently. A department head has requested a formal incident analysis for preventive measures. What should you do?

A) Generate an incident analysis report detailing the underlying problems, insights gained, individual accountability, and remedial tasks assigned to specific team members. Share it exclusively with the requesting department head.
B) Draft an incident analysis report highlighting the problems and insights. Share it across the organization's technical documentation repository for reference.
C) Prepare an incident analysis report summarizing the issues, insights, and a structured set of remedial tasks. Share it solely with the requesting department head.
D) Compile an incident analysis report summarizing the issues, insights, and a structured set of corrective actions. Disseminate it across the organization's technical documentation platform for broader access.

QUESTION 50

Your company is utilizing Spinnaker for managing deployments in a cloud-based SaaS application. A canary release phase is part of your deployment pipeline. What is the recommended setup for canary analysis in this SaaS environment?

A) Compare the canary with performance data from historical stable releases.
B) Evaluate the canary alongside the ongoing stable production release.
C) Analyze the canary in isolation without any performance comparison.
D) Assess the canary against a controlled user acceptance testing environment.

PRACTICE TEST 1 - ANSWERS ONLY

QUESTION 1

Answer - A) Deploy the application across multiple Google Cloud regions, implement Google Cloud CDN for content delivery, and use Google Cloud Storage for data backup and recovery.

Option A combines key services and strategies to ensure high availability and disaster recovery for the e-commerce application, aligning with Google's recommended DevOps practices.
Option B provides security and cost optimization but does not address high availability and disaster recovery comprehensively.
Options C, D, E, and F mention various services but do not directly cover the objectives of high availability and disaster recovery.

QUESTION 2

Answer - C) Set up individual CI/CD pipelines for each microservice, allowing independent builds and deployments.

Option C aligns with the goal of ensuring that each microservice is independently deployable and changes to one do not impact others. Individual CI/CD pipelines provide flexibility and isolation for microservices. This approach follows recommended DevOps practices.
Option A suggests a monolithic pipeline, which contradicts the goal of independence.
Option B proposes conditional deployment, which may lead to complex logic.
Option D mentions separate pipelines but does not emphasize independence.

QUESTION 3

Answer - A) 1 and 3

Options 1 and 3 are the recommended choices to implement a blue-green deployment strategy for a containerized web application on Google Kubernetes Engine (GKE). Using Helm charts for managing application versions facilitates controlled updates, and using Kubernetes Services for routing traffic between versions is essential for blue-green deployments.
Option 2, creating separate GKE clusters, is not typically used for blue-green deployments.
Option 4, implementing a DaemonSet, is not relevant for this type of deployment.

QUESTION 4

Answer - A) 1 and 2

To ensure effective communication and coordination among microservices in a Kubernetes-based microservices architecture, you should:
- Implement Kubernetes Services to enable DNS-based service discovery (Option 1).
- Utilize Ingress controllers to manage external access to microservices (Option 2).
These practices help with service discovery and external access management.
Option 3, setting up Kubernetes ConfigMaps, is useful for configuration management but does not directly address communication and coordination.

Option 4, deploying Kubernetes Network Policies, is important for network security but does not focus on communication and coordination.

QUESTION 5

Answer - C) Utilize the Terraform templates from the Cloud Foundation Toolkit. Implement the templates with the necessary parameters to establish the Google Cloud department and requisite infrastructure.

Option C is the correct choice as it recommends leveraging Terraform templates from the Cloud Foundation Toolkit, ensuring scalability and dependability while automating department creation.
Option A introduces a manual script which is less scalable,
Option B suggests Terraform but without templates and lacks scalability,
Option D is highly manual and not scalable.

QUESTION 6

Answer - B) Circulate the Incident Summary Document to every stakeholder immediately.

Option B is the correct choice as it suggests circulating the Incident Summary Document to every stakeholder immediately, providing a concise overview of the incident.
Option A delays communication,
Option C is inefficient for a large number of stakeholders,
Option D is not the initial step and focuses on personal apologies rather than incident summary.

QUESTION 7

Answer - A and B

Option A - Segmenting automation procedures into finer-grained components reduces redundancy and improves efficiency.
Option B - Implementing automatic progression confirmations streamlines the workflow by reducing manual interventions.
Options C, D, and E are not the most effective ways to optimize the workflow.

QUESTION 8

Answer - A) Implement a Horizontal Pod Autoscaler based on CPU utilization.

A) Correct - This ensures dynamic scaling of pods during varying workloads, maintaining performance and efficiency.
B) Incorrect - Vertical scaling might not be effective for bursty workloads.
C) Incorrect - Scheduled scaling may not align well with unpredictable workloads.
D) Incorrect - Node pool autoscaling is beneficial but needs to be complemented with pod-level scaling.
E) Incorrect - Manual adjustments are less efficient and may not respond timely to real-time demand changes.

QUESTION 9

Answer - D) Ensure the application's resource requirements do not exceed the allocated regional network and compute quotas.

A) Incorrect - Choosing a specific machine type is important, but not the first step in the planning process.
B) Incorrect - Regional autoscaling is vital but should follow initial resource and quota verification.
C) Incorrect - Testing in one region is useful, but the primary concern is verifying resource availability across regions.
D) Correct - Confirming that the application's demands are within Google Cloud's regional quotas is essential before deployment.
E) Incorrect - While monitoring is critical for ongoing management, it's not the first step in deployment planning.

QUESTION 10

Answer - D) Save the OAuth 2.0 token in Secret Manager and access it in Cloud Run through environment variables.

A) Incorrect - Hard-coding secrets in source code is a security risk.
B) Incorrect - Storing sensitive data in environment variables without encryption is not recommended.
C) Incorrect - While Cloud KMS is secure, this method adds unnecessary complexity compared to using Secret Manager.
D) Correct - Secret Manager is the ideal solution for managing sensitive data like OAuth tokens in cloud applications.
E) Incorrect - Storing sensitive tokens in Cloud Storage is not as secure as using Secret Manager and can lead to security vulnerabilities.

QUESTION 11

Answer - B) Assign the roles/storage.objectViewer role to a Google Group containing all security team members.

A) Incorrect - Assigning roles to individuals is not as efficient as assigning to a group.
B) Correct - This approach is efficient and adheres to the principle of least privilege, providing only the necessary access.
C) Incorrect - The storage.admin role provides more permissions than necessary for just viewing logs.
D) Incorrect - The logging.viewer role is not specific to Cloud Storage buckets.
E) Incorrect - While creating a custom role is an option, it is not necessary when a predefined role meets the requirements.

QUESTION 12

Answer - A) Push the images to Google Container Registry using a single global hostname like gcr.io.

A) Correct - GCR with a global hostname automatically manages the storage and distribution of images efficiently across regions.
B) Incorrect - Using separate regional hostnames is less efficient for a globally distributed application.
C) Incorrect - Third-party services might not offer the same level of integration and efficiency as GCR.

D) Incorrect - Cloud Storage is not optimized for container image distribution like GCR is.
E) Incorrect - Custom replication is unnecessary as GCR handles this efficiently with a global hostname.

QUESTION 13

Answer - C) Store the Cloud Build ID in the custom metadata of each GCS object.

A) Incorrect - Including the build ID in filenames can be cumbersome and challenging to manage.
B) Incorrect - Object versioning in GCS is not designed for mapping to external identifiers like Cloud Build IDs.
C) Correct - Storing the build ID in the object's metadata provides a clear and manageable way to track the association.
D) Incorrect - Using separate buckets for each build ID is not scalable and can lead to management difficulties.
E) Incorrect - While a database can track this information, it adds unnecessary complexity compared to using GCS metadata.

QUESTION 14

Answer - C) Create an aggregated log sink at the organization level, directing all logs to a single Pub/Sub topic for analysis.

A) Incorrect - Individual log sinks create fragmentation and are less efficient for centralized analysis.
B) Incorrect - Cloud Monitoring is primarily for metrics, not for centralized log collection.
C) Correct - An organization-level aggregated log sink provides a unified approach for collecting and analyzing logs across all projects.
D) Incorrect - Using Cloud Functions for log collection is less efficient and scalable than using aggregated log sinks.
E) Incorrect - Aggregated log sinks per project still require centralization for effective analysis.

QUESTION 15

Answer - B) Utilize Google Kubernetes Engine (GKE) with an Ingress controller for URL path-based routing and deploy new versions alongside old ones for blue-green deployment.

A) Incorrect - App Engine Standard Environment has limitations in URL path-based routing and version flexibility.
B) Correct - GKE with an Ingress controller allows for sophisticated URL path-based routing, and deploying new versions alongside old ones supports blue-green deployments.
C) Incorrect - Compute Engine with a custom NGINX setup requires significant manual configuration and maintenance.
D) Incorrect - Cloud Run supports traffic splitting but does not offer URL path-based routing in the same way as GKE with an Ingress controller.
E) Incorrect - Cloud Functions is not suited for multi-tier web applications requiring complex routing and deployment strategies.

QUESTION 16

Answer - C) Establish a Managed Instance Group with a single instance and configure health checks to monitor its status.

Option C is the correct choice because it aligns with Site Reliability Engineering (SRE) practices by automatically replacing the instance when it fails, ensuring high reliability.
 Option A - Option A is incorrect because it suggests notifying the application development team, which may not directly address the need for automated instance replacement.
 Option B - Option B is incorrect because while Load Balancers provide traffic distribution, they do not automatically replace instances in the event of failure.
 Option D - Option D is incorrect because manual tracking via a monitoring dashboard does not provide automated failover capabilities as needed for high reliability.

QUESTION 17

Answer - B) Use Cloud Pub/Sub to initiate a Cloud Build workflow.

Option B is the correct choice because using Cloud Pub/Sub to trigger a Cloud Build workflow when new code versions are committed provides automation while maintaining a straightforward setup.
 Option A - Option A introduces an additional layer of complexity with App Engine and Cloud Functions, which may not be necessary.
 Option C - Option C involves creating a custom orchestrator service, which may be more complex than needed for this task.
 Option D - Option D uses Cloud Scheduler, which is not the most suitable choice for triggering a build workflow when code changes occur.

QUESTION 18

Answer - B) Implement a CI/CD pipeline with Google Cloud Build and Google Cloud Deployment Manager templates, enabling automated deployments and version control.

Option B is the correct choice because it sets up a CI/CD pipeline with Google Cloud Build and Google Cloud Deployment Manager templates, ensuring automated, consistent deployments with version control and rollback capabilities.
 Option A - Option A involves manual deployment scripts, which are not as efficient and automated as a CI/CD pipeline.
 Option C - Option C suggests ad-hoc manual deployments, which lack consistency and automation.
 Option D - Option D proposes separate pipelines but doesn't address the need for an efficient CI/CD pipeline.

QUESTION 19

Answer - A) Temporarily relax the iam.disableServiceAccountKeyCreation policy constraint at the organization level, create the key, and then re-enforce the policy.

Option A is the correct choice.
 Option A - Temporarily relaxing the policy constraint at the organization level allows you to create the necessary service account key securely, following Google's recommended practices.
 Option B - Overriding the policy at the project level may not adhere to organizational policies and is not

the recommended approach.
 Option C - Enabling the default service account key may not provide the required security for the analytics platform.
 Option D - Modifying the project's IAM policy to disable the constraint is not recommended and can have unintended consequences.

QUESTION 20

Answer - B) Ensure the Maven Compute Engine instance is associated with a linked service account containing the required Identity and Access Management (1AM) roles.

Option B is the correct choice.
 Option B - Ensuring that the Maven Compute Engine instance is associated with a linked service account containing the necessary IAM roles aligns with Google Cloud's recommended practices for Ansible authorization.
 Option A - Implementing a Terraform module for Secret Manager is unrelated to Ansible authorization.
 Option C - Integrating the gcloud auth application-default login command is not the recommended practice for Ansible authorization.
 Option D - Creating a dedicated service account and setting GOOGLE_CREDENTIALS is a valid but more complex approach compared to Option B.

QUESTION 21

Answer - C) A detailed timeline of events leading up to and during the outage.
Answer - E) Identification of root causes and recommended actions to prevent future outages.

Explanation for Option C - A detailed timeline of events is essential for understanding the sequence of actions and events that led to the outage, which is crucial for identifying areas for improvement and prevention.
Explanation for Option E - Identification of root causes and recommended actions are key for preventing future outages. They provide insights into the underlying causes and steps to take to avoid similar incidents.
Explanation for Option A - While customer support tickets may be relevant, they are not typically the central focus of a post-incident report aimed at preventing future outages.
Explanation for Option B - Summarizing financial losses is important but is not typically the primary focus of a post-incident report for outage prevention.
Explanation for Option D - Personal assessments of team skills and expertise are not typically the primary content of a post-incident report for outage prevention.

QUESTION 22

Answer - B) Announce the update to users in advance, providing details about the changes, and roll out the new model gradually while monitoring its performance.

Explanation for Option B - Announcing the update in advance and gradually rolling out the new model while monitoring performance allows users to be informed and minimizes disruption. It aligns with best practices for managing updates.
Explanation for Option A - Updating the model without notice may lead to user dissatisfaction and concerns about changes in recommendations. Communication is essential.

Explanation for Option C - Updating the model during peak hours without notice can disrupt the user experience and is generally not recommended.
Explanation for Option D - Immediately retiring the old model without communication can lead to confusion and dissatisfaction among users.

QUESTION 23

Answer - A) hostNetwork: true

Option A) hostNetwork: true in the pod's YAML definition allows the containers within the pod to share the same network namespace and communicate with each other using localhost.
The other options are not valid configurations for achieving this specific requirement.

QUESTION 24

C) Implement Google Kubernetes Engine (GKE) Autopilot clusters for automated security and compliance management.

Option C is the correct choice as it suggests implementing GKE Autopilot clusters, which provide automated security and compliance management. This aligns with the goal of ensuring security and compliance effectively for a technology startup.
Option A recommends a single cluster with manual security configuration, which may be error-prone and time-consuming.
Option B suggests using unmanaged clusters without specific security configurations, which may not meet security requirements.
Option D promotes separate clusters without security controls, which is not aligned with security and compliance needs.

QUESTION 25

Answer - B) Count the number of API requests responded to within 200 ms and divide this by the total number of API requests.

Option A - This method does not accurately reflect instances where the response time may exceed the threshold.
Option B - This is the correct approach as it directly measures how often the service meets the defined threshold.
Option C - While percentile measurements are useful, they do not directly assess compliance with the specific threshold.
Option D - Timeout counts are a different metric and do not measure response speed.
Option E - Recording daily availability time is irrelevant to measuring response time.

QUESTION 26

Answer - B) Shared: System monitoring and SLI/SLO management; SRE team: Infrastructure maintenance; App Dev team: Feature development.

Option A - Limiting the App Dev team's role to code development without involvement in setting performance metrics can lead to misaligned goals.

Option B - This promotes a balanced approach with shared responsibilities for critical aspects, ensuring alignment between development and operations.
Option C - Excluding the App Dev team from defining SLIs/SLOs may not reflect the true capabilities of the system.
Option D - This approach can overburden the App Dev team and underutilize the SRE team's expertise.
Option E - While shared code review is beneficial, the SRE team should also be involved in performance analysis.

QUESTION 27

Answer - A) Response time metric with a window-based method of evaluation.

Option A - A window-based response time metric aligns with the weekly performance target.
Option B - Throughput does not directly relate to response time.
Option C - Error rate is not the correct metric for response time objectives.
Option D - While response time is correct, a request-based method may not effectively capture weekly performance.
Option E - Uptime is about availability, not response speed.

QUESTION 28

Answer - A) and B)

Option A - Increasing deployment frequency can drive innovation without necessarily impacting reliability.
Option B - Adding more nuanced SLIs provides a broader view of service quality and user satisfaction.
Option C - While beneficial, this doesn't directly relate to optimizing SLOs or utilizing the error budget.
Option D - Adjusting SLOs should be done cautiously to avoid setting unrealistic expectations.
Option E - Auto-scaling relates to cost and performance, but not directly to SLO optimization.

QUESTION 29

Answer - D) Include logging configuration commands in the App Engine app.yaml for each application.

Option A - Manually enabling logging for each instance is not scalable and prone to oversight.
Option B - Using an API script can be effective but requires maintenance and may not automatically apply to new instances.
Option C - Organization-wide policies for App Engine specific configurations are not typically available.
Option D - Including logging configurations in app.yaml ensures that all new and redeployed instances have the necessary settings.
Option E - Default settings may not provide the level of detail required for effective monitoring and compliance.

QUESTION 30

Answer - B) Install the Cloud Monitoring agent on the on-premises servers and use built-in GCP tools for the cloud portion, unifying the data.

Option A - Custom scripts can be labor-intensive and might not offer the real-time monitoring needed.

Option B - This approach ensures consistent monitoring across environments with minimal development effort.

Option C - External services may offer monitoring solutions, but integrating these with Cloud Monitoring might be complex.

Option D - While Cloud Trace is effective in GCP, setting up a similar tool on-premises and integrating data can be challenging.

Option E - Third-party APM tools could provide the necessary monitoring, but they may lack seamless integration with GCP services.

QUESTION 31

Answer - B) Grant the Cloud Run service account the role of roles/secretmanager.secretAccessor on the relevant Secret Manager secret.

Option A, modifying the service configuration to use environment variables, is not the recommended approach for accessing secrets.

Option C, creating a new Cloud Run service, may not address the permissions issue and is not a best practice.

Option D, disabling secret access, would render the service unable to access necessary secrets.

QUESTION 32

Answer - B) Invoke the curl -H "Authorization:Bearer $(gcloud auth print-identity-token)" command to authenticate. Use the https://api-financialxy.z.run.app URL for private testing.

Option A, assigning the roles/run.invoker role, does not involve authentication and private testing.

Option C, deploying with the dev tag, is related to deployment but not authentication.

Option D, updating traffic to the latest revision, does not address authentication for testing new revisions.

QUESTION 33

Answer - C) Impose organization-level constraints to prohibit service account key creation.

Option A, assigning specific IAM roles, may not effectively address the issue of minimizing key usage.

Option B, customizing predefined roles, could be complex and error-prone.

Option D, implementing guidelines, may not address the root concern of key creation.

QUESTION 34

Answer - A) Deploy a Cloud Identity-Aware Proxy (Cloud IAP) in front of your GKE application to enforce identity-based access control.

Explanation:

Option A is the correct choice because Cloud Identity-Aware Proxy (Cloud IAP) provides identity-based access control and integrates seamlessly with GKE, ensuring only authorized personnel can interact with the application effectively.

Option B, a custom OAuth2-based solution, may introduce complexity and is less streamlined.

Option C, Google Cloud Armor with a WAF, focuses on filtering traffic but does not provide fine-grained

access control.
 Option D, GKE Network Policies, is more about network-level control and does not address identity-based access control as effectively as Cloud IAP.

QUESTION 35

Answer - D) Utilize Google Cloud's Secret Manager service to securely store and manage sensitive information, integrating them into your Cloud Build deployment script.

Explanation:
 Option D is the correct choice as it leverages Google Cloud's Secret Manager to securely store and manage sensitive information, seamlessly integrating them into the Cloud Build deployment script with proper security.
 Option A suggests implementing encryption within application code, which may not be the best practice for managing secrets.
 Option B proposes storing secrets in environment variables, which is not as secure and manageable as Secret Manager.
 Option C suggests using a Cloud Storage bucket but lacks the security and management features of Google Cloud's Secret Manager.

QUESTION 36

Answer - A) Establish a custom log filter in Cloud Logging to identify the "AccessLogs" label, create a log sink directed to Cloud Storage, and then establish a log exclusion based on the "AccessLogs" filter.

Option A is the correct choice as it aligns with best practices. It involves setting up a custom log filter to identify sensitive logs, directing them to Cloud Storage for secure storage, and excluding them from regular Cloud Logging to prevent exposure.
 Option B is incorrect because it lacks the exclusion step, which is crucial for preventing exposure.
 Option C is incorrect because it uses a Fluentd filter plugin with the Cloud Logging Agent but doesn't mention log exclusion.
 Option D is incorrect because it lacks the customization required for secure storage and exclusion.

QUESTION 37

Answer - D) Utilize a green/blue deployment approach, and assess the new microservices once the deployment process is finalized.

Option D is the correct choice as it aligns with the requirement to enable a seamless rollback by keeping the current version (green) running alongside the new one (blue) until the deployment is finalized.
 Option A is incorrect as it focuses on continuous evaluations without a clear rollback strategy.
 Option B is incorrect as it lacks a blue/green approach for immediate rollback.
 Option C is incorrect as rolling updates may not provide the same level of safety in case of issues.

QUESTION 38

Answer - A) Adjust the associated Service Level Objective (SLO) to account for these frequent restarts within the error budget.

Option A is the correct choice as it aligns with SRE principles by adapting the SLO to account for frequent restarts, ensuring that these events do not exceed the error budget. This approach optimizes workflow while maintaining reliability.

Option B suggests creating comprehensive incident reports for every alert, which may be excessive for brief interruptions. Option C involves geographic distribution of alerts, which may not directly address the issue. Option D recommends escalating alerts to higher management, which may not optimize service reliability for this specific scenario.

QUESTION 39

Answer - B) Apply labels to each BigQuery dataset reflective of the project team, enable billing export to BigQuery, and perform cost analysis using SQL queries.

Option A - Incorrect: Using Cloud Storage and Dataflow for this task is less efficient than BigQuery.
Option B - Correct: Labeling datasets and using BigQuery for cost analysis is the most efficient method.
Option C - Incorrect: Using metadata and Cloud Logging is more complicated than necessary.
Option D - Incorrect: Manual tracking is time-consuming and error-prone.
Option E - Incorrect: Developing a custom application is unnecessary and less efficient.

QUESTION 40

Answer - A) Integrate Cloud Profiler and add the google-cloud-profiler library to your Python application.

Option A - Correct: Cloud Profiler is designed for low-overhead monitoring and is ideal for identifying inefficient code segments.
Option B - Incorrect: py-spy could provide insights, but its setup and analysis require more maintenance.
Option C - Incorrect: Setting up a separate VM for profiling adds complexity and maintenance overhead.
Option D - Incorrect: Cloud Monitoring tracks execution time but doesn't pinpoint inefficient code segments.

QUESTION 41

Answer - D) Suppress notifications for alerts that are transient and have minimal impact on the overall service.

Option A - Incorrect: While documentation is important, it doesn't reduce the frequency of alerts.
Option B - Incorrect: An on-call schedule helps distribute the load but doesn't reduce the number of alerts.
Option C - Incorrect: Adjusting SLOs can help, but it might not reduce the immediate impact of frequent alerts.
Option D - Correct: Suppressing low-impact, transient alerts can help focus on significant issues and reduce team fatigue.

QUESTION 42

Answer - C) Use a single repository for all Terraform configurations with folders for each environment, a shared repository for Anthos Config Management with environment-specific directories, and separate repositories for each application service with branches for development and production.

Option A - Incorrect: Consolidating everything into a single repository can lead to complexity and management challenges.
Option B - Incorrect: Individual repositories for each Terraform environment can cause duplication, and a monolithic repository for applications can become unwieldy.
Option C - Correct: This approach provides a balance between environment-specific configuration management and clear separation for application services.
Option D - Incorrect: Maintaining separate repositories for each environment's configurations can lead to duplication and increased maintenance.

QUESTION 43

Answer - A) Assign each department's primary project as the scoped project for their respective dashboards.

Option A - Correct: This approach ensures that each department's dashboard is scoped to display metrics from their primary project, aligning with best practices.
Option B - Incorrect: Creating new scoped projects can be unnecessary and complicate the existing infrastructure.
Option C - Incorrect: A centralized scoped project may not effectively segregate metrics by department.
Option D - Incorrect: While this provides granularity, it can be overly complex and against the simplicity principle in dashboard design.

QUESTION 44

Answer - A) Configure App Engine for automatic scaling to manage varying loads efficiently.

Option A - Correct: Automatic scaling in App Engine is designed to handle load variations effectively, making it ideal for seasonal spikes.
Option B - Incorrect: While Kubernetes offers scalability, it may not be necessary for this scenario.
Option C - Incorrect: High availability improves redundancy but not necessarily performance under high load.
Option D - Incorrect: Upgrading storage class may improve access times but doesn't address the core issue of high CPU usage.

QUESTION 45

Answer - C) Distribute the processing load across a cluster of Compute Engine instances using a load balancer.

Option A - Incorrect: Adjusting the SLO may not solve the underlying issue and could compromise service quality.
Option B - Incorrect: Simply upgrading the instance might not be sufficient for peak load times.
Option C - Correct: Using a cluster with a load balancer can effectively distribute the load and enhance processing efficiency.
Option D - Incorrect: Backup instances are more of a failover solution and might not provide continuous load handling.

QUESTION 46

Answer - D) Store encryption keys in Cloud Key Management Service (KMS) and enable automatic key rotation.

Option A - Incorrect: Hard-coding credentials is a security risk and not recommended.
Option B - Correct: Using an IAM provider ensures secure and controlled access to sensitive data.
Option C - Incorrect: Regularly generating new credentials can be complex and error-prone.
Option D - Correct: Utilizing Cloud KMS for key management with rotation enhances data security.

QUESTION 47

Answer - B) Configure a liveness probe for the microservice in question, which restarts the pod when it becomes unresponsive.

Option A - Incorrect: Readiness probes are used to determine if a pod is ready to serve traffic, not to handle performance issues.
Option B - Correct: A liveness probe can automatically restart pods that are experiencing issues, offering a temporary workaround.
Option C - Incorrect: Custom scripts require additional maintenance and are less integrated with Kubernetes' native functionalities.
Option D - Incorrect: Periodic restarts via the CI/CD pipeline do not directly address the unpredictable nature of the latency issue.

QUESTION 48

Answer - E) Enable automated container image updates in your CI/CD pipeline to keep dependencies current.

Option A focuses on traffic inspection and doesn't directly address code vulnerabilities or dependencies.
Option B is a valid practice but may not be efficient for containerized microservices at scale.
Option C is the recommended approach as it integrates scanning into the CI/CD pipeline to address vulnerabilities.
Option D provides runtime protection but doesn't directly handle code vulnerabilities and dependency updates.

QUESTION 49

C) Prepare an incident analysis report summarizing the issues, insights, and a structured set of remedial tasks. Share it solely with the requesting department head.

Option C is the correct choice because it provides a summarized incident analysis report with issues, insights, and structured remedial tasks, shared exclusively with the requesting department head.
Option A includes detailed information and accountability but has a narrow distribution.
Option B summarizes the issues and insights but lacks individual accountability and corrective actions, with broader distribution.
Option D is similar to Option B but lacks individual accountability and corrective actions, making Option C the most appropriate choice.

QUESTION 50

Answer - B) Evaluate the canary alongside the ongoing stable production release.

Option B is the recommended setup for canary analysis in a SaaS environment as it allows you to evaluate the canary alongside the ongoing stable production release, providing real-time performance insights.
Options A, C, and D do not offer the same real-time context for analysis, making option B the preferred choice.

PRACTICE TEST 2 - QUESTIONS ONLY

QUESTION 1

Your company is managing a complex multi-cloud environment with resources spread across Google Cloud, AWS, and Azure. You need to implement a unified monitoring and alerting solution for all these environments. What approach should you take to achieve this, considering the Google Cloud DevOps best practices?

A) Use Google Cloud Operations for monitoring Google Cloud resources, set up AWS CloudWatch for AWS resource monitoring, and implement Azure Monitor for Azure resource monitoring

B) Leverage Google Cloud Monitoring for AWS and Azure resources, utilize Google Cloud Pub/Sub for cross-cloud event streaming, and implement Google Cloud Security Command Center for cross-cloud security

C) Implement Google Cloud VPN for secure cross-cloud communication, configure Google Cloud Identity and Access Management (IAM) for access control, and use Google Cloud Armor for DDoS protection

D) Set up Google Cloud Spanner for distributed database management, utilize Google Cloud CDN for content delivery, and deploy Google Cloud Load Balancing for traffic distribution

E) Use Google Cloud Deployment Manager for multi-cloud resource provisioning, implement Google Cloud Dataprep for data transformation, and configure Google Cloud Functions for serverless computing

F) Implement Google Cloud Cost Management tools for cost optimization, set up Google Cloud Storage for cross-cloud data backup, and deploy Google Cloud Memorystore for caching across clouds.

QUESTION 2

Your organization is managing a large-scale application on Google Cloud. You want to improve security by ensuring that all Compute Engine instances use authorized and verified container images. Which approach should you take to achieve this goal while minimizing manual efforts and ensuring compliance with company policies?

A) Transfer the container monitoring reports from Operations Suite to BigQuery.

B) Assemble a dashboard in Data Studio.

C) Circulate the dashboard to your team members.

QUESTION 3

You are planning to deploy a critical update to your microservices-based application running on Google Kubernetes Engine (GKE). To minimize potential disruptions, you want to implement a canary deployment strategy. Which two Kubernetes concepts or techniques should you consider for this purpose? I. Use a Helm chart for package management. 2. Implement a DaemonSet for controlling pod placement. 3. Utilize Istio for traffic routing. 4. Configure a Deployment with a subset of pods for testing.

A) 1 and 2

B) 2 and 4

C) 3 and 4

D) 1 and 3

QUESTION 4

You are responsible for optimizing the CI/CD pipeline for your organization's cloud-native applications on Google Cloud. Which two practices should you prioritize to achieve this? I. Implement containerization using Docker to create consistent and portable build artifacts. 2. Utilize Jenkins as the sole CI/CD tool to centralize all pipeline tasks. 3. Integrate automated testing into the pipeline to catch issues early. 4. Leverage Google Kubernetes Engine (GKE) for container orchestration and deployment.

A) 1 and 2
B) 2 and 3
C) 3 and 4
D) 1 and 4

QUESTION 5

As the manager of a high-traffic media streaming service on GKE with various microservices, how can you best determine which containers are consuming the most CPU and memory resources?

A) Deploy Prometheus to collect and aggregate container logs, then analyze data in Grafana.
 B) Implement Cloud Logging to funnel application logs into BigQuery, cluster logs by container, and analyze resource usage for CPU and memory.
 C) Leverage the Cloud Monitoring API to create custom metrics and categorize containers into clusters.
 D) Utilize Cloud Monitoring with GKE support.

QUESTION 6

In the aftermath of a significant network disruption, you're required to brief key stakeholders as per Site Reliability Engineering practices. What should be your initial action?

A) Craft a comprehensive incident report for distribution among the stakeholders.
 B) Circulate the Incident Summary Document to every stakeholder immediately.
 C) Individually phone each stakeholder to detail the events that transpired.
 D) Instruct the network engineer at fault to compose a personal apology letter to every stakeholder.

QUESTION 7

You're examining your media processing workflow in Google Cloud's Dataflow with the aim of minimizing repetitive tasks and shortening job execution times. What strategies should you consider? (Choose two.)

A) Segment the automation procedures into finer-grained components.
 B) Implement automatic progression confirmations transferring from the staging area to the production zone.
 C) Run a script to facilitate the setup of the media processing workflow in Google Cloud Dataflow.
 D) Set up an alert to inform the designated team to proceed with the next phase when human input is needed.
 E) Increase the number of personnel to execute hands-on steps.

QUESTION 8

Your team is deploying a new video processing application on Google Cloud, expected to have fluctuating demand, with an estimated average CPU utilization of 30%. The application runs on a GKE Autopilot cluster, with critical importance on cost optimization and high availability across two zones. Considering the variable workloads and the need to ensure uninterrupted service, how would you configure the resources?

A) Rely on GKE Autopilot's default settings as it automatically adjusts resources based on demand.
B) Set up a vertical pod autoscaler and a custom node pool with larger machine types to handle potential spikes in demand.
C) Implement a horizontal pod autoscaler and enable multi-zone replication to ensure availability.
D) Increase the cluster size by 50% to handle potential spikes and employ a horizontal pod autoscaler.
E) Manually adjust node pools based on weekly demand forecasts and implement a vertical pod autoscaler.

QUESTION 9

You are planning to deploy a resource-intensive machine learning application that requires real-time data processing and autoscaling in multiple regions on Google Cloud. The application demands high memory and CPU resources. What should be your initial step to ensure smooth deployment?

A) Choose high-memory machine types for the Managed Instance Group configuration.
B) Utilize Google Cloud's Monitoring and Logging services to predict resource usage based on simulations.
C) Start with deployment in one region, using a global load balancer to manage traffic.
D) Verify that your resource needs are within Google Cloud's per-region CPU and memory quota limits.
E) Implement a custom script to automatically adjust resources based on real-time data processing demands.

QUESTION 10

You are deploying a Cloud Run service that interacts with a database hosted on Cloud SQL. The database connection requires a username and password for access. What is the most secure way to store and access these credentials in line with Google Cloud best practices?

A) Store the username and password as plaintext environment variables in the Cloud Run service.
B) Encrypt the credentials using Cloud KMS and store them in a Compute Engine instance for retrieval by Cloud Run.
C) Save the credentials in Secret Manager and reference them in Cloud Run using the Secret Manager API.
D) Keep the credentials in a configuration file within the Cloud Source Repositories and pull them into Cloud Run during deployment.
E) Use Application Layer Encryption with Cloud KMS to encrypt the credentials and then store them as environment variables in Cloud Run.

QUESTION 11

Your cloud-based CRM system frequently faces disruptions due to developers deploying untested features directly to production. You need to revise the deployment process to prevent these disruptions. Which approach would you recommend?

A) Require all new features to undergo a peer review process before being deployed to the production environment.

B) Establish a multi-stage deployment pipeline, including a pre-production environment for integration and stress testing.

C) Limit production deployments to once a month to ensure thorough testing and review of all new features.

D) Mandate that all development be done in a production-like environment using containerized microservices.

E) Introduce a policy of rolling back any update that causes issues, relying on rapid response rather than pre-deployment testing.

QUESTION 12

Your organization's development team is working on a microservices-based application hosted on GKE in the asia-southeast1 region. The CI/CD pipeline is located in the us-central1 region. To ensure efficient deployment of container images to your GKE clusters, where should you store these images?

A) Store the images in a Compute Engine instance within the asia-southeast1 region.

B) Use Google Container Registry with the us.gcr.io hostname for image storage.

C) Push the images to Google Container Registry using the asia.gcr.io hostname.

D) Store the images in a third-party container registry service located in the us-central1 region.

E) Implement a custom solution using Cloud Storage in the asia-southeast1 region for image storage.

QUESTION 13

As part of your CI/CD pipeline, processed data files are generated by a machine learning model and stored in GCS. Each data file must be traceable to the specific commit in your version control that triggered the model run. How should you implement this traceability?

A) Embed the commit hash in the filename of each data file stored in GCS.

B) Utilize GCS object versioning and map each version to the corresponding commit hash in your version control.

C) Store the commit hash as a label on each GCS object when the data file is uploaded.

D) Create separate GCS buckets for each commit, storing the relevant data files within them.

E) Maintain a separate database that maps the commit hashes to the corresponding GCS object URLs.

QUESTION 14

Your organization is scaling its use of Google Cloud services and requires a robust IaC approach to manage a growing number of Compute Engine instances. The goal is to ensure configuration consistency and automate the provisioning process. What solution should you adopt?

A) Set up a GitLab CI/CD pipeline that triggers Terraform scripts to provision and configure Compute Engine instances on code commits.

B) Develop a custom application on App Engine that periodically checks and aligns the Compute Engine instances with Terraform configurations.

C) Implement a series of Cloud Functions that are triggered by Pub/Sub messages to apply Terraform configurations to Compute Engine instances.

D) Configure a Cloud Build pipeline that runs Terraform scripts to manage Compute Engine instances upon detecting changes in the configuration repository.

E) Use a manually triggered Jenkins job on a Compute Engine VM to apply Terraform configurations for provisioning and managing instances.

QUESTION 15

Your organization is planning to migrate a web application to Google Cloud, requiring the ability to route traffic based on user roles and to support multiple versions for A/B testing. Which deployment approach and infrastructure would best meet these needs?

A) Deploy the application to Google Kubernetes Engine (GKE) with Anthos Service Mesh, using HTTP headers for role-based routing and supporting multiple versions for A/B testing.

B) Migrate the application to App Engine and utilize its traffic splitting feature to manage different versions based on user roles.

C) Host the application on Compute Engine and implement a custom load balancer to route traffic based on user roles and manage versioning.

D) Use Cloud Run to deploy the application, leveraging its traffic splitting capabilities to route different user roles to specific revisions.

E) Move the application to Cloud Functions, creating separate functions for each user role and version for A/B testing.

QUESTION 16

Your team has developed a custom dashboard in Google Cloud Operations Suite to monitor a critical application. You need to provide read-only access to the dashboard for an external auditor. What's the most appropriate way to share the dashboard while maintaining data integrity?

A) Share the dashboard with the auditor's Google account and grant full access rights.

B) Export the dashboard as a JSON file and send it to the auditor.

C) Create a temporary access link to the dashboard with view-only permissions for the auditor.

D) Duplicate the dashboard and provide a copy to the auditor.

QUESTION 17

Your organization stores data processing scripts in Cloud Source Repositories, and you want to create an automated workflow to run the latest script version on Google Compute Engine (GCE) instances whenever a new version is committed. You aim to minimize setup complexity. What should you do?

A) Deploy a custom service in App Engine to invoke Cloud Functions.

B) Utilize Cloud Pub/Sub to trigger a Cloud Build workflow.

C) Implement Cloud Pub/Sub to trigger a custom orchestrator service hosted on Compute Engine.

D) Configure Cloud Scheduler to trigger a Cloud Build workflow.

QUESTION 18

Your team is responsible for managing a large-scale web application on Google Cloud. You want to ensure that the application is highly available and can recover quickly from failures. What architectural approach should you follow to achieve this goal effectively?

A) Deploy the application on a single instance in a single zone to minimize complexity.
B) Use Google Cloud Load Balancing to distribute traffic across multiple instances in multiple zones with autohealing enabled.
C) Implement a backup strategy to periodically replicate data to an on-premises data center.
D) Set up separate instances for different application components to achieve isolation.

QUESTION 19

Your healthcare technology firm is deploying a patient management system for a national health event, expecting a substantial increase in user traffic. To prepare for potential outages due to high demand, what steps should you take? (Choose two.)

A) Implement continuous monitoring using Cloud Monitoring to track essential system metrics and set up alerts for critical thresholds.
B) Configure Cloud Monitoring to send notifications for each common failure observed in your system's operations.
C) Monitor database performance and storage utilization regularly.
D) Employ a serverless architecture to handle the surge in traffic efficiently.
E) Assess the anticipated traffic increase and request necessary quota adjustments ahead of time.

QUESTION 20

Your organization relies on Apache Maven running on Google Cloud Compute Engine instances for software build automation. You are tasked with introducing configuration management automation using Ansible, and it's essential to ensure that the Ansible Maven instance has the necessary authorization to manage Google Cloud assets while adhering to Google Cloud's recommended practices. What should you do?

A) Implement a Terraform module to enable Secret Manager to obtain credentials.
B) Ensure that the Maven Compute Engine instance is associated with a linked service account containing the required Identity and Access Management (1AM) roles.
C) Add the gcloud auth application-default login command to the Maven build process before executing Ansible playbooks.
D) Create a dedicated service account exclusively for the Ansible host, download the service account key, and set the GOOGLE_CREDENTIALS environment variable within the Maven environment.

QUESTION 21

Your team experienced a critical application outage that disrupted customer services. You are tasked with creating a post-mortem report to prevent similar outages in the future. What should you include in the report?

A) A list of customer complaints received during the outage.
B) An analysis of the impact of the outage on revenue.

C) A detailed timeline of events leading up to and during the outage.
D) Personal assessments of team members' performance.
E) Root cause analysis and recommended actions to prevent future outages.

QUESTION 22

Your team is launching a web application on Google Cloud that must be available across multiple geographic regions to ensure low-latency access for users worldwide. Which strategy should you adopt to achieve this goal?

A) Deploy the application in a single region with a global load balancer to handle traffic distribution.
B) Utilize the smallest available instance type to minimize costs while ensuring scalability.
C) Continuously monitor resource utilization and adjust instance counts to meet varying traffic demands.
D) Implement the application in multiple regions and configure a global load balancer to distribute traffic based on proximity to users.

QUESTION 23

You are responsible for managing a Google Kubernetes Engine (GKE) cluster used for your company's e-commerce platform. To meet security requirements, you need to restrict external access to the Kubernetes API server. Which GKE feature should you use?

A) Node pools
B) VPC Peering
C) Master Authorized Networks
D) GKE Private Clusters

QUESTION 24

You oversee a network of Kubernetes clusters on Google Cloud for a retail company, and ensuring the security and compliance of these clusters is a top priority. What steps should you take to meet these requirements effectively?

A) Use separate clusters for each application without specific security configurations to simplify management.
B) Implement Google Kubernetes Engine (GKE) Autopilot clusters for automated security and compliance management.
C) Manually configure Kubernetes clusters to meet security and compliance standards and periodically audit the configurations.
D) Deploy unmanaged clusters without any additional security measures for cost-effectiveness.

QUESTION 25

Your company uses Google Cloud to host its internal applications. You've been asked to set up access for a new operational team that needs to monitor application performance but should not modify any configurations. Which approach aligns best with the principle of least privilege while meeting the team's needs?

A) Assign the Project Editor role to the operational team.

B) Provide the operational team with the Monitoring Viewer role.
C) Grant the operational team the Monitoring Admin role.
D) Allocate the Custom Role with tailored permissions for monitoring.
E) Give the operational team the Project Viewer role.

QUESTION 26

In a cloud-based enterprise software company, the SRE team and the Application Development team are tasked with collaborative management of a CRM system. How should responsibilities be allocated between these teams for optimal operation and development?

A) SRE team: Manage cloud infrastructure; App Dev team: Code development and set SLIs/SLOs.
B) SRE team: Infrastructure and on-call duties; Shared: Code critique and SLI/SLO development; App Dev team: Code deployment.
C) SRE team: On-call and SLI/SLO setting; App Dev team: Code development and performance monitoring.
D) Shared: Infrastructure management and code deployment; SRE team: SLI/SLO setting; App Dev team: On-call duties.
E) SRE team: Cloud resource management; App Dev team: Code development; Shared: On-call duties and SLI/SLO development.

QUESTION 27

As a cloud architect, you are setting up an SLO for a cloud storage service, aiming for at least 99.9% data availability over a calendar year. Which metric and evaluation method would best suit this objective?

A) Availability metric with a window-based method of evaluation.
B) Data retrieval time metric with a request-based method of evaluation.
C) Data integrity metric with a window-based method of evaluation.
D) Availability metric with a request-based method of evaluation.
E) Data replication metric with a window-based method of evaluation.

QUESTION 28

As a DevOps engineer, you are tasked with setting up a CI/CD pipeline for an application hosted on Google Kubernetes Engine. The application utilizes several microservices, each managed by different teams. How should you structure the CI/CD process to ensure efficient and error-free deployments?

A) Configure Jenkins to deploy all microservices simultaneously after a weekly code review.
B) Set up individual Cloud Build triggers for each microservice, executing tests upon pull requests to their respective branches.
C) Mandate that all microservices be deployed manually by their respective teams to allow for thorough testing.
D) Implement a single GitHub Actions workflow that tests and deploys all microservices together for every commit.
E) Use Cloud Build to run integration tests nightly, aggregating all microservices changes made during the day.

QUESTION 29

Your organization requires centralized logging for its multi-regional Google Kubernetes Engine (GKE) clusters to enhance monitoring and compliance. How do you ensure all GKE nodes automatically forward logs to Cloud Operations?

A) Manually install the logging agent on each GKE node using kubectl commands.
 B) Use a DaemonSet to deploy the Stackdriver Logging Agent to each node in your GKE clusters.
 C) Rely on GKE's default logging mechanism, assuming it automatically integrates with Cloud Operations.
 D) Create a custom GKE node image with the logging agent pre-installed and use it for all future cluster deployments.
 E) Schedule a Cloud Function to periodically install the logging agent on new GKE nodes.

QUESTION 30

You are overseeing a hybrid cloud environment with applications running on Google Cloud and on-premises data centers. To ensure effective capacity planning, you need to monitor disk usage and I/O operations across both environments. What is the best approach to streamline this monitoring process?

A) Set up individual monitoring solutions for each environment and manually compile reports for analysis.
 B) Implement Cloud Monitoring agents across both cloud and on-premises environments to collect disk metrics.
 C) Use native tools for disk monitoring in Google Cloud and third-party tools for on-premises, integrating data via custom scripts.
 D) Install a comprehensive APM solution that supports hybrid environments and configure it to send data to Cloud Monitoring.
 E) Rely solely on Cloud Monitoring for Google Cloud and perform periodic audits for on-premises disk usage.

QUESTION 31

You are tasked with enhancing the monitoring strategy for a cloud-based service. What approach should you consider?

A) Implementing manual log analysis for identifying issues.
B) Setting up alerts based solely on CPU utilization.
C) Implementing distributed tracing to track requests across microservices.
D) Reducing the frequency of monitoring checks to conserve resources.

QUESTION 32

Your team relies on WebSocket connections to interact with a public Cloud Run service hosted at the https://api-financialxy.z.run.app URL. To ensure smooth validation of new service revisions before client access, what approach should you take?

A) Assign the roles/run.invoker role to the development team members for testing, using the https://api-financialxy.private.run.app URL.
B) Use the curl -H "Authorization:Bearer $(gcloud auth print-identity-token)" command to authenticate, and test using the https://api-financialxy.z.run.app URL in a private manner.

C) Deploy the report-service with the --no-traffic --tag dev options, and test it at https://dev-api-financialxy.z.run.app.

D) Update the traffic for the report-service using the gcloud run services update-traffic command, targeting the latest revision, and test at https://api-financialxy.z.run.app.

QUESTION 33

You are tasked with establishing a new Google Cloud setup for a telecommunications company. The company has voiced concerns regarding security risks associated with the utilization of persistent credentials within Google Cloud. Your responsibility is to devise a strategy that completely mitigates the hazards linked to JSON service account key usage while also minimizing operational overhead. What approach should you employ?

A) Allocate specific IAM roles to designated teams for service account key management.

B) Tailor predefined roles to remove permissions related to creating service account keys.

C) Impose organization-level constraints to prevent service account key creation.

D) Enact policies to control service account key uploads.

QUESTION 34

Your organization is managing a Google Kubernetes Engine (GKE) cluster that hosts a mission-critical application. You want to ensure that the application can recover quickly from node failures. Which GKE feature should you leverage, and how should you configure it for optimal resilience?

A) Use Regional Clusters to span multiple zones within a region, ensuring that the application can continue running even if one zone experiences issues.

B) Deploy a separate standby cluster in a different region to serve as a failover option in case of regional outages.

C) Implement Vertical Pod Autoscaling to adjust the resource requests of pods dynamically, optimizing their performance during node failures.

D) Set up Node Pools with different instance types and distribution strategies to maximize the likelihood of a healthy node in the event of a failure.

QUESTION 35

Your organization is deploying a healthcare service using Cloud Build and needs to handle sensitive information like API keys securely within the build process. What is the best approach to integrate these secrets with minimal disruption to your existing workflows?

A) Implement encryption and decryption logic within your application code to handle sensitive information securely.

B) Store API keys in environment variables and configure Cloud Build to access them directly.

C) Create a new Cloud Storage bucket and store sensitive information with object-level permissions configured for Cloud Build access.

D) Utilize Google Cloud's Secret Manager service to securely store and manage sensitive information, integrating them into your Cloud Build deployment script.

QUESTION 36

Your role involves managing a cloud-based e-commerce platform on Google Cloud Platform (GCP). You've noticed that confidential customer purchase data is unintentionally being logged and is collected through Cloud Logging. This sensitive information is marked with the label "PurchaseData." What should you do to securely store these logs for compliance reasons and prevent their exposure through Cloud Logging?

A) Configure a custom log filter in Cloud Logging to detect the "PurchaseData" label, create a log sink directed to Cloud Storage, and set up a log exclusion based on the "PurchaseData" filter.
 B) Define a basic log filter in Cloud Logging to identify the "PurchaseData" label and set up a log sink targeted at a Cloud Storage bucket to archive these entries.
 C) Utilize a Fluentd filter plugin with the Cloud Logging Agent to filter out log entries tagged with "PurchaseData," and route the filtered entries to a dedicated Cloud Storage bucket for secure storage.
 D) Implement a custom log sink in Cloud Logging to route logs with the "PurchaseData" label directly to Cloud Storage while excluding them from regular Cloud Logging processing.

QUESTION 37

You are managing a cloud-based HR management system, and a recent system disruption has prompted a postmortem review to prevent similar incidents. How should you allocate responsibility for postmortem resolution tasks?

A) Assign a dedicated task owner for each resolution task and involve collaborators as needed.
 B) Nominate collaborators without assigning explicit ownership to promote a non-punitive postmortem atmosphere.
 C) Allocate multiple task owners for each issue to ensure swift problem resolution.
 D) Designate the head of HR as the primary owner of all resolution tasks due to their overall responsibility for system stability.

QUESTION 38

Your video processing service on Google Cloud encounters recurrent brief interruptions, where instances briefly become unresponsive but recover automatically within seconds. You receive alerts for each occurrence. To improve service reliability following Site Reliability Engineering (SRE) principles, what should you do?

A) Modify the Service Level Objective (SLO) to accommodate these frequent restarts within the error budget.
 B) Generate a detailed incident report for every alert received to analyze the root cause.
 C) Distribute alert notifications among team members across different geographical regions.
 D) Implement a mechanism to suppress notifications for events that do not require immediate intervention.

QUESTION 39

You are tasked with overseeing the expenditure of various App Engine applications deployed for different departments. Each department's application is hosted on its unique set of App Engine instances within the same project. What approach should you take to determine the cost for each department's application usage?

A) Assign a specific naming convention to each App Engine instance based on the department, export usage reports to a Cloud Storage bucket, and analyze costs using Dataflow.
B) Utilize department-specific labels for each App Engine instance, configure BigQuery for billing export, and analyze costs by querying labels.
C) Attach metadata to each App Engine instance indicative of the department, set up Cloud Monitoring to export data to BigQuery, and use that data for cost analysis.
D) In the Google Cloud Console, manually track and calculate each department's App Engine usage and associated costs.
E) Develop a custom Cloud Function that monitors usage metrics of App Engine instances per department and calculates costs, storing the data in Firestore.

QUESTION 40

As an SRE, you are responsible for the operational success of a cloud-based data processing service on Google Cloud. The development team is creating a new version of the service. When and how should you provide your operational expertise?

A) Lead an alpha testing phase focusing on system resilience and scalability, then share the test results with the development team for improvements.
B) Get involved after the service passes the initial development phase, deploy it in a controlled environment, and identify any operational inefficiencies.
C) Participate in the initial design discussions, offering insights on system scalability, reliability, and cloud resource optimization.
D) Review the service's operational performance once it's in use by a specific team, and then provide recommendations based on the collected data.

QUESTION 41

Your team manages a cloud-based API that frequently experiences short-lived spikes in traffic, leading to a high volume of non-critical performance alerts. This is affecting team morale. How should you optimize alert handling to reduce fatigue while maintaining service reliability?

A) Create comprehensive reports for each spike in traffic and alert.
B) Rotate alert responsibilities among team members in different time zones.
C) Refine the Service Level Indicators (SLIs) to better reflect critical performance thresholds.
D) Filter out alerts that are resolved automatically within a predefined timeframe.

QUESTION 42

As part of a DevOps initiative, a company is setting up isolated environments for development, QA, and production using Terraform and GKE. Anthos Config Management is used for Kubernetes configurations. What is the recommended structure for the source control repositories to ensure efficient management and deployment?

A) One repository for Terraform scripts with sub-directories for each environment, another repository for Anthos Config Management with branches for each environment, and separate repositories for application code with development and release branches.

B) Separate repositories for each environment's Terraform scripts, a unified repository for Anthos Config Management with directories for each environment, and one repository for all application code with feature flags.

C) Unified repository for all Terraform and Anthos configurations with branches for different environments, and separate repositories for each application service with branches for features and releases.

D) Distinct repositories for Terraform configurations per environment, individual repositories for Anthos Config Management per environment, and separate repositories for each application service with feature-based branching.

QUESTION 43

You're overseeing the infrastructure management of a cloud-based healthcare application using Terraform. The team is expanding, and you need a robust method to handle configuration changes and document updates effectively. What approach should you implement?

A) Adopt a shared cloud drive for storing Terraform configuration files, with a folder structure based on the environment. Use a manual versioning system and document changes in a shared log.

B) Use a centralized version control system like Git for Terraform files, incorporating a workflow with feature branches, pull requests, and code reviews for all changes.

C) Maintain Terraform configurations on individual developer machines, synchronizing changes to a central server at the end of each day. Use a log file to track changes.

D) Store Terraform configurations in a collaborative online code editor, allowing real-time editing by team members. Back up configurations to a version-controlled repository periodically.

QUESTION 44

You oversee an online booking system on App Engine, which recently experienced slowdowns during peak usage hours. The system uses Cloud SQL for data storage and Cloud Storage for additional resources. You need to prepare for future spikes in user activity. What measure should you implement to improve system performance?

A) Increase the number of App Engine instances to handle higher loads.

B) Migrate the booking system from App Engine to Compute Engine for better control over the infrastructure.

C) Implement read replicas for the Cloud SQL database to distribute the query load.

D) Change the Cloud Storage class to regional storage to enhance data access speed.

QUESTION 45

Your cloud-based data analysis service occasionally experiences downtime due to CPU overutilization on its Compute Engine instance. This affects your ability to meet the defined SLO. Which approach should you consider to ensure more consistent uptime?

A) Lower the Service Level Objective to match the current capabilities of the service.

B) Upgrade the Compute Engine instance to a more powerful machine type with additional CPU resources.

C) Implement an autoscaling group of Compute Engine instances across multiple zones to handle varying loads.

D) Create additional fixed Compute Engine instances in various zones as failovers for the primary instance.

QUESTION 46

As a cloud engineer, you need to implement a system where your team receives instant messaging alerts for high-priority incidents identified by Cloud Monitoring. What is the most effective method to set up these alerts?

A) Directly integrate Cloud Monitoring with a messaging app to send alerts to team members.
B) Configure Cloud Monitoring alerts to use a Webhook that connects to an external service, which then sends messages to a team messaging app.
C) Set up Cloud Monitoring to send alerts to an email address that is configured to forward messages to a team messaging app.
D) Use a third-party alert forwarding service that takes Cloud Monitoring alerts and sends them to your chosen instant messaging platform.

QUESTION 47

You are managing a GKE-based application consisting of several microservices. One of the services occasionally crashes after a specific duration of activity. While a permanent fix is in progress, you need an interim solution to ensure continuous operation. What action should you take?

A) Add a liveness probe to the Deployment configuration of the affected microservice to automatically restart it upon failure.
B) Set up a Cloud Function to monitor the service and restart it when it becomes unresponsive.
C) Implement a monitoring alert to notify the team whenever the service goes down, so they can manually restart it.
D) Configure a cron job within the cluster to periodically restart the service before it reaches its failure point.

QUESTION 48

Your company has adopted a microservices architecture for its applications, deployed in containers via a CI/CD pipeline. You've been tasked with enhancing security by addressing code vulnerabilities and outdated dependencies. What is your recommended approach?

A) Utilize traditional security tools to scan the container images for vulnerabilities.
B) Implement a continuous monitoring solution to detect and respond to security threats in real-time.
C) Automate the process of updating container images and their dependencies in the CI/CD pipeline.
D) Conduct periodic penetration testing on the live microservices environment.
E) Deploy a network intrusion detection system (NIDS) to protect against external threats.

QUESTION 49

In a DevOps-oriented transition, your application faced sporadic performance issues recently. A leader from a different department asks for a formal rundown of the incident to facilitate preventive measures. What action should you take?

A) Create an incident report outlining the problems and insights gained, and distribute it exclusively to the department leader who requested it.
B) Generate an incident report summarizing the issues and insights, and share it across the company's technical documentation repository for reference.
C) Formulate an incident report detailing the problems, insights, individual accountability, and a structured set of remedial tasks. Share it solely with the inquiring department leader.
D) Develop an incident report detailing the problems, insights, and a structured set of corrective actions. Disseminate it across the company's technical documentation platform for broader access.

QUESTION 50

Your team is using Spinnaker to manage deployments in a cloud-native microservices application. A canary release phase has been integrated into your deployment pipeline. What is the appropriate configuration for canary analysis in this microservices environment?

A) Compare the canary with a baseline performance from a pre-defined stable release.
B) Evaluate the canary alongside the existing stable production release.
C) Analyze the canary in isolation without any performance comparison.
D) Assess the canary against a synthetic test environment.

PRACTICE TEST 2 - ANSWERS ONLY

QUESTION 1

Answer - B) Leverage Google Cloud Monitoring for AWS and Azure resources, utilize Google Cloud Pub/Sub for cross-cloud event streaming, and implement Google Cloud Security Command Center for cross-cloud security.

Option B aligns with best practices for implementing a unified monitoring and alerting solution across multi-cloud environments, including the use of Google Cloud services and cross-cloud event streaming. Option A suggests using different monitoring solutions for each cloud provider, which does not provide a unified approach.
Options C, D, E, and F mention various services but do not directly address the unified monitoring requirements.

QUESTION 2

Answer - A) Transfer the container monitoring reports from Operations Suite to BigQuery.

Option A is the recommended approach. By transferring container monitoring reports to BigQuery, you can analyze the data, create interactive dashboards in Data Studio, and share them with your team members. This ensures improved security and compliance without extensive manual efforts.
Options B and C focus on dashboard creation and distribution but do not address the data transfer and analysis aspects.

QUESTION 3

Answer - D) 1 and 3

Options 1 and 3 are the recommended choices to implement a canary deployment strategy for a microservices-based application on Google Kubernetes Engine (GKE). Using Helm charts for package management allows for controlled updates, and utilizing Istio for traffic routing enables gradual deployment of the update.
Option 2, implementing a DaemonSet, is not typically used for canary deployments.
Option 4, configuring a Deployment with a subset of pods for testing, is a valid choice but not as relevant as the other options for canary deployments.

QUESTION 4

Answer - D) 1 and 4

To optimize the CI/CD pipeline for cloud-native applications on Google Cloud, you should:
- Implement containerization using Docker to create consistent and portable build artifacts (Option 1).
- Leverage Google Kubernetes Engine (GKE) for container orchestration and deployment (Option 4).
These practices ensure consistency, portability, and efficient deployment of cloud-native applications.
Option 2, using Jenkins as the sole tool, may not cover all pipeline tasks efficiently.
Option 3, integrating automated testing, is important but does not address containerization and orchestration.

QUESTION 5

Answer - B) Implement Cloud Logging to funnel application logs into BigQuery, cluster logs by container, and analyze resource usage for CPU and memory.

Option B is the correct choice as it efficiently allows you to analyze resource usage by aggregating application logs using Cloud Logging.
Option A introduces Prometheus and Grafana, which are not the most suitable for this scenario,
Option C suggests creating custom metrics, which may not be necessary,
Option D is too vague and doesn't provide a clear solution.

QUESTION 6

Answer - B) Circulate the Incident Summary Document to every stakeholder immediately.

Option B is the correct choice as it suggests circulating the Incident Summary Document to every stakeholder immediately, providing a concise overview of the incident.
Option A delays communication,
Option C is inefficient for a large number of stakeholders,
Option D is not the initial step and focuses on personal apologies rather than incident summary.

QUESTION 7

Answer - A and B

Option A - Segmenting automation procedures into finer-grained components reduces redundancy and streamlines the workflow, making it a valid optimization strategy.
Option B - Implementing automatic progression confirmations reduces the need for manual interventions, contributing to a more efficient workflow.
Options C, D, and E are not directly related to optimizing the workflow.

QUESTION 8

Answer - C) Implement a horizontal pod autoscaler and enable multi-zone replication to ensure availability.

A) Incorrect - GKE Autopilot's default settings may not be sufficient for cost optimization in fluctuating demand scenarios.
B) Incorrect - Vertical scaling alone might not be effective in handling variable workloads efficiently.
C) Correct - This approach ensures scalability for fluctuating workloads and high availability across zones.
D) Incorrect - A fixed increase in cluster size isn't cost-effective and may not align with actual demand.
E) Incorrect - Manual adjustments are less efficient and may not respond quickly to real-time demand changes.

QUESTION 9

Answer - D) Verify that your resource needs are within Google Cloud's per-region CPU and memory quota limits.

A) Incorrect - While high-memory machine types are important, verifying quota limits is the first step.

B) Incorrect - Monitoring services are useful but not the initial step in resource planning.

C) Incorrect - Starting in one region might not fulfill the requirement for multi-regional scaling.

D) Correct - Ensuring that the application's resource demands are within quota limits is crucial before deployment.

E) Incorrect - Custom scripts are helpful for managing resources but not the primary concern at the initial planning stage.

QUESTION 10

Answer - C) Save the credentials in Secret Manager and reference them in Cloud Run using the Secret Manager API.

A) Incorrect - Storing sensitive information as plaintext in environment variables is not secure.

B) Incorrect - Using a Compute Engine instance for storing credentials adds unnecessary complexity and potential security risks.

C) Correct - Secret Manager provides a secure and efficient way to manage sensitive information like database credentials.

D) Incorrect - Storing sensitive information in source code repositories, even in a configuration file, is not secure.

E) Incorrect - While Application Layer Encryption is secure, it's an overly complex solution for this scenario.

QUESTION 11

Answer - B) Establish a multi-stage deployment pipeline, including a pre-production environment for integration and stress testing.

A) Incorrect - While peer review is important, it does not replace the need for thorough testing in a controlled environment.

B) Correct - A multi-stage deployment pipeline allows for comprehensive testing and validation before features reach production.

C) Incorrect - Limiting deployment frequency does not necessarily ensure quality if adequate testing environments are not used.

D) Incorrect - Developing in a production-like environment is beneficial but should be part of a broader testing and deployment strategy.

E) Incorrect - Relying on rapid response is risky and can lead to frequent disruptions in the production environment.

QUESTION 12

Answer - C) Push the images to Google Container Registry using the asia.gcr.io hostname.

A) Incorrect - Using a Compute Engine instance for image storage is inefficient and not scalable.

B) Incorrect - Storing images in the us.gcr.io region may result in slower image pulls in the asia-southeast1 region.

C) Correct - Using the asia.gcr.io hostname ensures that images are stored closer to the GKE clusters, improving pull efficiency.

D) Incorrect - A third-party service in us-central1 might lead to slower image delivery due to regional distance.

E) Incorrect - While Cloud Storage is scalable, GCR is optimized for container image storage and delivery.

QUESTION 13

Answer - C) Store the commit hash as a label on each GCS object when the data file is uploaded.

A) Incorrect - Embedding the hash in the filename can lead to management complexities.
B) Incorrect - Object versioning in GCS does not provide a direct way to map to version control commits.
C) Correct - Using labels on GCS objects for commit hashes is an efficient way to maintain traceability.
D) Incorrect - Creating separate buckets for each commit is not scalable or practical.
E) Incorrect - Maintaining a separate database adds unnecessary complexity and potential for errors.

QUESTION 14

Answer - D) Configure a Cloud Build pipeline that runs Terraform scripts to manage Compute Engine instances upon detecting changes in the configuration repository.

A) Incorrect - While GitLab CI/CD is a valid approach, Cloud Build is more integrated with Google Cloud for IaC practices.
B) Incorrect - An App Engine custom application is not the ideal tool for managing infrastructure as code.
C) Incorrect - Cloud Functions are typically used for lighter, event-driven tasks, not for comprehensive infrastructure management.
D) Correct - Cloud Build automates the process of applying IaC practices, ensuring consistency and efficiency in managing Compute Engine instances.
E) Incorrect - A manually triggered Jenkins job does not fully automate the provisioning process and can lead to inconsistencies.

QUESTION 15

Answer - A) Deploy the application to Google Kubernetes Engine (GKE) with Anthos Service Mesh, using HTTP headers for role-based routing and supporting multiple versions for A/B testing.

A) Correct - GKE with Anthos Service Mesh offers advanced routing capabilities based on HTTP headers and supports multiple service versions for A/B testing.
B) Incorrect - App Engine's traffic splitting is based on IP address or cookie, not user roles.
C) Incorrect - Custom load balancers on Compute Engine are complex to set up for role-based routing and version management.
D) Incorrect - Cloud Run's traffic splitting does not support routing based on user roles.
E) Incorrect - Cloud Functions is not ideal for complex web applications requiring role-based traffic routing and version management.

QUESTION 16

Answer - C) Create a temporary access link to the dashboard with view-only permissions for the auditor.

Option C is the correct choice because it allows you to provide secure read-only access to the dashboard without compromising data integrity. Temporary access ensures that the auditor can review the data while maintaining control.
 Option A - Option A is incorrect because granting full access rights may not be appropriate for an

external auditor.
 Option B - Option B is incorrect because exporting as a JSON file may not provide real-time access and is not the most secure option.
 Option D - Option D is incorrect because duplicating the dashboard may lead to synchronization and maintenance challenges.

QUESTION 17

Answer - B) Utilize Cloud Pub/Sub to trigger a Cloud Build workflow.

Option B is the correct choice because using Cloud Pub/Sub to trigger a Cloud Build workflow when new code versions are committed provides automation while minimizing setup complexity.
 Option A - Option A introduces an additional layer of complexity with App Engine and Cloud Functions, which may not be necessary.
 Option C - Option C involves creating a custom orchestrator service, which may be more complex than needed for this task.
 Option D - Option D uses Cloud Scheduler, which is not the most suitable choice for triggering a build workflow when code changes occur.

QUESTION 18

Answer - B) Use Google Cloud Load Balancing to distribute traffic across multiple instances in multiple zones with autohealing enabled.

Option B is the correct choice because it leverages Google Cloud Load Balancing to distribute traffic across multiple instances in multiple zones, ensuring high availability and quick recovery from failures with autohealing.
 Option A - Option A deploys the application on a single instance, which lacks high availability.
 Option C - Option C mentions replicating data to an on-premises data center, which is not an effective approach for achieving high availability.
 Option D - Option D suggests isolating components but doesn't address high availability and failure recovery.

QUESTION 19

Answer - A) Implement continuous monitoring using Cloud Monitoring to track essential system metrics and set up alerts for critical thresholds.
 Answer - B) Configure Cloud Monitoring to send notifications for each common failure observed in your system's operations.

Option A and Option B are the correct choices.
 Option A - Implementing continuous monitoring with Cloud Monitoring helps track essential system metrics and set alerts for critical thresholds, ensuring robustness during high demand.
 Option C - Monitoring database performance and storage utilization is important but not directly related to addressing potential outages.
 Option D - Employing a serverless architecture is relevant but not specific to handling outages.
 Option E - Assessing traffic and requesting quota adjustments is a good practice but doesn't directly address ensuring system robustness during outages.

QUESTION 20

Answer - B) Ensure that the Maven Compute Engine instance is associated with a linked service account containing the required Identity and Access Management (1AM) roles.

Option B is the correct choice.
 Option B - Ensuring that the Maven Compute Engine instance is associated with a linked service account containing the necessary IAM roles aligns with Google Cloud's recommended practices for Ansible authorization.
 Option A - Implementing a Terraform module for Secret Manager is not directly related to Ansible authorization.
 Option C - Adding the gcloud auth application-default login command to the Maven build process is not a recommended practice for Ansible authorization.
 Option D - Creating a dedicated service account and setting GOOGLE_CREDENTIALS is a valid but more complex approach compared to Option B.

QUESTION 21

Answer - C) A detailed timeline of events leading up to and during the outage.
Answer - E) Root cause analysis and recommended actions to prevent future outages.

Explanation for Option C - A detailed timeline of events is crucial in understanding the sequence of actions and events that led to the outage, which is essential for identifying areas for improvement and prevention.
Explanation for Option E - Root cause analysis and recommended actions are vital for preventing future outages. They provide insights into the underlying causes and steps to take to avoid similar incidents.
Explanation for Option A - While customer complaints may be relevant, they are not the central focus of a post-mortem report aimed at preventing future outages.
Explanation for Option B - Analyzing the impact on revenue, while important, is not typically the primary focus of a post-mortem report focused on preventing outages.
Explanation for Option D - Personal assessments of team members' performance are not typically the primary content of a post-mortem report for outage prevention.

QUESTION 22

Answer - D) Implement the application in multiple regions and configure a global load balancer to distribute traffic based on proximity to users.

Explanation for Option D - Implementing the application in multiple regions and using a global load balancer that considers user proximity ensures low-latency access and aligns with the requirement for global availability.
Explanation for Option A - Deploying the application in a single region with a global load balancer may provide high availability but doesn't address the need for regional presence and low-latency access.
Explanation for Option B - Utilizing the smallest instance type for cost control is a valid consideration but doesn't ensure global availability or low-latency access.
Explanation for Option C - Monitoring resource utilization and adjusting instance counts is important for optimization but doesn't directly address the initial planning for global availability and low-latency access.

QUESTION 23

Answer - C) Master Authorized Networks

Option A) Node pools control worker nodes, not API server access.
Option B) VPC Peering connects VPC networks but doesn't directly restrict API server access.
Option D) GKE Private Clusters provide network isolation but are not focused on API server access control.
Option C) Master Authorized Networks allows you to restrict external access to the Kubernetes API server by specifying IP ranges that are allowed to connect, enhancing security for your GKE cluster.

QUESTION 24

B) Implement Google Kubernetes Engine (GKE) Autopilot clusters for automated security and compliance management.

Option B is the correct choice as it recommends implementing GKE Autopilot clusters, which provide automated security and compliance management. This aligns with the goal of ensuring security and compliance effectively for a retail company.
Option A suggests using separate clusters without specific security configurations, which may not meet security requirements.
Option C promotes manual configuration and auditing, which can be time-consuming and error-prone.
Option D advocates deploying unmanaged clusters without additional security measures, which can pose security risks.

QUESTION 25

Answer - B) Provide the operational team with the Monitoring Viewer role.

A) The Project Editor role offers broad permissions that include the ability to modify configurations, which is unnecessary for monitoring purposes.
B) This role is the most appropriate as it allows the team to monitor application performance without the ability to modify configurations.
C) The Monitoring Admin role includes permissions to modify monitoring configurations, which exceeds the team's requirements.
D) Creating a custom role might be unnecessary when a predefined role like Monitoring Viewer fits the requirement perfectly.
E) The Project Viewer role provides broader access to the project than necessary for the specific task of monitoring application performance.

QUESTION 26

Answer - B) SRE team: Infrastructure and on-call duties; Shared: Code critique and SLI/SLO development; App Dev team: Code deployment.

Option A - Separating SLI/SLO setting from SRE responsibilities is not optimal for integrated cloud operations.
Option B - This structure promotes collaborative development and operational excellence, aligning with best practices.
Option C - Excluding the App Dev team from SLI/SLO setting might lead to unrealistic service levels.

Option D - Shared infrastructure management can dilute accountability.
Option E - Excluding the App Dev team from on-call duties may lead to a disconnect between development and operational realities.

QUESTION 27

Answer - A) Availability metric with a window-based method of evaluation.

Option A - Availability measured over a set time window accurately reflects the year-long objective.
Option B - Data retrieval time is a performance metric, not directly related to availability.
Option C - Data integrity, while important, does not directly reflect availability.
Option D - A request-based method may not capture the long-term availability goal.
Option E - Data replication is a factor in availability but not a direct measure of it.

QUESTION 28

Answer - B) Set up individual Cloud Build triggers for each microservice, executing tests upon pull requests to their respective branches.

Option A - Simultaneous deployment of all microservices can be risky and does not allow for independent testing.
Option B - This approach allows for independent and automated testing of each microservice, ensuring that each team's changes are validated.
Option C - Manual deployment can lead to inconsistencies and delays.
Option D - A single workflow for all microservices might not cater to the specific needs of each service.
Option E - Nightly integration tests delay the feedback loop, potentially slowing down the development process.

QUESTION 29

Answer - B) Use a DaemonSet to deploy the Stackdriver Logging Agent to each node in your GKE clusters.

Option A - Manual installation is not scalable for large or dynamic GKE environments.
Option B - Deploying the logging agent via a DaemonSet ensures consistent and automated installation across all nodes.
Option C - GKE's default logging may not meet specific organizational requirements for centralized logging.
Option D - Custom images require maintenance and may not be as dynamic as a DaemonSet approach.
Option E - Cloud Functions are not designed for managing infrastructure agents and may not provide the necessary consistency.

QUESTION 30

Answer - B) Implement Cloud Monitoring agents across both cloud and on-premises environments to collect disk metrics.

Option A - Individual solutions create additional work and can lead to inconsistent reporting.
Option B - Cloud Monitoring agents can provide a unified and automated approach to gathering disk metrics in both environments.

Option C - While this approach is feasible, it may require additional effort to ensure consistent and integrated reporting.
Option D - A comprehensive APM solution might work but could introduce complexity and additional costs.
Option E - Periodic audits are not as effective as continuous monitoring for capacity planning.

QUESTION 31

Answer - C) Implementing distributed tracing to track requests across microservices.

Option A, manual log analysis, is time-consuming and less efficient than automated solutions.
Option B, setting up alerts based solely on CPU utilization, may not provide a comprehensive view of service health.
Option D, reducing the frequency of monitoring checks, can lead to delayed issue detection and is not recommended.

QUESTION 32

Answer - B) Use the curl -H "Authorization:Bearer $(gcloud auth print-identity-token)" command to authenticate, and test using the https://api-financialxy.z.run.app URL in a private manner.

Option A, assigning roles/run.invoker, does not involve authentication and private testing.
Option C, deploying with the dev tag, is related to deployment but not authentication.
Option D, updating traffic to the latest revision, does not address authentication for testing new revisions.

QUESTION 33

Answer - C) Impose organization-level constraints to prevent service account key creation.

Option A, allocating specific IAM roles, may not effectively address the issue of minimizing key usage.
Option B, tailoring predefined roles, could be complex and error-prone.
Option D, enacting policies, may not address the root concern of key creation.

QUESTION 34

Answer - A) Use Regional Clusters to span multiple zones within a region, ensuring that the application can continue running even if one zone experiences issues.

Option A is the correct choice because it suggests using Regional Clusters in GKE, which span multiple zones within a region, providing resilience to zone failures. This is a best practice for ensuring high availability without the complexity of deploying a separate standby cluster (Option B) or introducing complexities (Options C and D) that may not directly address node failures.

QUESTION 35

Answer - D) Utilize Google Cloud's Secret Manager service to securely store and manage sensitive information, integrating them into your Cloud Build deployment script.

Explanation:

Option D is the correct choice as it leverages Google Cloud's Secret Manager to securely store and manage sensitive information, seamlessly integrating them into the Cloud Build deployment script with proper security.
Option A suggests implementing encryption within application code, which may not be the best practice for managing secrets.
Option B proposes storing secrets in environment variables, which is not as secure and manageable as Secret Manager.
Option C suggests using a Cloud Storage bucket but lacks the security and management features of Google Cloud's Secret Manager.

QUESTION 36

Answer - A) Configure a custom log filter in Cloud Logging to detect the "PurchaseData" label, create a log sink directed to Cloud Storage, and set up a log exclusion based on the "PurchaseData" filter.

Option A is the correct choice as it aligns with best practices. It involves configuring a custom log filter to identify sensitive logs, directing them to Cloud Storage for secure storage, and excluding them from regular Cloud Logging to prevent exposure.
Option B is incorrect because it lacks the exclusion step, which is crucial for preventing exposure.
Option C is incorrect because it uses a Fluentd filter plugin with the Cloud Logging Agent but doesn't mention log exclusion.
Option D is incorrect because it lacks the customization required for secure storage and exclusion.

QUESTION 37

Answer - A) Assign a dedicated task owner for each resolution task and involve collaborators as needed.

Option A is the correct choice as it aligns with effective postmortem practices by assigning clear ownership while allowing collaboration.
Option B is incorrect as it lacks explicit ownership, which can lead to accountability issues.
Option C is incorrect as multiple owners may create confusion and delays.
Option D is incorrect as placing sole ownership on one individual may not involve the necessary expertise for resolution.

QUESTION 38

Answer - A) Modify the Service Level Objective (SLO) to accommodate these frequent restarts within the error budget.

Option A is the correct choice as it aligns with SRE principles by adjusting the SLO to account for frequent restarts, ensuring they fall within the error budget. This approach optimizes service reliability while maintaining stability.
Option B suggests generating detailed incident reports for every alert, which may be excessive for brief interruptions. Option C involves geographic distribution of alerts, which may not directly address the issue. Option D recommends suppressing notifications for non-intervention events, which may not optimize service reliability for this specific scenario.

QUESTION 39

Answer - B) Utilize department-specific labels for each App Engine instance, configure BigQuery for billing export, and analyze costs by querying labels.

Option A - Incorrect: This method is less direct and efficient compared to using BigQuery.
Option B - Correct: Labeling instances and using BigQuery for cost analysis is the most streamlined approach.
Option C - Incorrect: Attaching metadata and using Cloud Monitoring is more complex than necessary.
Option D - Incorrect: Manual tracking is inefficient and prone to errors.
Option E - Incorrect: Developing a custom function is overly complex for this task.

QUESTION 40

Answer - C) Participate in the initial design discussions, offering insights on system scalability, reliability, and cloud resource optimization.

Option A - Incorrect: Alpha testing is important but secondary to influencing the initial design.
Option B - Incorrect: Involvement after initial development may not address fundamental design challenges.
Option C - Correct: Providing input during the design phase allows for a more robust and efficient system from the start.
Option D - Incorrect: Feedback after deployment is reactive rather than proactive, missing early intervention opportunities.

QUESTION 41

Answer - D) Filter out alerts that are resolved automatically within a predefined timeframe.

Option A - Incorrect: Generating detailed reports for each spike can be unnecessary and time-consuming.
Option B - Incorrect: Rotating responsibilities may help but doesn't address the frequency of non-critical alerts.
Option C - Incorrect: Refining SLIs is useful but does not directly address alert fatigue.
Option D - Correct: Filtering out quickly resolved alerts can significantly reduce unnecessary notifications and team exhaustion.

QUESTION 42

Answer - A) One repository for Terraform scripts with sub-directories for each environment, another repository for Anthos Config Management with branches for each environment, and separate repositories for application code with development and release branches.

Option A - Correct: This setup maintains a clear organizational structure, ensuring that configurations for different environments are easily manageable while keeping application code separate.
Option B - Incorrect: Separate repositories for each environment's Terraform scripts can lead to fragmentation and duplication.
Option C - Incorrect: A unified repository for all configurations can become unwieldy and difficult to manage.
Option D - Incorrect: While this approach offers isolation, it may result in significant duplication and maintenance overhead.

QUESTION 43

Answer - B) Use a centralized version control system like Git for Terraform files, incorporating a workflow with feature branches, pull requests, and code reviews for all changes.

Option A - Incorrect: Shared cloud drives do not offer robust mechanisms for concurrent version control and change documentation.
Option B - Correct: A centralized version control system like Git, with a structured workflow, is ideal for collaborative and documented Terraform configuration management.
Option C - Incorrect: Individual management of configurations can lead to conflicts and lacks a reliable change tracking system.
Option D - Incorrect: While collaborative code editors are useful for real-time collaboration, they do not provide structured version control and review processes for Terraform files.

QUESTION 44

Answer - A) Increase the number of App Engine instances to handle higher loads.

Option A - Correct: Increasing App Engine instances can effectively handle increased load and improve performance.
Option B - Incorrect: Migrating to Compute Engine is a more complex solution and may not be necessary.
Option C - Incorrect: Read replicas can help with database loads but won't address overall system slowdowns.
Option D - Incorrect: Changing storage classes may not significantly impact the performance issues observed.

QUESTION 45

Answer - C) Implement an autoscaling group of Compute Engine instances across multiple zones to handle varying loads.

Option A - Incorrect: Reducing the SLO may not be acceptable for maintaining service quality.
Option B - Incorrect: A more powerful instance provides more resources but doesn't address demand spikes.
Option C - Correct: Autoscaling provides a dynamic way to adjust resources based on demand, improving uptime.
Option D - Incorrect: Fixed failover instances may not be as effective in managing fluctuating loads as autoscaling.

QUESTION 46

Answer - B) Configure Cloud Monitoring alerts to use a Webhook that connects to an external service, which then sends messages to a team messaging app.

Option A - Incorrect: Direct integration of Cloud Monitoring with messaging apps is not typically available.
Option B - Correct: Utilizing a Webhook to connect Cloud Monitoring with an external service for messaging is an efficient solution.
Option C - Incorrect: Email forwarding to a messaging app is less direct and may introduce delays.
Option D - Incorrect: While feasible, using a third-party forwarding service may not be as efficient as a

direct Webhook setup.

QUESTION 47

Answer - A) Add a liveness probe to the Deployment configuration of the affected microservice to automatically restart it upon failure.

Option A - Correct: Liveness probes in Kubernetes automatically restart containers that are no longer responsive, ensuring service continuity.
Option B - Incorrect: While possible, using Cloud Functions adds complexity and is not as efficient as Kubernetes-native solutions.
Option C - Incorrect: Manual intervention for restarts is not a scalable or reliable interim solution.
Option D - Incorrect: Scheduling periodic restarts might not align with the unpredictable timing of the service failure.

QUESTION 48

Answer - C) Automate the process of updating container images and their dependencies in the CI/CD pipeline.

Option A is not the best choice for microservices, as traditional tools may not be optimized for containerized environments.
Option B focuses on monitoring but doesn't directly address code vulnerabilities and outdated dependencies.
Option D is a valid practice but is not the most efficient way to address these specific issues.
Option E provides network-level protection but doesn't directly handle code vulnerabilities and dependency updates.

QUESTION 49

C) Formulate an incident report detailing the problems, insights, individual accountability, and a structured set of remedial tasks. Share it solely with the inquiring department leader.

Option C is the correct choice because it provides a comprehensive incident report with insights, individual accountability, and structured remedial tasks, which is shared with the department leader who requested it.
Option A lacks details on individual accountability and relies on a narrower distribution.
Option B distributes to the company's technical documentation repository but lacks individual accountability details.
Option D is similar to Option B but lacks individual accountability, making Option C more comprehensive.

QUESTION 50

Answer - B) Evaluate the canary alongside the existing stable production release.

Option B is the appropriate configuration for canary analysis in a microservices environment as it allows you to evaluate the canary alongside the existing stable production release, providing a real-world performance comparison.
Options A, C, and D do not offer the same real-world context, making option B the suitable choice.

PRACTICE TEST 3 - QUESTIONS ONLY

QUESTION 1

Your organization is planning to migrate a legacy monolithic application to a microservices architecture on Google Cloud. As the DevOps engineer, you are tasked with designing a secure and scalable CI/CD pipeline for this migration. Which combination of Google Cloud services and practices should you consider to meet these requirements?

A) Use Google Kubernetes Engine (GKE) for container orchestration, implement Google Cloud Build for automated builds, and set up Google Cloud Endpoints for API management
 B) Implement Google Cloud Security Command Center for vulnerability scanning, leverage Google Cloud Monitoring for resource monitoring, and use Google Artifact Registry for secure image storage
 C) Utilize Google Cloud Dataprep for data transformation, configure Google Cloud VPN for secure cross-cloud communication, and deploy Google Cloud Armor for DDoS protection
 D) Set up Google Cloud Identity-Aware Proxy (IAP) for access control, employ Google Cloud Pub/Sub for event-driven architecture, and utilize Google Cloud Memorystore for caching
 E) Implement Google Cloud Deployment Manager for multi-cloud resource provisioning, enable Google Cloud Logging for centralized logging, and utilize Google Cloud Storage for data backup and recovery
 F) Leverage Google Cloud Pub/Sub for real-time event streaming, configure Google Cloud Spanner for distributed database management, and utilize Google Cloud Functions for serverless computing.

QUESTION 2

Your organization is managing a large-scale application on Google Cloud. You want to improve security by ensuring that all Compute Engine instances use authorized and verified container images. Which approach should you take to achieve this goal while minimizing manual efforts and ensuring compliance with company policies?

A) Manually inspect and validate each container image before deployment, and update instances accordingly.
 B) Use Google Cloud IAM to restrict access to container images and enforce strict permissions.
 C) Implement Google Cloud Security Command Center to scan and verify container images, then use deployment manager to update instances.
 D) Configure a Binary Authorization policy that enforces image verification for Compute Engine instances.

QUESTION 3

Your team manages a containerized application running on Google Kubernetes Engine (GKE). Recently, you observed that the application experiences performance degradation and increased response times during peak usage hours. The GKE cluster runs in a multi-zone configuration. After analyzing metrics, you find the following deviations: - CPU utilization: Typical state: 40% Current state during peak hours: 90% - Memory usage: Typical state: 50% Current state during peak hours: 80% - Latency: Typical state: 20 milliseconds Current state during peak hours: 500 milliseconds - Error rate: Typical state: 2% Current state during peak hours: 10% To improve performance during peak hours while following Google's recommended DevOps practices, what action should you take?

A) Manually add additional nodes to the GKE cluster during peak hours.
B) Implement vertical pod autoscaling (VPA) to adjust resource requests for containers dynamically.
C) Optimize the application code to reduce CPU and memory usage.
D) Deploy a global load balancer to distribute traffic evenly across multiple GKE clusters.

QUESTION 4

Your organization is transitioning to a microservices architecture on Google Kubernetes Engine (GKE). You want to ensure effective communication and coordination among microservices. Which two Kubernetes features should you use to achieve this goal? I. Implement Kubernetes Services to enable DNS-based service discovery. 2. Utilize Ingress controllers to manage external access to microservices. 3. Set up Kubernetes ConfigMaps for sharing configuration data. 4. Deploy Kubernetes Network Policies to control network traffic between microservices.

A) 1 and 2
B) 2 and 3
C) 3 and 4
D) 1 and 4

QUESTION 5

Your team manages a media streaming service on a GKE cluster spanning both on-premises and Google Cloud infrastructure. How should you pinpoint containers consuming the most CPU and memory resources?

A) Deploy Prometheus to collect and aggregate container logs, then analyze data in Grafana.
B) Implement Cloud Logging to funnel application logs into BigQuery, cluster logs by container, and analyze resource usage for CPU and memory.
C) Leverage the Cloud Monitoring API to create custom metrics and categorize containers into clusters.
D) Utilize Cloud Monitoring with GKE support.

QUESTION 6

As the administrator of a video streaming platform on GKE with varying viewer traffic, how can you best optimize resource usage by auto-adjusting Pods and nodes based on demand?

A) Configure the Horizontal Pod Autoscaler and enable the cluster autoscaler.
B) Configure the Horizontal Pod Autoscaler but fix the size of the node pool.
C) Configure the Vertical Pod Autoscaler and enable the cluster autoscaler.
D) Configure the Vertical Pod Autoscaler but fix the size of the node pool.

QUESTION 7

In the context of optimizing your media processing workflow in Google Cloud's Dataflow, which actions should you prioritize? (Choose two.)

A) Segment the automation procedures into finer-grained components.
B) Implement automatic progression confirmations transferring from the staging area to the production

zone.

C) Run a script to facilitate the setup of the media processing workflow in Google Cloud Dataflow.

D) Increase the number of personnel to execute hands-on steps.

E) Rely on manual intervention for complex processing steps.

QUESTION 8

You are overseeing the deployment of a critical financial service application on Google Cloud, which requires strict compliance with regulatory standards for data security and high availability. The application will be hosted on a GKE regional cluster with expected steady growth in user base. What measures would you take to ensure compliance and scalability?

A) Utilize GKE Autopilot for automatic resource management and enforce network policies for security.

B) Set up dedicated node pools with Shielded VMs for enhanced security and a horizontal pod autoscaler for scalability.

C) Implement a manual scaling strategy for the nodes and pods, focusing on regulatory compliance checks.

D) Configure a vertical pod autoscaler and use preemptible VMs to reduce costs while ensuring compliance.

E) Rely solely on the GKE standard cluster's default security settings and enable cluster autoscaler.

QUESTION 9

Your team is considering using preemptible VMs for certain workloads to optimize cloud costs in Google Cloud. Which scenario would be most appropriate for using preemptible VM instances?

A) An online retail store's website handling constant customer transactions.

B) Background processing of geospatial data for a research project, where interruptions are acceptable.

C) A critical system for monitoring and managing urban traffic in real-time.

D) Hosting a continuous and interactive virtual training environment.

E) A patient record system for a hospital that requires high reliability and data integrity.

QUESTION 10

Your team has developed a web application hosted on Cloud Run that requires access to a third-party email service API. The API requires a secure API key for integration. Following Google Cloud best practices, how should you securely store and use this API key?

A) Encrypt the API key using Cloud KMS and store the encrypted key in a Cloud Storage bucket. Retrieve and decrypt the key in the Cloud Run service.

B) Store the API key in Cloud Datastore, and retrieve it directly within the Cloud Run service when needed.

C) Keep the API key in Secret Manager and reference it as an environment variable in the Cloud Run service.

D) Embed the API key in the application code, and deploy it to Cloud Run, relying on Cloud Run's inherent security.

E) Use Cloud KMS to encrypt the API key and pass the encrypted key as an environment variable to Cloud Run.

QUESTION 11

As a DevOps engineer, you are addressing issues caused by simultaneous development and testing in the production environment of a cloud-based analytics platform. What strategy would you recommend to improve the development and testing process?

A) Implement a blue/green deployment strategy to ensure that all testing is done on the 'blue' environment while the 'green' environment remains untouched.
B) Instruct developers to conduct more comprehensive unit testing on their local machines to reduce the need for testing in the production environment.
C) Establish a dedicated testing environment that mirrors production and integrate it into a CI/CD pipeline for pre-production validation.
D) Schedule regular maintenance windows where developers can test new features in production without impacting users.
E) Move all development and testing activities to a cloud environment with less stringent performance requirements.

QUESTION 12

A real-time data processing application on GKE needs to be scaled effectively to maintain performance. The application processes a large stream of data and writes to a BigQuery dataset. What SLI should you use for optimal scaling of the processing pods?

A) Scale based on the CPU utilization of the pods processing the data stream.
B) Implement autoscaling based on the memory usage of the pods to ensure efficient data processing.
C) Use the throughput of data processed (e.g., records per second) as the metric for horizontal pod autoscaling.
D) Monitor the latency of data writes to BigQuery and scale the pods accordingly.
E) Employ a custom metric based on the number of data processing errors and scale the pods when errors increase.

QUESTION 13

Your team uses Cloud Dataflow for processing large datasets and stores the output in GCS. Each dataset version correlates with a specific release of the processing algorithm. You need to link the processed data with the corresponding algorithm version. What is the best approach?

A) Store the algorithm version in the metadata of the GCS object.
B) Name the GCS buckets according to the algorithm version.
C) Include the algorithm version directly in the filenames of the stored data.
D) Use GCS object versioning, correlating each data version with the algorithm's release tag.
E) Implement a custom labeling system in your version control to track both the data and the algorithm version.

QUESTION 14

As part of your IaC strategy, you are tasked with ensuring that the network configurations in Google Cloud are consistently applied and maintained. Your team uses Terraform for defining network resources. How should you automate the process of applying these configurations?

A) Schedule a Cron job in a Compute Engine VM to run Terraform apply at regular intervals.
B) Utilize Cloud Build to automatically execute Terraform apply when changes are pushed to the network configurations in the repository.
C) Manually run Terraform apply from a local machine whenever network configuration changes are made.
D) Deploy a dedicated GKE cluster to run Terraform scripts as part of a continuous deployment process.
E) Set up a Cloud Scheduler job to trigger a Cloud Function that runs Terraform apply for network configurations.

QUESTION 15

A six-month marketing campaign is planned to be supported by a series of Compute Engine instances for running various analytics and reporting tasks. The instances will be used heavily throughout the campaign and require stable performance. What is the most cost-effective approach to manage these instances?

A) Deploy the instances in a Managed Instance Group with autoscaling to adjust resources as per demand.
B) Configure the instances as preemptible VMs to benefit from lower pricing during the campaign.
C) Acquire Committed Use Discounts for the duration of the marketing campaign for the required instances.
D) Regularly monitor and optimize the instance sizes based on utilization metrics to manage costs.
E) Use a combination of regular and preemptible VMs to balance cost and availability throughout the campaign.

QUESTION 16

You need to collaborate with a third-party consultant who will provide insights based on your Google Cloud Operations Suite custom dashboard data. What's the best approach to share the dashboard with the consultant while ensuring data security?

A) Share your dashboard with the consultant's Google account with full edit access.
B) Export the dashboard as a PDF and send it to the consultant via email.
C) Create a new Google Cloud project and replicate the dashboard there for the consultant.
D) Share the dashboard with the consultant via a temporary access link with view-only permissions.

QUESTION 17

Your company embraces DevOps principles, and you're the Incident Coordinator for a critical issue affecting clients. To ensure efficient incident resolution, which two roles would you assign immediately?

A) Technical Lead
B) Third-party Legal Advisor
C) Communications Coordinator
D) Operations Coordinator
E) Client Impact Analyst.

QUESTION 18

Your organization uses a microservices architecture deployed on Google Kubernetes Engine (GKE). You want to ensure that services can scale dynamically based on traffic and resource utilization. What should you do to achieve this goal efficiently?

A) Set a fixed number of replicas for each service to ensure predictability in scaling.
B) Implement custom scripts to manually adjust the number of replicas based on monitoring data.
C) Utilize Kubernetes Horizontal Pod Autoscalers (HPAs) to automatically adjust the number of replicas based on resource metrics and custom metrics.
D) Create a separate GKE cluster for each service to isolate scaling concerns.

QUESTION 19

Your company is launching an e-commerce platform for a special promotion event, anticipating a surge in user traffic. You want to ensure system robustness to handle potential outages during high demand. What actions should you take? (Choose two.)

A) Employ monitoring through Cloud Monitoring to continuously monitor essential system parameters and configure alerts for critical thresholds.
B) Configure Cloud Monitoring to generate notifications for each common failure observed in your system's operations.
C) Monitor server CPU and memory usage on a regular basis.
D) Implement a Content Delivery Network (CDN) to enhance content delivery performance.
E) Evaluate the expected traffic surge and plan for necessary quota adjustments in advance.

QUESTION 20

Your Python web service running on Google Kubernetes Engine (GKE) interacts extensively with external APIs. To identify potential performance degradation due to these integrations, what action should you take?

A) Apply Cloud Profiler across all services.
B) Modify the Python service to record API call durations and log this data. Use Cloud Logging to identify slow-response external APIs.
C) Instrument all services with Cloud Trace and analyze span timings for external API calls.
D) Deploy Cloud Debugger to inspect the runtime state and execution flow across services.

QUESTION 21

Your company encountered a major security breach in its cloud infrastructure. You are tasked with creating a post-incident report to prevent similar security incidents. What two sections should be included in the report?

A) A list of security tools used in the cloud infrastructure.
B) A timeline of events leading up to and during the security breach.
C) A summary of employee performance during the incident.
D) A review of the organization's financial performance in the past year.
E) An analysis of vulnerabilities in the cloud infrastructure.

QUESTION 22

Your team is deploying a web application on Google Cloud that requires global availability and scalability. You want to ensure that traffic is efficiently distributed to the nearest data center. Which approach should you take?

A) Use a single region with a global load balancer to manage traffic distribution.
B) Deploy the application in multiple regions and utilize a regional load balancer.
C) Select a small instance type to minimize costs while ensuring scalability.
D) Monitor resource utilization continuously and adjust instance counts as needed to meet traffic demands.

QUESTION 23

Your company is deploying a new web application on Google Cloud that needs to handle varying levels of traffic throughout the day. You want to optimize resource utilization and cost-efficiency. What should you do?

A) Maintain a fixed number of virtual machines (VMs) to handle peak traffic at all times.
B) Implement autoscaling based on predefined traffic patterns and resource utilization metrics.
C) Use on-demand instances and manually add more VMs as needed.
D) Schedule regular resource scaling based on a fixed daily schedule.

QUESTION 24

You manage a network of Kubernetes clusters on Google Cloud for a healthcare organization. Security and compliance are critical. What actions should you take to meet these requirements effectively?

A) Utilize unmanaged clusters without specific security configurations to simplify management.
B) Implement Google Kubernetes Engine (GKE) Autopilot clusters for automated security and compliance management.
C) Deploy a single cluster for all applications and manually configure security settings.
D) Use separate clusters for each application without implementing security controls.

QUESTION 25

As a DevOps engineer, you've set up a Cloud SQL instance for a new project in Google Cloud. You need to enable your database administrators to monitor database performance without granting them full administrative privileges. What is the most appropriate role assignment to meet this requirement?

A) Grant the Database Administrators the SQL Admin role.
B) Assign the Cloud SQL Viewer role to the Database Administrators.
C) Provide the Project Viewer role to the Database Administrators.
D) Allocate the Custom Monitoring role with specific permissions to the Database Administrators.
E) Assign the Database Administrators the role of Monitoring Editor.

QUESTION 26

Your team is managing a cloud service that logs user login attempts in Google Cloud Logging. You need to identify trends in failed login attempts to enhance security measures. Which method would you use to visualize these trends over time?

A) Utilize Google Cloud Monitoring to create a dashboard based on a logs-based metric for failed login attempts.

B) Configure a BigQuery sink in Google Cloud Logging to analyze and visualize failed login attempts using Data Studio.

C) Export login attempt logs to a third-party analytics service and use its tools to create visual trend analyses.

D) Set up Google Cloud Profiler to trace and visualize the pattern of failed login attempts.

E) Integrate Google Cloud Logging with a machine learning model to predict and chart future login attempt trends.

QUESTION 27

You are configuring an SLO for a cloud-based e-commerce platform. The goal is to ensure that the checkout process completes within 3 seconds for 99% of transactions each month. Which metric and evaluation method is most suitable?

A) Latency metric with a request-based method of evaluation.

B) Throughput metric with a request-based method of evaluation.

C) Latency metric with a window-based method of evaluation.

D) Error rate metric with a window-based method of evaluation.

E) Transaction completion metric with a request-based method of evaluation.

QUESTION 28

You are overseeing the deployment of a large-scale web application on Google Cloud. The application uses Cloud SQL and Cloud Storage, and you want to ensure the infrastructure code is robust and error-free. What CI/CD strategy should you adopt for testing infrastructure changes?

A) Implement Travis CI to execute infrastructure tests after each deployment to production.

B) Use Cloud Build to automatically run infrastructure tests on pull requests against the development branch.

C) Require manual execution of infrastructure tests by the QA team before approving any deployment.

D) Configure CircleCI to perform infrastructure testing only on the release branch.

E) Set up a Spinnaker pipeline to test infrastructure changes during off-peak hours only.

QUESTION 29

You have added a vendor-provided network monitoring tool to your GKE cluster. This tool logs network events to a non-standard directory and cannot be reconfigured. You need to ensure these logs are incorporated into Stackdriver for analysis and alerting. What is the best course of action?

A) Directly edit the tool's configuration files to change the logging directory to a Stackdriver-compatible path.

B) Deploy a logging agent as a DaemonSet in GKE to capture and forward logs from the custom path to Stackdriver.

C) Rely on GKE's built-in logging capabilities to automatically detect and send these logs to Stackdriver.

D) Develop a custom Kubernetes service to periodically scan the log directory and push entries to

Stackdriver.

 E) Manually check the logs at regular intervals and upload relevant entries to Stackdriver.

QUESTION 30

Your company's application is deployed on both Google Kubernetes Engine (GKE) and on-premises servers. You need to monitor network traffic and latency metrics consistently across both environments. How should you set up monitoring to achieve this with minimal additional development?

A) Utilize Cloud Monitoring's built-in capabilities for GKE and implement similar monitoring tools on-premises, then integrate the data.
 B) Deploy the Cloud Operations agent on both GKE and on-premises servers to collect and send network metrics to Cloud Monitoring.
 C) Develop a custom monitoring solution for on-premises and use Cloud Monitoring for GKE, consolidating data through an API.
 D) Install third-party network monitoring software on both GKE and on-premises servers, exporting data to a common analytics platform.
 E) Rely on GKE's default monitoring for cloud infrastructure and manually monitor the on-premises servers.

QUESTION 31

You are responsible for a CI/CD pipeline for a cloud-based application. To ensure reliable and efficient delivery, what should you prioritize?

A) Reducing the frequency of pipeline executions to avoid resource consumption.
B) Implementing automated testing at various stages of the pipeline.
C) Removing automated deployment to avoid potential errors.
D) Limiting the number of developers with access to the pipeline configuration.

QUESTION 32

You are tasked with deploying a mission-critical service on Google Cloud. The staging environment had limited load testing, and you need to ensure an automated and seamless production deployment while closely monitoring performance. What strategy should you employ?

A) Deploy the service through a continuous delivery pipeline using blue/green deployment patterns. Shift all traffic to the new version and monitor performance with Cloud Monitoring.
B) Use kubectl to roll out the service and employ Config Connector to incrementally shift traffic between versions. Monitor performance with Cloud Monitoring and detect anomalies.
C) Implement the deployment with kubectl and configure the spec.updateStrategy.type to RollingUpdate. Use Cloud Monitoring to watch for performance issues, and if necessary, perform a rollback using kubectl.
D) Deploy the service using a continuous delivery pipeline with canary releases. Monitor the service performance using Cloud Monitoring, and gradually increase traffic based on the observed metrics.

QUESTION 33

You have been tasked with configuring a new Google Cloud environment for a healthcare organization.

The organization is concerned about potential security vulnerabilities related to the usage of JSON service account keys within Google Cloud. Your objective is to develop a strategy that fully mitigates the risks associated with JSON service account key usage while keeping operational efforts to a minimum. What approach should you adopt?

A) Assign specific IAM roles to dedicated teams for managing service account keys.
B) Customize predefined roles to eliminate permissions related to service account key management.
C) Enforce organization-level constraints to prohibit service account key creation.
D) Implement guidelines to control service account key uploads.

QUESTION 34

Your organization is migrating a monolithic application to a microservices architecture on Google Kubernetes Engine (GKE). You want to implement a CI/CD pipeline that includes automated testing, staging, and deployment of microservices. Which GKE features and practices should you incorporate into your pipeline to achieve this goal?

A) Use GKE Autopilot to automatically manage and scale the microservices, reducing the need for manual intervention.
B) Implement Canary deployments to gradually roll out new microservices versions and monitor their performance before full deployment.
C) Set up VPC peering to isolate the testing and staging environments, ensuring data separation.
D) Apply Helm charts for managing the deployment configurations of microservices, simplifying versioning and release management.

QUESTION 35

Your organization runs a critical API service on Google Compute Engine instances. You need to monitor incoming HTTP requests and capture the source IP addresses for compliance and security analysis. What should you do to accomplish this with minimal effort?

A) Enable VPC Flow Logs for the network subnet.
B) Implement custom logging in the API service code.
C) Deploy a reverse proxy server to capture IP addresses.
D) Install a third-party intrusion detection system on each instance.

QUESTION 36

You are responsible for managing a cloud-based IoT platform on Google Cloud Platform (GCP). You've observed that confidential IoT device data is mistakenly being logged and is collected through Cloud Logging. This sensitive information is marked with the label "IoTData." What action should you take to securely store these logs for compliance purposes and prevent their exposure through Cloud Logging?

A) Set up a custom log filter in Cloud Logging to identify the "IoTData" label, create a log sink directed to Cloud Storage, and then establish a log exclusion based on the "IoTData" filter.
B) Define a basic log filter in Cloud Logging to detect the "IoTData" label and configure a log sink directed at a Cloud Storage bucket to archive these entries.
C) Employ a Fluentd filter plugin with the Cloud Logging Agent to filter out log entries tagged with "IoTData," and route the filtered entries to a dedicated Cloud Storage bucket for secure storage.

D) Create a custom log sink in Cloud Logging to direct logs with the "IoTData" label to Cloud Storage while excluding them from regular Cloud Logging processing.

QUESTION 37

You are responsible for a cloud-based customer support system, and a recent incident necessitates a postmortem to prevent reoccurrence. What's the best way to allocate responsibility for postmortem resolution tasks?

A) Appoint a dedicated owner for each resolution task and involve collaborators as needed.
B) Designate collaborators without assigning explicit ownership to maintain a non-punitive postmortem atmosphere.
C) Assign multiple task owners for each issue to ensure swift problem resolution.
D) Designate the head of customer support as the primary owner of all resolution tasks due to their overall responsibility for system uptime.

QUESTION 38

You oversee a Cloud Run service that produces semi-structured plain text logs sent to Cloud Logging. The need is to transition to structured logging in JSON format. What action should you take?

A) Develop a custom logging library for your Cloud Run service, ensuring that log records are created in JSON format with the necessary attributes.
B) Incorporate a third-party log processing tool with your Cloud Run service, configuring it to convert plain text logs into structured JSON.
C) Adjust the Cloud Run service's log settings to automatically convert plain text logs into structured JSON format.
D) Implement a log transformation script within the Cloud Run service's container image, converting logs to JSON and forwarding them to Cloud Logging.

QUESTION 39

As a cloud engineer, you are responsible for analyzing the costs of Cloud Spanner instances used by different business units in your organization. Each unit has its own set of instances within the same Google Cloud project. How would you most effectively determine the cost incurred by each business unit's Cloud Spanner usage?

A) Create a unique identifier for each Cloud Spanner instance corresponding to its business unit, export usage data to BigQuery, and perform cost analysis using SQL queries.
B) Label each Cloud Spanner instance with a business unit-specific tag, set up BigQuery billing export, and query the costs by label.
C) Add business unit-specific metadata to each Cloud Spanner instance, configure Stackdriver Logging to export logs to BigQuery, and analyze costs using metadata.
D) Manually review each business unit's Cloud Spanner usage and costs using the Google Cloud Console's Cost Breakdown tool.
E) Implement a custom script to extract usage metrics from Cloud Spanner API, correlate with business units, and calculate costs, storing results in a Cloud SQL database.

QUESTION 40

You are tasked as an SRE with guiding the development of a new cloud-native application deployment tool on Google Cloud. How should you best participate in this project to ensure operational efficiency and reliability?

A) Conduct a thorough beta test of the tool in a non-production environment, focusing on user experience and scalability, then relay findings to the developers.
B) Begin involvement after the tool meets initial development milestones, implement it in a test environment, and monitor for any functional issues.
C) Collaborate with the development team during the planning phase, providing insights on deployment strategies and cloud resource management.
D) Observe the tool's performance in an actual operational setting post-deployment, then deliver feedback based on real-world usage data.

QUESTION 41

As a cloud administrator for an online media streaming service, you are tasked with overseeing operational efficiency and issue detection on the live streaming infrastructure. Considering best practices for access control, how should you configure Google Cloud Operations Suite for targeted monitoring and minimal privilege access?

A) Initiate a centralized monitoring project in Google Cloud, create a Cloud Operations Workspace, and connect only live streaming infrastructure projects, providing appropriate team members with read access.
B) Assign the Project Viewer IAM role for all streaming service projects to the team, and configure separate Cloud Operations workspaces for each.
C) Grant read permissions to your team on all streaming service projects, with individual Cloud Operations workspaces configured per project.
D) Choose an existing live streaming project to act as the central point for the Cloud Operations monitoring workspace.

QUESTION 42

You are configuring a CI/CD pipeline for a company that uses Terraform for cloud infrastructure provisioning and Anthos for Kubernetes configurations. The company has separate environments for development, staging, and production. How should the source control repositories be organized for optimal management and deployment?

A) Single repository for Terraform configurations with branches for each environment, separate repositories for Anthos Config Management with environment-specific directories, and individual repositories for each microservice with feature branching.
B) Unified repository for all Terraform and Anthos configurations with directory separation for environments, and separate repositories for each microservice application.
C) Separate repositories for Terraform configurations for each environment, unified repository for Anthos Config Management with environment overlays, and a single repository for all microservices with feature-based branches.
D) Shared repository for both Terraform and Anthos configurations, with directory-based separation for environments, and separate repositories for each microservice with branches for each environment.

QUESTION 43

In an e-commerce company, you're responsible for updating Terraform configurations for cloud infrastructure with a team of developers. To ensure efficient collaboration and accurate tracking of changes, what strategy should be adopted?

A) Keep Terraform configurations in a synchronized folder accessible by all team members, with a standard folder naming system for version control. Regularly, back up these folders to a cloud storage service.
B) Store Terraform configurations in a cloud-based document management system, with a structured directory. Manually log each change in a shared document.
C) Manage Terraform configurations using a Git-based repository, with a branching strategy and pull requests for peer reviews. Track changes via commit history.
D) Utilize a network-shared drive for Terraform configurations, allowing direct edits by team members. Implement a daily process for updating a central version control document.

QUESTION 44

Managing logs for a financial service application on Google Cloud, you discover that logs contain unintended sensitive customer data. You need a solution to quickly filter this data from logs. What method should you employ to address this issue effectively?

A) Modify the application code to prevent logging of sensitive data and wait for the next deployment cycle.
B) Set up a Cloud Dataflow pipeline to cleanse the logs of sensitive data before they reach Cloud Logging.
C) Utilize the fluent-plugin-grep Fluentd filter plugin to exclude log entries containing sensitive data.
D) Implement a Cloud Storage staging area for logs where a Cloud Function redacts sensitive data before forwarding to Cloud Logging.

QUESTION 45

You are managing a cloud-based image processing service on Google Cloud, and you've noticed periodic service disruptions due to high demand overloading the current Compute Engine instance. What action should you take to improve service reliability and meet your SLO?

A) Modify the SLO to align with the current performance of the Compute Engine instance.
B) Upgrade the existing Compute Engine instance to a type with higher CPU and memory capacity.
C) Deploy additional Compute Engine instances and implement a load balancer to distribute the image processing load.
D) Set up standby Compute Engine instances in different zones to handle excess load during peak times.

QUESTION 46

Your team operates a critical infrastructure on Google Cloud and requires immediate SMS notifications for specific Cloud Monitoring alarms. What approach should you take to configure these SMS alerts efficiently?

A) Configure Cloud Monitoring to send alerts to team members' phones directly via SMS.
B) Set up Cloud Monitoring alerts to trigger a Webhook, which is linked to a third-party SMS notification service where team members have registered their phone numbers.

C) Create Cloud Monitoring alerts that send messages to a dedicated Microsoft Teams channel, with an add-on in Teams to forward these as SMS.
D) Employ a custom script in Cloud Monitoring that interfaces with an external SMS gateway to deliver notifications to team members.

QUESTION 47

You are troubleshooting a network issue where a compute instance in Google Cloud VPC-1 is unable to reach a database service in VPC-2. Your task is to locate the problem in the network setup. What method can you employ to diagnose the issue effectively?

A) Check the VPC peering connections between VPC-1 and VPC-2 for any misconfigurations or disruptions.
B) Run a Connectivity Test from the Network Intelligence Center to analyze the network path between the compute instance and the database service.
C) Implement custom network logging on both the compute instance and database service to capture detailed traffic data.
D) Create a temporary firewall rule in both VPCs to log and analyze all traffic attempting to reach the database service.

QUESTION 48

Your organization utilizes a microservices architecture deployed in containers with a CI/CD pipeline. Security concerns have arisen due to potential vulnerabilities in the microservices' dependencies. What should you do?

A) Use a traditional vulnerability scanning tool designed for monolithic applications to assess the microservices.
B) Employ a runtime application security protection (RASP) tool to monitor and protect the microservices.
C) Incorporate automated dependency updates in the CI/CD pipeline to keep dependencies up-to-date.
D) Conduct manual code reviews of the microservices to identify vulnerabilities.
E) Deploy a web application firewall (WAF) in front of the microservices to block potential threats.

QUESTION 49

In a DevOps-oriented transition, your application faced sporadic performance issues recently. A leader from a different department asks for a formal rundown of the incident to facilitate preventive measures. What action should you take?

A) Develop an incident report detailing the problems, insights, and a structured set of corrective actions. Share it exclusively with the department leader who requested it.
B) Create a summary incident report highlighting the issues and insights gained, and distribute it across the company's technical documentation repository for reference.
C) Formulate an incident report outlining the problems, insights, and individual accountability, then share it solely with the inquiring department leader.
D) Generate an incident report outlining the problems, insights, and a structured set of corrective actions. Disseminate it across the company's technical documentation platform for broader access.

QUESTION 50

Your organization is facing a critical security incident, and you are responsible for managing communications.

A) Forward all internal team member messages to the Communication Lead and let them handle internal communications, prioritizing direct communications with external stakeholders.

B) Respond promptly to internal team members, aiming for updates every 30 minutes. Commit to 'next update' times.

C) Delegate the task of replying to internal team member messages to a trusted team member while focusing on direct communications with external stakeholders.

D) Provide regular updates to all parties involved, maintaining a 'next update' time commitment in all communications.

PRACTICE TEST 3 - ANSWERS ONLY

QUESTION 1

Answer - A) Use Google Kubernetes Engine (GKE) for container orchestration, implement Google Cloud Build for automated builds, and set up Google Cloud Endpoints for API management.

Option A combines key services for container orchestration, automated builds, and API management, aligning with the requirements for a secure and scalable CI/CD pipeline in a microservices migration.
 Option B provides vulnerability scanning and monitoring but does not address CI/CD pipeline components.
 Option C and D involve services that are not directly related to CI/CD pipelines.
 Option E and F mention various services, but they do not provide a cohesive solution for the CI/CD pipeline for microservices.

QUESTION 2

Answer - D) Configure a Binary Authorization policy that enforces image verification for Compute Engine instances.

Option D is the recommended approach. Binary Authorization allows you to enforce policies on container images, ensuring that only authorized and verified images can be used for Compute Engine instances, thus improving security and compliance while minimizing manual efforts.
 Option A involves manual inspection, which can be time-consuming and error-prone.
 Option B focuses on access control but does not enforce image verification.
 Option C includes security scanning but lacks the direct enforcement of image policies during instance updates.

QUESTION 3

Answer - B) Implement vertical pod autoscaling (VPA) to adjust resource requests for containers dynamically.

Option B is the recommended action to improve performance during peak hours while following Google's recommended DevOps practices. Implementing vertical pod autoscaling (VPA) allows for dynamic adjustment of resource requests for containers based on their actual usage. This ensures efficient resource allocation and better performance during peak usage, aligning with DevOps principles of automation and optimization.
 Option A suggests manual node addition, which is not as automated or efficient.
 Option C mentions code optimization, which is important but may not fully address resource scaling.
 Option D proposes a global load balancer, which helps with traffic distribution but does not directly address resource scaling.

QUESTION 4

Answer - A) 1 and 2

To ensure effective communication and coordination among microservices in a Kubernetes-based

microservices architecture, you should:
 - Implement Kubernetes Services to enable DNS-based service discovery (Option 1).
 - Utilize Ingress controllers to manage external access to microservices (Option 2).
 These practices help with service discovery and external access management.
 Option 3, setting up Kubernetes ConfigMaps, is useful for configuration management but does not directly address communication and coordination.
 Option 4, deploying Kubernetes Network Policies, is important for network security but does not focus on communication and coordination.

QUESTION 5

Answer - B) Implement Cloud Logging to funnel application logs into BigQuery, cluster logs by container, and analyze resource usage for CPU and memory.

Option B is the correct choice as it efficiently allows you to analyze resource usage by aggregating application logs using Cloud Logging.
 Option A introduces Prometheus and Grafana, which are not the most suitable for this scenario,
 Option C suggests creating custom metrics, which may not be necessary,
 Option D is too vague and doesn't provide a clear solution.

QUESTION 6

Answer - A) Configure the Horizontal Pod Autoscaler and enable the cluster autoscaler.

Option A is the correct choice as it recommends configuring the Horizontal Pod Autoscaler and enabling the cluster autoscaler to dynamically adjust the number of Pods and nodes based on demand, optimizing resource usage.
 Option B fixes the node pool size, limiting scalability,
 Option C introduces the Vertical Pod Autoscaler, which is not necessary for this scenario,
 Option D also fixes the node pool size, limiting scalability.

QUESTION 7

Answer - A and B

Option A - Segmenting automation procedures into finer-grained components reduces redundancy and improves efficiency.
 Option B - Implementing automatic progression confirmations streamlines the workflow by reducing manual interventions.
 Options C, D, and E are not the most effective ways to optimize the workflow.

QUESTION 8

Answer - B) Set up dedicated node pools with Shielded VMs for enhanced security and a horizontal pod autoscaler for scalability.

A) Incorrect - While GKE Autopilot provides automatic management, it may not meet specific regulatory compliance requirements.
B) Correct - This approach ensures both security compliance with Shielded VMs and scalability with

horizontal autoscaling.

C) Incorrect - Manual scaling is less efficient and may not promptly address growth in user base.

D) Incorrect - Preemptible VMs may not be suitable for critical financial services due to their ephemeral nature.

E) Incorrect - Default settings may not suffice for the specific compliance and security requirements of a financial service application.

QUESTION 9

Answer - B) Background processing of geospatial data for a research project, where interruptions are acceptable.

A) Incorrect - Constant customer transactions on a retail website require stable, uninterrupted service.

B) Correct - Background processing tasks that tolerate interruptions are ideal for cost-saving preemptible VMs.

C) Incorrect - Urban traffic management requires real-time, reliable processing, not suitable for preemptible VMs.

D) Incorrect - A continuous virtual training environment needs stable, uninterrupted hosting.

E) Incorrect - Patient record systems demand high reliability and cannot afford interruptions, unsuited for preemptible VMs.

QUESTION 10

Answer - C) Keep the API key in Secret Manager and reference it as an environment variable in the Cloud Run service.

A) Incorrect - Storing encrypted keys in Cloud Storage is not as secure as using Secret Manager.

B) Incorrect - Cloud Datastore is not designed for storing sensitive information like API keys.

C) Correct - Secret Manager is specifically designed for securely managing and accessing secrets like API keys.

D) Incorrect - Embedding secrets in application code is not a secure practice.

E) Incorrect - While Cloud KMS is secure, it's more complex and not as streamlined as using Secret Manager for this purpose.

QUESTION 11

Answer - C) Establish a dedicated testing environment that mirrors production and integrate it into a CI/CD pipeline for pre-production validation.

A) Incorrect - Blue/green deployment is primarily a deployment strategy, not a testing strategy.

B) Incorrect - While unit testing is important, it cannot replace testing in an environment similar to production.

C) Correct - A dedicated testing environment in a CI/CD pipeline allows for thorough testing without impacting production.

D) Incorrect - Maintenance windows still pose a risk of impacting users and do not provide continuous testing capabilities.

E) Incorrect - Moving to a less stringent environment does not address the need to test in conditions similar to production.

QUESTION 12

Answer - C) Use the throughput of data processed (e.g., records per second) as the metric for horizontal pod autoscaling.

A) Incorrect - CPU utilization may not directly correlate with the data processing needs of the application.
B) Incorrect - Memory usage is important but doesn't directly reflect the data processing throughput.
C) Correct - Throughput of data processed is a direct indicator of the performance and scaling needs of a data processing application.
D) Incorrect - Latency of data writes is more of a data output metric and may not directly influence processing scaling.
E) Incorrect - While error rates are important, they are not a primary metric for scaling a data processing application.

QUESTION 13

Answer - A) Store the algorithm version in the metadata of the GCS object.

A) Correct - Storing the version in the object's metadata allows for easy tracking and correlation without affecting the data itself.
B) Incorrect - Using buckets for versioning is inefficient and not scalable.
C) Incorrect - Including versions in filenames can be cumbersome and less flexible.
D) Incorrect - GCS object versioning is used for tracking changes to objects, not for correlating with external systems.
E) Incorrect - While custom labeling in version control is useful, it does not directly link data stored in GCS.

QUESTION 14

Answer - B) Utilize Cloud Build to automatically execute Terraform apply when changes are pushed to the network configurations in the repository.

A) Incorrect - Cron jobs on VMs require manual setup and do not fully leverage cloud-native IaC practices.
B) Correct - This ensures that changes to network configurations are consistently and automatically applied in line with IaC principles.
C) Incorrect - Manual application of Terraform is error-prone and does not align with automated IaC practices.
D) Incorrect - Using a dedicated GKE cluster for this purpose is overkill and not cost-effective.
E) Incorrect - Cloud Scheduler and Cloud Functions are not typically used for complex infrastructure management tasks.

QUESTION 15

Answer - C) Acquire Committed Use Discounts for the duration of the marketing campaign for the required instances.

A) Incorrect - Autoscaling is not necessary for a workload with constant demand and may lead to increased costs.

B) Incorrect - Preemptible VMs may not provide the stable performance required for the campaign.
C) Correct - Committed Use Discounts offer an ideal cost-saving solution for stable, uninterrupted usage over a fixed period.
D) Incorrect - Constantly adjusting instance sizes can be time-consuming and may not offer significant cost benefits.
E) Incorrect - The unpredictability of preemptible VMs could affect the stability and performance of the campaign's analytics tasks.

QUESTION 16

Answer - D) Share the dashboard with the consultant via a temporary access link with view-only permissions.

Option D is the correct choice because it allows you to securely share the dashboard with the consultant without providing full edit access. This ensures data security and control.
 Option A - Option A is incorrect because granting full edit access to an external consultant may pose a security risk.
 Option B - Option B is incorrect because exporting as a PDF doesn't provide real-time access to the dashboard.
 Option C - Option C is incorrect because replicating the dashboard in a new project might be unnecessary and complex.

QUESTION 17

Answer - A) Technical Lead, C) Communications Coordinator

The Technical Lead (Option A) is vital for providing technical guidance during incident resolution. The Communications Coordinator (Option C) is essential for managing communications and ensuring stakeholders are informed during the incident.
 Option B - Third-party Legal Advisor is not typically a core role during internal incident resolution.
 Option D - Operations Coordinator is important but may not be as pivotal as the Technical Lead and Communications Coordinator in the initial phase of incident resolution.
 Option E - Client Impact Analyst, while valuable, may not be among the two most pivotal roles during the initial incident response.

QUESTION 18

Answer - C) Utilize Kubernetes Horizontal Pod Autoscalers (HPAs) to automatically adjust the number of replicas based on resource metrics and custom metrics.

Option C is the correct choice because it leverages Kubernetes Horizontal Pod Autoscalers (HPAs) to automate the scaling process based on both resource metrics and custom metrics, ensuring efficient scaling.
 Option A - Option A suggests using a fixed number of replicas, which doesn't enable dynamic scaling.
 Option B - Option B involves manual adjustments, which are not efficient in a microservices environment.
 Option D - Option D proposes creating separate clusters, which can lead to complexity and resource inefficiency.

QUESTION 19

Answer - A) Employ monitoring through Cloud Monitoring to continuously monitor essential system parameters and configure alerts for critical thresholds.
Answer - B) Configure Cloud Monitoring to generate notifications for each common failure observed in your system's operations.

Option A and Option B are the correct choices.
Option A - Employing monitoring with Cloud Monitoring helps continuously monitor essential system parameters and set alerts for critical thresholds, ensuring system robustness.
Option C - Monitoring server CPU and memory usage is important but not directly related to addressing potential outages.
Option D - Implementing a CDN is relevant but not specific to handling outages.
Option E - Evaluating expected traffic and planning for quota adjustments is a good practice but doesn't directly address ensuring system robustness during outages.

QUESTION 20

Answer - B) Modify the Python service to record API call durations and log this data. Use Cloud Logging to identify slow-response external APIs.

Option B is the correct choice.
Option B - Modifying the Python service to record API call durations and using Cloud Logging to identify slow-response external APIs is an effective approach for identifying performance degradation due to API integrations.
Option A - Applying Cloud Profiler is more focused on profiling code performance and may not capture external API issues.
Option C - Instrumenting services with Cloud Trace focuses on tracing but may not capture API performance nuances.
Option D - Deploying Cloud Debugger is more for debugging code and may not specifically address API integration performance.

QUESTION 21

Answer - B) A timeline of events leading up to and during the security breach.
Answer - E) An analysis of vulnerabilities in the cloud infrastructure.

Explanation for Option B - A timeline of events is crucial to understanding the sequence of actions leading to the security breach, which helps in identifying areas for improvement. It is a key component of post-incident reporting.
Explanation for Option E - An analysis of vulnerabilities in the cloud infrastructure is essential to determine the weaknesses that led to the security breach and how to address them to prevent similar incidents in the future.
Explanation for Option A - While listing security tools may be informative, it does not provide the same level of insight into the incident's causes and prevention as the other options.
Explanation for Option C - A summary of employee performance is not typically the focus of a post-incident report aimed at preventing security incidents.
Explanation for Option D - Reviewing the organization's financial performance is not directly relevant to a post-incident report focused on security incidents.

QUESTION 22

Answer - B) Deploy the application in multiple regions and utilize a regional load balancer.

Explanation for Option B - Deploying the application in multiple regions and using a regional load balancer ensures global availability and efficient traffic distribution to the nearest data center, aligning with the requirements.
Explanation for Option A - Using a single region with a global load balancer may provide high availability but doesn't address the need for regional presence and efficient traffic distribution.
Explanation for Option C - Selecting a small instance type to minimize costs is a cost optimization consideration but doesn't ensure global availability or scalability.
Explanation for Option D - Monitoring resource utilization and adjusting instance counts is important for optimization but doesn't directly address the initial planning for global availability and efficient traffic distribution.

QUESTION 23

Answer - B) Implement autoscaling based on predefined traffic patterns and resource utilization metrics.

Explanation for Option B - Implementing autoscaling allows resources to automatically adjust to traffic patterns, optimizing resource utilization and cost-efficiency.
Explanation for Option A - Maintaining a fixed number of VMs may lead to over-provisioning during off-peak times, increasing costs.
Explanation for Option C - Manually adding VMs is not as efficient as autoscaling and may result in delayed responses to traffic changes.
Explanation for Option D - Scheduling resource scaling based on a fixed daily schedule may not align with actual traffic patterns and can lead to suboptimal resource utilization.

QUESTION 24

B) Implement Google Kubernetes Engine (GKE) Autopilot clusters for automated security and compliance management.

Option B is the correct choice as it suggests implementing GKE Autopilot clusters, which provide automated security and compliance management. This aligns with the goal of ensuring security and compliance effectively in a healthcare organization.
Option A recommends using unmanaged clusters without specific security configurations, which may not meet security requirements.
Option C promotes manual configuration for security settings, which can be error-prone and time-consuming.
Option D suggests separate clusters without security controls, which is not aligned with security and compliance needs.

QUESTION 25

Answer - B) Assign the Cloud SQL Viewer role to the Database Administrators.

A) The SQL Admin role provides extensive privileges that go beyond monitoring, which is not in line with the least privilege principle.
 B) This role allows the Database Administrators to monitor the database performance without

unnecessary administrative privileges, adhering to the least privilege principle.
 C) The Project Viewer role provides broader access than necessary for the specific task of monitoring database performance.
 D) While a custom role can be configured, it's more complex and may not be necessary when a predefined role fits the requirement.
 E) The Monitoring Editor role grants permissions for editing monitoring configurations, which is more than what's needed for just monitoring.

QUESTION 26

Answer - A) Utilize Google Cloud Monitoring to create a dashboard based on a logs-based metric for failed login attempts.

Option A - Creating a logs-based metric and using Cloud Monitoring for visualization is a direct and effective approach for trend analysis.
 Option B - Using BigQuery and Data Studio is a robust solution but may be more complex than necessary for this task.
 Option C - While third-party services can be used, they lack the integration and simplicity of Google Cloud tools.
 Option D - Cloud Profiler is not the ideal tool for analyzing login attempt patterns.
 Option E - Employing machine learning is an advanced approach but may not be required for simple trend analysis.

QUESTION 27

Answer - C) Latency metric with a window-based method of evaluation.

Option A - While latency is the correct metric, a request-based method might not accurately capture the monthly performance.
 Option B - Throughput is not the relevant metric for measuring transaction completion time.
 Option C - A window-based latency metric aligns with the need to ensure performance over a defined period, like a month.
 Option D - Error rate does not directly measure transaction completion time.
 Option E - Transaction completion metric is relevant, but the window-based method is more appropriate for a monthly evaluation.

QUESTION 28

Answer - B) Use Cloud Build to automatically run infrastructure tests on pull requests against the development branch.

Option A - Post-deployment testing can be risky for production environments.
 Option B - This strategy ensures that infrastructure code is thoroughly and automatically tested before merging, minimizing risks.
 Option C - Manual testing is error-prone and might not be consistent.
 Option D - Testing should occur before reaching the release branch to catch issues earlier.
 Option E - Limiting testing to off-peak hours might delay the identification of critical issues.

QUESTION 29

Answer - B) Deploy a logging agent as a DaemonSet in GKE to capture and forward logs from the custom path to Stackdriver.

Option A - Direct editing of the tool's configuration is not possible as the application cannot be altered.
Option B - Deploying a logging agent as a DaemonSet is a scalable solution to ensure logs from a custom path are sent to Stackdriver.
Option C - GKE's default logging might not capture logs from non-standard directories.
Option D - While a custom service could work, it's more complex and less efficient than using a DaemonSet.
Option E - Manual processes are error-prone and not scalable for continuous operations.

QUESTION 30

Answer - B) Deploy the Cloud Operations agent on both GKE and on-premises servers to collect and send network metrics to Cloud Monitoring.

Option A - While built-in capabilities are useful, they may not provide consistent metrics across environments.
Option B - The Cloud Operations agent is designed to work in both cloud and on-premises environments, offering a unified solution.
Option C - Developing custom solutions can be resource-intensive and may lead to inconsistencies.
Option D - Third-party tools can be used, but they might not integrate seamlessly with Google Cloud services.
Option E - Manual monitoring is not efficient and does not provide the necessary integration for comprehensive analysis.

QUESTION 31

Answer - B) Implementing automated testing at various stages of the pipeline.

Option A, reducing the frequency of pipeline executions, can slow down the development process and is not recommended.
Option C, removing automated deployment, is counterproductive as automation is key to efficient CI/CD.
Option D, limiting developer access to the pipeline configuration, may hinder collaboration and transparency in the development process.

QUESTION 32

Answer - D) Deploy the service using a continuous delivery pipeline with canary releases. Monitor the service performance using Cloud Monitoring, and gradually increase traffic based on the observed metrics.

Option A, using blue/green deployment, switches all traffic immediately and doesn't allow for gradual monitoring.
Option B, using Config Connector, doesn't align with the concept of canary releases and gradual traffic increase.
Option C, using RollingUpdate, is a valid approach but doesn't leverage canary releases for gradual traffic

increase and monitoring.

QUESTION 33

Answer - C) Enforce organization-level constraints to prohibit service account key creation.

Option A, assigning specific IAM roles, may not effectively address the issue of minimizing key usage.
Option B, customizing predefined roles, could be complex and error-prone.
Option D, implementing guidelines, may not address the root concern of key creation.

QUESTION 34

Answer - B) Implement Canary deployments to gradually roll out new microservices versions and monitor their performance before full deployment.

Option B is the correct choice because implementing Canary deployments allows you to gradually roll out new microservices versions, monitor their performance, and test them before full deployment, which is a best practice for microservices in a CI/CD pipeline.
Option A, GKE Autopilot, is focused on cluster management and doesn't address deployment strategies.
Option C, VPC peering, is about network isolation and doesn't directly relate to CI/CD or microservices deployment.
Option D, Helm charts, is useful for managing configurations but doesn't specifically address deployment strategies or testing.

QUESTION 35

Answer - A) Enable VPC Flow Logs for the network subnet.

Explanation:
Option A is the correct choice because enabling VPC Flow Logs for the network subnet allows you to monitor incoming HTTP requests and capture source IP addresses with minimal effort and without modifying the API service code or introducing additional components.
Option B, implementing custom logging, requires code changes and may not capture all incoming requests.
Option C, deploying a reverse proxy server, adds complexity and may not be the most straightforward solution.
Option D, installing a third-party intrusion detection system, is a more comprehensive approach that may introduce additional complexity and resource overhead.

QUESTION 36

Answer - A) Set up a custom log filter in Cloud Logging to identify the "IoTData" label, create a log sink directed to Cloud Storage, and then establish a log exclusion based on the "IoTData" filter.

Option A is the correct choice as it aligns with best practices. It involves setting up a custom log filter to identify sensitive logs, directing them to Cloud Storage for secure storage, and excluding them from regular Cloud Logging to prevent exposure.
Option B is incorrect because it lacks the exclusion step, which is crucial for preventing exposure.
Option C is incorrect because it uses a Fluentd filter plugin with the Cloud Logging Agent but doesn't

mention log exclusion.
 Option D is incorrect because it lacks the customization required for secure storage and exclusion.

QUESTION 37

Answer - A) Appoint a dedicated owner for each resolution task and involve collaborators as needed.

Option A is the correct choice as it aligns with effective postmortem practices by assigning clear ownership while allowing collaboration.
 Option B is incorrect as it lacks explicit ownership, which can lead to accountability issues.
 Option C is incorrect as multiple owners may create confusion and delays.
 Option D is incorrect as placing sole ownership on one individual may not involve the necessary expertise for resolution.

QUESTION 38

Answer - A) Develop a custom logging library for your Cloud Run service, ensuring that log records are created in JSON format with the necessary attributes.

Option A is the correct choice as it involves developing a custom logging library within the Cloud Run service to create log records in JSON format with the required attributes, meeting the requirement for structured logging.
 Option B, C, and D suggest external solutions or configurations that may not be needed for achieving structured logging within Cloud Run.

QUESTION 39

Answer - B) Label each Cloud Spanner instance with a business unit-specific tag, set up BigQuery billing export, and query the costs by label.

Option A - Incorrect: While feasible, using unique identifiers without labels is less efficient for segregating costs.
Option B - Correct: Using labels for instances and BigQuery for cost analysis is the most efficient method.
Option C - Incorrect: Using metadata and logs is overly complex for cost analysis.
Option D - Incorrect: Manual tracking is time-consuming and error-prone.
Option E - Incorrect: Creating a custom script is unnecessary and less efficient than existing tools.

QUESTION 40

Answer - C) Collaborate with the development team during the planning phase, providing insights on deployment strategies and cloud resource management.

Option A - Incorrect: Beta testing is valuable but does not influence early design decisions.
Option B - Incorrect: Engagement after initial development may miss critical design considerations.
Option C - Correct: Early involvement in planning ensures that operational efficiencies are embedded from the start.
Option D - Incorrect: Post-deployment feedback is useful but less proactive than early stage collaboration.

QUESTION 41

Answer - A) Initiate a centralized monitoring project in Google Cloud, create a Cloud Operations Workspace, and connect only live streaming infrastructure projects, providing appropriate team members with read access.

Option A - Correct: This method ensures focused monitoring of critical infrastructure and adheres to the least privilege principle.
Option B - Incorrect: Granting broad access to all projects can lead to information overload and access control issues.
Option C - Incorrect: Multiple workspaces per project can complicate monitoring and access management.
Option D - Incorrect: Relying on an existing project may not provide the targeted and centralized monitoring needed.

QUESTION 42

Answer - A) Single repository for Terraform configurations with branches for each environment, separate repositories for Anthos Config Management with environment-specific directories, and individual repositories for each microservice with feature branching.

Option A - Correct: This approach offers a clear separation of concerns and allows for independent versioning and rollback mechanisms for each environment and service.
Option B - Incorrect: A unified repository can become complex and difficult to manage.
Option C - Incorrect: Separate repositories for each Terraform environment can lead to duplication and inconsistency.
Option D - Incorrect: Having a shared repository for both Terraform and Anthos configurations can lead to complexity and confusion.

QUESTION 43

Answer - C) Manage Terraform configurations using a Git-based repository, with a branching strategy and pull requests for peer reviews. Track changes via commit history.

Option A - Incorrect: A synchronized folder lacks proper mechanisms for handling concurrent modifications and version tracking.
Option B - Incorrect: Manual logging in a document management system is not efficient for tracking changes in Terraform configurations.
Option C - Correct: A Git-based repository with a branching strategy and pull requests is the most effective way to manage collaborative changes and maintain an accurate history.
Option D - Incorrect: Network-shared drives do not provide an efficient way to manage concurrent edits and version history.

QUESTION 44

Answer - C) Utilize the fluent-plugin-grep Fluentd filter plugin to exclude log entries containing sensitive data.

Option A - Incorrect: Application code changes may not be immediate.
Option B - Incorrect: While Dataflow is powerful, it may not be the quickest solution.

Option C - Correct: fluent-plugin-grep can quickly filter out sensitive data from logs, addressing the issue in real-time.
Option D - Incorrect: This approach introduces additional steps and potential delays in log processing.

QUESTION 45

Answer - C) Deploy additional Compute Engine instances and implement a load balancer to distribute the image processing load.

Option A - Incorrect: Adjusting the SLO might not address the underlying performance issue.
Option B - Incorrect: While upgrading the instance can help, it may not suffice during peak demand.
Option C - Correct: Adding more instances and load balancing can efficiently distribute the workload, enhancing reliability.
Option D - Incorrect: Standby instances may improve availability but don't efficiently address constant high demand.

QUESTION 46

Answer - B) Set up Cloud Monitoring alerts to trigger a Webhook, which is linked to a third-party SMS notification service where team members have registered their phone numbers.

Option A - Incorrect: Cloud Monitoring does not support direct SMS notifications.
Option B - Correct: Using a Webhook with a third-party SMS service is an efficient way to set up SMS notifications.
Option C - Incorrect: Relying on Microsoft Teams for SMS forwarding adds unnecessary steps.
Option D - Incorrect: Custom scripting is more complex and not necessary when third-party services can be integrated more simply.

QUESTION 47

Answer - B) Run a Connectivity Test from the Network Intelligence Center to analyze the network path between the compute instance and the database service.

Option A - Incorrect: While checking VPC peering is important, it might not provide complete diagnostics for connectivity issues.
Option B - Correct: The Connectivity Test can help identify the exact location of the network issue between the VPCs.
Option C - Incorrect: Custom logging requires access to instances and may not pinpoint network path issues.
Option D - Incorrect: Temporary firewall rules can help monitor traffic but are less effective in diagnosing path-related connectivity problems.

QUESTION 48

Answer - C) Incorporate automated dependency updates in the CI/CD pipeline to keep dependencies up-to-date.

Option A is not the best choice as traditional scanning tools may not be well-suited for microservices.
Option B is focused on runtime protection, which is important but doesn't directly address dependency

vulnerabilities.
Option D is a valid practice but may not be efficient for microservices at scale.
Option E provides a layer of protection but doesn't directly address dependency vulnerabilities.

QUESTION 49

A) Develop an incident report detailing the problems, insights, and a structured set of corrective actions. Share it exclusively with the department leader who requested it.

Option A is the correct choice because it provides a detailed incident report with insights and a structured set of remedial tasks, which is distributed to the department leader who requested it.
Option B lacks individual accountability details and relies on a broader distribution.
Option C distributes to the department leader but lacks structured remedial tasks.
Option D is similar to Option B but lacks individual accountability, making Option A more comprehensive.

QUESTION 50

Answer - D) Provide regular updates to all parties involved, maintaining a 'next update' time commitment in all communications.

Option D is the most appropriate strategy as it emphasizes providing regular updates to all parties involved and commits to 'next update' times during a critical security incident, ensuring effective communication.
Options A, B, and C prioritize direct communications with external stakeholders but do not address the need for regular updates and commitment to update times, which are crucial during such incidents.
Explanation:
Option A: Forwarding messages to the Communication Lead may lead to delays in communication with internal team members. Option B: While responding promptly to internal team members is important, it doesn't emphasize regular updates to all parties. Option C: Delegating tasks may not guarantee timely updates to internal team members. Option D: Provides a balanced approach with regular updates and a commitment to update times for effective communication with all parties involved.

PRACTICE TEST 4 - QUESTIONS ONLY

QUESTION 1

Your organization is deploying a microservices-based application on Google Kubernetes Engine (GKE). You want to ensure that all container images used in the application are scanned for vulnerabilities before deployment. Which approach should you take to achieve this, following Google's recommended DevOps practices?

A) Use Google Cloud Security Command Center for post-deployment vulnerability scanning, and configure alerts for vulnerabilities.
 B) Set up a Binary Authorization policy for GKE that requires images to pass vulnerability scans before deployment.
 C) Employ Google Cloud Pub/Sub for real-time event streaming of image vulnerabilities and take manual action for resolution.
 D) Implement Google Cloud Armor for DDoS protection to prevent vulnerabilities from being exploited.

QUESTION 2

Your team is responsible for managing a large-scale web application on Google Cloud. You need to ensure that the application can handle unexpected traffic spikes and maintain high availability. What Google Cloud services and strategies should you consider to achieve this, following Google's recommended DevOps practices?

A) Use Google Cloud Functions for serverless compute and Google Cloud Memorystore for caching to optimize application performance.
 B) Implement Google Cloud CDN for content delivery and set up auto-scaling with Google Kubernetes Engine (GKE) to handle traffic spikes.
 C) Deploy Google Cloud Armor for DDoS protection and use Google Cloud Trace for performance monitoring.
 D) Utilize Google Cloud Endpoints to create APIs and implement Google Cloud Pub/Sub for event-driven scaling.

QUESTION 3

Your team is responsible for managing a complex microservices architecture on Google Kubernetes Engine (GKE). You need to ensure high availability and reliability for your application. Which two Kubernetes concepts or techniques should you consider for achieving this goal? I. Implement PodDisruptionBudgets to control disruptions during maintenance. 2. Use Horizontal Pod Autoscaling (HPA) to adjust resources dynamically. 3. Deploy multi-cluster clusters across different regions for redundancy. 4. Set up Network Policies for fine-grained network control between microservices.

A) 1 and 2
 B) 2 and 3
 C) 3 and 4
 D) 1 and 4

QUESTION 4

When integrating Cloud Build with GKE for container deployments, what's the optimal way to handle authentication efficiently?

A) Create a separate service account with the Kubernetes Engine Developer role for Cloud Build.
B) Implement a manual step in Cloud Build to get service account credentials for kubectl.
C) Embed Kubernetes Engine Developer role into Cloud Build's configuration.
D) Grant Cloud Build's service account the Kubernetes Engine Developer role.
E) Utilize the default Cloud Build service account.

QUESTION 5

Your organization has shifted its operations to Google Cloud, and you're tasked with creating an automated and scalable method for setting up new departments and infrastructure. What's the best approach?

A) Develop a script using the gcloud command-line tool to insert the required parameters from the submission. Archive the script in a version control system.
B) Construct a Terraform configuration and store it in your version control system. Duplicate and execute the terraform apply instruction to generate the new department.
C) Utilize the Terraform templates from the Cloud Foundation Toolkit. Implement the templates with the necessary parameters to establish the Google Cloud department and requisite infrastructure.
D) Manually configure each department through the Google Cloud console.

QUESTION 6

Following a significant network disruption, you're obligated to brief key stakeholders in adherence to Site Reliability Engineering best practices. What's the initial course of action you should take?

A) Craft a comprehensive incident report for distribution among the stakeholders.
B) Circulate the Incident Summary Document to every stakeholder immediately.
C) Individually phone each stakeholder to detail the events that transpired.
D) Instruct the network engineer at fault to compose a personal apology letter to every stakeholder.

QUESTION 7

Your organization has implemented a review committee to oversee all changes to the existing financial systems. What actions should you take to modify this process while maintaining the efficiency of the software deployment workflow? (Choose two.)

A) Authorize developers to integrate their updates autonomously, but ensure the application deployment environment can roll back changes if issues arise.
B) Implement a peer-review system for each modification submitted as part of the source code, backed by automated checks.
C) Replace the review committee with a high-ranking executive for continuous oversight throughout the development and release cycle.
D) Ensure the software development environment provides developers with rapid feedback on the consequences of their changes.
E) Consolidate changes into more substantial, albeit less frequent, application updates.

QUESTION 8

You are overseeing a Regional GKE deployment for a large-scale data analytics service. The service processes complex data queries and experiences unpredictable peaks in usage. Ensuring low latency and efficient resource use during peak and non-peak periods is crucial. What approach should you take for resource management?

A) Configure a Vertical Pod Autoscaler to adjust resources as per demand.
B) Set up node pool autoscaling and a Horizontal Pod Autoscaler.
C) Employ a cron job to increase pod count during expected peak times.
D) Rely on GKE's default settings for automatic resource adjustment.
E) Implement custom scripts to manually scale resources based on real-time monitoring.

QUESTION 9

You are tasked with setting up a distributed data analysis service on Google Cloud, requiring substantial compute resources and autoscaling across several regions. The service will process large datasets quickly. What should be your primary action to ensure successful deployment?

A) Opt for Compute Engine instances with high-CPU machine types to ensure fast data processing.
B) Start with a pilot deployment in a single region, then scale out to additional regions based on the pilot's success.
C) Confirm that your service's compute and storage demands are within the resource quotas for each intended region.
D) Set up an elaborate monitoring system to track performance metrics across different regions.
E) Implement autoscaling based on custom metrics tailored to the data processing workload.

QUESTION 10

Your organization has deployed a set of microservices using Cloud Run and needs to optimize the cost. You are tasked with analyzing the performance and resource usage of these services. What approach should you take?

A) Enable Cloud Debugger on each microservice to continuously monitor performance and resource usage.
B) Use Cloud Trace to monitor the request latency and number of requests per microservice.
C) Implement Cloud Monitoring to track CPU and memory metrics and analyze the scalability of each service.
D) Set up Cloud Logging to log detailed performance metrics and manually calculate resource usage.
E) Deploy Cloud Profiler to profile the microservices and optimize the resource allocation based on usage patterns.

QUESTION 11

Your organization requires certain team members to have read-only access to the VM instance logs in Google Compute Engine for audit purposes, following Google Cloud's best practices. What is the most appropriate action to take?

A) Grant each team member the roles/compute.viewer role individually.
B) Assign the roles/logging.viewer role to a Google Group that includes all relevant team members.

C) Create a custom role with minimal permissions necessary for accessing Compute Engine logs and assign it to the team.
D) Grant the roles/compute.admin role to a Google Group containing all team members for comprehensive access.
E) Assign the roles/logging.logViewer role to each team member individually.

QUESTION 12

Your company is developing a large-scale analytics application with GKE clusters in multiple regions, including us-west1 and europe-north1. You need to manage container image distribution for these regions effectively. Which strategy should you adopt for storing and serving these images?

A) Utilize a single global Cloud Storage bucket to store all container images and configure GKE to pull images from this bucket.
B) Push the container images to Google Container Registry using region-specific hostnames like us.gcr.io and eu.gcr.io.
C) Store the container images in Google Container Registry using a global hostname such as gcr.io.
D) Create regional Compute Engine instances in each region and store the container images on their local storage.
E) Implement a custom image replication service across multiple Google Cloud Storage buckets in each region.

QUESTION 13

Your company's cloud-based image processing service recently experienced a slowdown after a new algorithm update. Users are reporting longer processing times. You need to identify and address the cause of the slowdown as quickly as possible. What should be your initial action?

A) Roll back the service to the previous version before the algorithm update.
B) Review the Cloud Monitoring metrics for the service to identify any anomalies since the update.
C) Immediately deploy additional Compute Engine instances to increase processing capacity.
D) Inform users about the slowdown and promise a fix in the next scheduled update.
E) Conduct a detailed code review of the new algorithm to identify potential inefficiencies.

QUESTION 14

As a part of enhancing security measures, your organization requires real-time analysis of access logs from a set of Cloud Storage buckets used across various Google Cloud projects. The goal is to detect and respond to any unauthorized access. What is the best way to achieve this?

A) Enable Access Transparency logs for each Cloud Storage bucket and analyze them using Cloud Functions.
B) Set up Data Loss Prevention (DLP) scans on each bucket and monitor the scan results for unauthorized access.
C) Create a log sink for each bucket, forwarding access logs to a central Cloud Logging bucket for analysis.
D) Configure an aggregated log sink at the folder level for all projects, directing Cloud Storage access logs to a single Pub/Sub topic.
E) Use Cloud Audit Logs to monitor access to the Cloud Storage buckets and analyze them using Cloud

Security Command Center.

QUESTION 15

As part of its cloud strategy, your company needs to deploy an API service on Google Cloud that can route traffic to different backend versions based on the API version requested by the client. The deployment should also allow for gradual rollout of new versions. Which solution aligns with these requirements?

A) Deploy the API service on Cloud Endpoints, using its version management features to route requests based on the API version and gradual rollout of new versions.
B) Use Cloud Run to host the API service, configuring the service to route requests to different revisions based on the API version and employing traffic splitting for version rollouts.
C) Implement the API service on Google Kubernetes Engine (GKE) with Anthos Service Mesh, setting up routing rules based on the API version in the request and managing version rollouts with traffic splitting.
D) Host the API service on App Engine, utilizing services and versions to route requests based on the API version and using traffic splitting for gradual version rollout.
E) Set up the API service on Compute Engine with a custom load balancer, manually configuring routing based on API versions and managing new version deployments.

QUESTION 16

Your organization relies on a single Google Cloud Compute Engine instance to run a critical service. You want to enhance the service's reliability by automatically replacing the instance if it becomes unhealthy while following Site Reliability Engineering (SRE) principles. What's the most suitable approach?

A) Notify the application development team when the instance becomes unhealthy so they can take appropriate action.
B) Implement a Load Balancer to distribute traffic and provide failover capabilities for the Compute Engine instance.
C) Create a Managed Instance Group with a single instance and configure health checks to monitor its status.
D) Set up a Google Cloud Monitoring dashboard to manually monitor the instance's health and initiate replacements when needed.

QUESTION 17

Your organization stores data processing scripts in Cloud Source Repositories and aims to establish an automated workflow that executes the latest script version on Google Compute Engine (GCE) instances whenever a new version is committed, with minimal setup complexity. What's the recommended approach?

A) Use a custom service in App Engine to invoke Cloud Functions.
B) Utilize Cloud Pub/Sub to trigger a Cloud Build workflow.
C) Implement Cloud Pub/Sub to trigger a custom orchestrator service hosted on Compute Engine.
D) Configure Cloud Scheduler to trigger a Cloud Build workflow.

QUESTION 18

Your team is responsible for managing containerized applications in a multi-cloud environment. You need a solution to securely store and manage container images with consistent access controls across all clouds. What approach should you take to achieve this efficiently?

A) Use a different container registry service for each cloud provider to maintain flexibility.
B) Implement Google Cloud Artifact Registry and leverage its multi-cloud support with consistent access controls.
C) Develop custom access control scripts for each cloud's container registry.
D) Rely on the default access controls provided by each cloud's container registry.

QUESTION 19

You are trying to generate a service account key for a partner analytics platform, but you receive an organization policy constraint error: 'iam.disableServiceAccountKeyCreation is enforced.' What is the most secure approach in line with Google's recommendations to address this issue?

A) Temporarily relax the iam.disableServiceAccountKeyCreation policy constraint at the organization level, create the key, and then re-enforce the policy.
B) Override the policy prohibiting service account key creation at the department level within the project and generate a key for use.
C) Enable the default service account key and retrieve it for the partner analytics platform.
D) Add a clause to your project's IAM policy to deactivate the iam.disableServiceAccountKeyCreation constraint, then proceed to create the necessary key.

QUESTION 20

Your organization uses Apache Maven on Google Cloud Compute Engine instances for software build automation. You are responsible for introducing configuration management automation through Ansible, while ensuring that the Ansible Maven instance has the necessary authorization to manage Google Cloud assets in compliance with Google Cloud's recommended practices. What is the appropriate action to take in this scenario?

A) Implement a Terraform module to enable Secret Manager to acquire credentials.
B) Ensure the Maven Compute Engine instance is equipped with a linked service account that has the necessary Identity and Access Management (1AM) roles.
C) Add the gcloud auth application-default login command to the Maven build process before executing Ansible playbooks.
D) Create a dedicated service account exclusively for the Ansible host, download the service account key, and set the GOOGLE_CREDENTIALS environment variable within the Maven environment.

QUESTION 21

Your e-commerce platform is approaching a major shopping event, and you want to ensure its reliability and scalability. What should be your first action to prepare for the anticipated surge in traffic?

A) Increase the server capacity by doubling the number of servers.
B) Implement an auto-scaling solution to dynamically adjust resources based on traffic.
C) Conduct performance monitoring to identify bottlenecks and areas for optimization.

D) Develop a contingency plan for handling unexpected outages during the event.

QUESTION 22

Your team is responsible for maintaining a critical machine learning model that is utilized by various departments in your organization. You've developed an improved version of the model and need to update it without causing disruptions to ongoing operations. What should you do?

A) Implement the new model without informing anyone to prevent potential resistance. Notify users after the update is complete.
B) Announce the update to all stakeholders, provide training on the new model, and gradually transition to the improved version while monitoring its performance.
C) Update the model during off-peak hours to minimize the impact on users. Notify users after the update is complete.
D) Replace the old model with the new one without any prior communication to users to avoid resistance to change.

QUESTION 23

You are tasked with implementing a CI/CD pipeline for your microservices-based application on Google Kubernetes Engine (GKE). Which Google Cloud service is most suitable for automating the building, testing, and deployment of containerized applications to GKE?

A) Google Cloud Storage
B) Google Cloud Functions
C) Google Cloud Build
D) Google Cloud Pub/Sub

QUESTION 24

You are developing a cloud-native application on Google Cloud, where ensuring zero downtime and collecting extensive user feedback is crucial. The application experiences varying loads, with occasional spikes. Which strategy would best suit your deployment needs while allowing for real-time performance analysis and immediate rollback if issues arise?

A) Implement a rolling update during off-peak hours.
B) Use blue/green deployment with load balancers.
C) Apply canary testing by routing a portion of traffic to the new version.
D) Conduct shadow testing by mirroring production traffic.
E) Perform A/B testing targeting specific demographic groups.

QUESTION 25

Your team is managing a cloud-based document processing service and aims to set an SLI for the time taken to open a document. The acceptable performance threshold is set at 300 ms. What is the recommended way to calculate this SLI in accordance with Google's guidelines?

A) Measure the average time taken to open documents.
B) Count the number of documents opened within 300 ms, then divide by the total number of

document open requests.
 C) Compute the median and 90th percentiles of document opening times.
 D) Record the number of user complaints about slow document openings and divide by the total number of users.
 E) Monitor the frequency of server errors during document opening.

QUESTION 26

For a cloud-based video streaming service, how should the SRE and Application Development teams divide their responsibilities to ensure service reliability and continuous improvement?

A) SRE team: Cloud infrastructure management and setting SLIs/SLOs; App Dev team: Feature development and code optimization.
 B) App Dev team: Full stack development and deployment; SRE team: SLI/SLO monitoring and incident management.
 C) Shared: Incident response and SLI/SLO development; SRE team: Infrastructure scaling; App Dev team: Code development.
 D) SRE team: Entire system maintenance and on-call duties; App Dev team: Code development and performance tuning.
 E) Shared: Code deployment and performance metrics setting; SRE team: System monitoring; App Dev team: New feature development.

QUESTION 27

A cloud service company plans to upgrade its storage systems to reduce data retrieval times, costing $10,000. The service generates $2,000,000 annually. The upgrade is expected to improve revenue by enhancing user experience. How should you assess whether this investment is financially justifiable?

A) Estimate a 5% increase in revenue due to improved performance, justifying the investment.
 B) Project a 0.5% increase in revenue, concluding the investment is not justified.
 C) Predict a 1% increase in user retention, determining the investment is justifiable.
 D) Calculate a potential revenue increase of $20,000, concluding the investment is not justified.
 E) Forecast an increase in new customer acquisition by 2%, justifying the investment.

QUESTION 28

As the head of IT for a cloud-based customer relationship management (CRM) service, you notice the service has been performing well within its error budget. To align the SLOs with actual performance and encourage innovation, what two steps should you take?

A) Introduce more complex features more frequently to test the service's limits.
 B) Expand the scope of SLIs to include metrics from the sales and marketing modules.
 C) Increase the error budget to allow for more risky updates and experiments.
 D) Tighten the SLOs to reflect the high performance observed in recent times.
 E) Conduct additional user experience surveys to directly incorporate customer feedback.

QUESTION 29

Your team manages a fleet of Virtual Machines on Google Compute Engine (GCE) tasked with processing sensitive data. You need to implement a solution to ensure all VMs, including those created in the future, are monitored consistently with Cloud Operations. What approach should you take?

A) Create a custom VM image with the Cloud Operations agent pre-installed for all future VM deployments.
B) Use the gcloud CLI to set up an instance template that includes the installation of the Cloud Operations agent in the startup script.
C) Manually install the Cloud Operations agent on each existing VM and any new VMs upon creation.
D) Rely on the default logging and monitoring settings of GCE, as they automatically integrate with Cloud Operations.
E) Develop a script to use the Compute Engine API to periodically check for VMs without the agent and install it.

QUESTION 30

Your organization runs a large-scale data analytics service on Google Cloud and wants to optimize BigQuery resource usage. You aim to choose the best approach to efficiently manage BigQuery slots while minimizing manual intervention. What should you do?

A) Regularly review query performance in the Cloud Monitoring dashboard and manually adjust slot allocation.
B) Use the BigQuery Slot Recommender to automatically receive recommendations for optimal slot allocation.
C) Set a fixed number of slots for all queries and adjust based on monthly usage reports.
D) Implement a custom script that adjusts slots based on daily query load.
E) Rely on BigQuery's default slot allocation and manually intervene only during peak usage times.

QUESTION 31

You are responsible for managing a Cloud Function that interacts with Cloud Pub/Sub. After deploying a new version of the function, you notice that it's not processing messages from the Pub/Sub topic as expected. The error logs indicate a permissions issue. What should you do to resolve this while adhering to Google Cloud recommended practices?

A) Grant the Cloud Function service account the role of roles/pubsub.subscriber on the relevant Pub/Sub topic.
B) Disable the Cloud Function and revert to the previous version.
C) Reconfigure the Cloud Function to use a different Pub/Sub topic.
D) Increase the allocated memory and CPU for the Cloud Function.

QUESTION 32

Your organization utilizes WebSocket connections to interact with a public Cloud Run service at https://api-financialxy.z.run.app. Developers need to validate new revisions of this service before making them generally available. What is the recommended approach for this?

A) Deploy the service through a continuous delivery pipeline with canary releases. Shift all traffic to the new version and monitor performance with Cloud Monitoring.
B) Use the curl -H "Authorization:Bearer $(gcloud auth print-identity-token)" command for

authentication. Test the service at https://api-financialxy.z.run.app privately.
C) Deploy the report-service with the --no-traffic --tag dev options and test it at https://dev-api-financialxy.z.run.app.
D) Update the traffic for the report-service using the gcloud run services update-traffic command, targeting the latest revision, and test at https://api-financialxy.z.run.app.

QUESTION 33

Your team manages multiple Google Kubernetes Engine (GKE) clusters across different regions. You want to ensure that container images are securely scanned for vulnerabilities before deployment. Which approach should you adopt to achieve this security objective effectively?

A) Manually scan container images before deployment.
B) Enable automated image vulnerability scanning in Google Container Registry.
C) Rely on GKE's built-in security measures without additional scanning.
D) Use third-party scanning tools to check container images.

QUESTION 34

Your organization is managing a large-scale containerized application on Google Kubernetes Engine (GKE). You want to implement a CI/CD pipeline that includes automated testing, staging, and deployment of microservices. Which GKE features and practices should you incorporate into your pipeline to achieve this goal?

A) Use GKE Autopilot to automatically manage and scale the microservices, reducing the need for manual intervention.
B) Implement Canary deployments to gradually roll out new microservices versions and monitor their performance before full deployment.
C) Set up VPC peering to isolate the testing and staging environments, ensuring data separation.
D) Apply Helm charts for managing the deployment configurations of microservices, simplifying versioning and release management.

QUESTION 35

You are responsible for managing secrets in a healthcare application deployed using Cloud Build. What is the most effective approach to securely integrate these secrets into your build process with minimal workflow disruption?

A) Utilize a secret management tool to store and retrieve secrets securely within your build process.
B) Store secrets in plaintext files within your version control system and grant Cloud Build access to these files.
C) Create a new Cloud Storage bucket and store secrets with object-level permissions configured for Cloud Build access.
D) Utilize Google Cloud's Secret Manager service to securely store and manage secrets, integrating them into your Cloud Build deployment script.

QUESTION 36

You are responsible for managing a cloud-based document collaboration platform on Google Cloud

Platform (GCP). This platform relies on n2-highcpu-4 Compute Engine instances for handling real-time document editing. Users have reported delays in document updates, and your Cloud Monitoring dashboard shows that network capacity is consistently at its limit. What step should you take to enhance network performance for the document collaboration platform?

A) Upgrade the Compute Engine instances to n2-highcpu-16 for improved network performance.
 B) Implement a content delivery network (CDN) to cache and deliver frequently accessed documents closer to users.
 C) Optimize the database queries used by the platform to reduce network traffic.
 D) Deploy additional firewalls to ensure network security and minimize traffic congestion.

QUESTION 37

You are managing the deployment of a real-time data processing system on Google Kubernetes Engine (GKE). You want to ensure the ability to revert to the previous system version in case of unexpected issues with the update. What deployment strategy is most appropriate?

A) Opt for a dark launch strategy, and continuously monitor the new data processing system's performance.
 B) Use a rolling update approach, and evaluate the new system after the deployment stage is completed.
 C) Implement a canary release method, and assess the new system periodically after its release.
 D) Adopt a blue/green deployment strategy, and evaluate the new system once the deployment is finalized.

QUESTION 38

Your media streaming service on Google Cloud experiences recurrent brief interruptions where instances temporarily become unresponsive but recover within seconds. Alerts are triggered for each occurrence. To optimize service reliability in line with Site Reliability Engineering (SRE) principles, what should you do?

A) Revise the associated Service Level Objective (SLO) to incorporate these frequent restarts within the error budget.
 B) Document detailed incident reports for each alert received to investigate the root causes.
 C) Disseminate alert notifications among team members situated in various geographic regions.
 D) Establish a protocol for automatic resolution of alerts without human intervention.

QUESTION 39

Your company is preparing its e-commerce website for an anticipated spike in traffic during a major sales event. The website is hosted on Google Cloud. What should be your initial step to ensure the website can handle the increased load, in accordance with Google's best practices?

A) Migrate the website to Cloud Run and enable automatic scaling.
B) Develop an Ansible playbook for quick deployment of additional resources in different regions.
C) Conduct stress testing on the website to evaluate its current performance and scalability.
D) Pre-provision additional Compute Engine resources based on previous sales event data plus an extra buffer for anticipated growth.

E) Implement a Cloud Function to dynamically adjust resources in response to traffic changes.

QUESTION 40

As a Site Reliability Engineer, you are addressing sporadic performance issues in a Node.js application that processes data streams from IoT devices using Cloud IoT Core and Dataflow. The goal is to continuously monitor the application in production to identify bottlenecks. Which method aligns with this requirement and ensures low overhead?

A) Deploy Cloud Profiler and integrate Node.js profiling capabilities within your application.
B) Regularly execute the Node.js --inspect flag on your instances and analyze the reports.
C) Set up a standalone profiling server in Compute Engine to collect detailed performance data from your application.
D) Monitor the Dataflow job metrics and Cloud IoT Core logs through Cloud Monitoring for performance insights.

QUESTION 41

You're managing a Google Cloud-based e-commerce platform and are experiencing frequent, short-duration performance issues, leading to a high volume of alerts. This is causing alert fatigue among your SRE team. How can you optimize the alert system to maintain operational efficiency without overwhelming the team?

A) Analyze each performance issue in depth and create a detailed incident report.
B) Establish a global team rotation for handling alerts to ensure continuous coverage.
C) Modify your alerting thresholds to only notify for prolonged or critical performance issues.
D) Redefine the error budgets to be more lenient with these frequent, short-duration issues.

QUESTION 42

You're overseeing a global web application on GKE, and users in one specific region are reporting slow response times. What should be your initial step to diagnose and address this issue, adhering to SRE principles?

A) Analyze the region-specific GKE clusters using Cloud Logging to identify any error patterns or service disruptions.
B) Increase the size of the node pool in the affected region to immediately boost performance and capacity.
C) Redirect user traffic from the affected region to other regions that are operating normally.
D) Examine the resource usage like CPU and memory in the impacted region using Cloud Monitoring for anomalies.

QUESTION 43

In a multinational corporation with distinct operations divisions, each with their own Google Cloud projects, you are tasked with setting up Cloud Monitoring to reflect division-specific metrics. What is the most effective way to achieve this, ensuring clear separation of data?

A) Implement a master dashboard for the entire corporation, with filters to select metrics from specific divisions.

B) Designate a primary project for each division and configure their dashboards to scope metrics from these projects.

C) Establish a new, overarching project for Cloud Monitoring and integrate all divisional projects under this for unified monitoring.

D) Create separate dashboards for each project in every division, grouping them under division-specific folders in Cloud Monitoring.

QUESTION 44

Your healthcare portal, hosted on App Engine and using Cloud SQL and Cloud Storage, faces performance issues during patient registration peaks. The system remains sluggish even after the peak. What steps should you take to enhance responsiveness and prepare for future high-traffic periods?

A) Increase the minimum number of instances in App Engine's automatic scaling configuration.

B) Transition the healthcare portal to a Compute Engine-based setup for more granular control.

C) Implement caching for frequently accessed data in Cloud SQL to reduce database load.

D) Opt for faster access Cloud Storage classes to improve file retrieval times.

QUESTION 45

You manage a set of GKE clusters and need to automate the enforcement of security policies, which are stored in a GitHub repository. The policies must be applied consistently across all clusters. What approach should you take for automatic policy updates and enforcement?

A) Use Config Connector to synchronize with the GitHub repository and automatically apply policy changes.

B) Trigger a Cloud Function upon GitHub repository changes to update policies in GKE clusters.

C) Configure Anthos Config Management with the GitHub repository to enforce policy updates.

D) Set up a GitHub Actions workflow to run Cloud Build jobs, applying policy updates via gcloud CLI commands.

QUESTION 46

As a cloud architect, you are designing a system for a legal firm that will handle confidential client information. What security practices should you implement to protect this sensitive data in the cloud environment?

A) Encrypt sensitive data at rest and in transit, using a robust encryption service like Cloud KMS.

B) Store sensitive client information in plaintext within cloud storage for ease of access.

C) Implement a system where client data is directly embedded into the application code.

D) Use a third-party encryption tool to manage keys outside of Google Cloud's infrastructure.

QUESTION 47

Your GKE cluster hosts a critical application that has recently started experiencing outages in one of its microservices due to memory leaks. Until a permanent solution is deployed, you need a stopgap measure to keep the service running. What is the best practice to temporarily mitigate this issue?

A) Adjust the microservice's Deployment to increase its memory allocation as a temporary buffer against the leak.
B) Use a liveness probe in the Kubernetes Deployment to restart the pod when it reaches a certain memory threshold.
C) Schedule a nightly restart of the microservice's pods using a cron job within Kubernetes to clear the memory leak.
D) Monitor the microservice with Cloud Monitoring and manually restart pods when a memory leak is detected.

QUESTION 48

You manage a Python-based streaming application on Google Cloud's Dataflow service. Recently, the workers have been shutting down every 20 minutes with memory spikes. What action should you take to address this issue?

A) Enable Cloud Debugger to analyze the application's memory usage and then restart the workers.
B) Increase the number of worker nodes in the Dataflow job's configuration.
C) Reduce the parallelism in the Dataflow pipeline to lower memory usage.
D) Adjust the Dataflow job's memory allocation to a higher value.

QUESTION 49

Your organization is transitioning to a DevOps culture, and your software application encountered intermittent performance issues recently. A department head has requested a formal incident analysis for preventive measures. What should you do?

A) Create an incident analysis report detailing the underlying problems, insights gained, individual responsibilities, and remedial tasks assigned to specific team members. Share it exclusively with the requesting department head.
B) Draft an incident analysis report summarizing the problems and insights. Share it across the organization's technical documentation repository for reference.
C) Formulate an incident analysis report outlining the issues, insights, and a structured set of corrective actions. Share it solely with the requesting department head.
D) Develop an incident analysis report highlighting the problems, insights, and a structured set of corrective actions. Disseminate it across the organization's technical documentation platform for broader access.

QUESTION 50

You are responsible for managing deployments using Spinnaker in a containerized application. A canary release phase is included in your deployment pipeline. What is the appropriate configuration for canary analysis in this containerized environment?

A) Compare the canary with performance metrics from previous canary releases.
B) Evaluate the canary alongside the latest stable production release.
C) Analyze the canary in isolation without any performance comparison.
D) Assess the canary against a containerized test environment.

PRACTICE TEST 4 - ANSWERS ONLY

QUESTION 1

Answer - B) Set up a Binary Authorization policy for GKE that requires images to pass vulnerability scans before deployment.

Option B aligns with best practices by using Binary Authorization to enforce image vulnerability scanning before deployment in GKE.
Option A suggests post-deployment scanning, which is not proactive.
Option C involves manual actions and is not fully automated.
Option D addresses DDoS protection, not vulnerability scanning.

QUESTION 2

Answer - B) Implement Google Cloud CDN for content delivery and set up auto-scaling with Google Kubernetes Engine (GKE) to handle traffic spikes.

Option B aligns with the goal of handling unexpected traffic spikes and maintaining high availability by using Google Cloud CDN for content delivery and auto-scaling with GKE. This strategy follows Google's recommended DevOps practices for scalability and availability.
Option A mentions serverless compute and caching but does not directly address traffic spikes.
Option C focuses on DDoS protection and monitoring but does not emphasize handling traffic spikes.
Option D mentions APIs and event-driven scaling but does not provide a comprehensive strategy for high availability.

QUESTION 3

Answer - A) 1 and 2

Options 1 and 2 are the recommended choices to ensure high availability and reliability for a complex microservices architecture on Google Kubernetes Engine (GKE). Implementing PodDisruptionBudgets helps control disruptions during maintenance, and using Horizontal Pod Autoscaling (HPA) ensures dynamic resource adjustment for high availability.
Option 3, deploying multi-cluster clusters across different regions, is relevant for disaster recovery but may not address day-to-day high availability concerns.
Option 4, setting up Network Policies, is important for network security but not directly related to availability and reliability.

QUESTION 4

Answer - D) Grant Cloud Build's service account the Kubernetes Engine Developer role.

Option D is correct as it directly assigns the required role to Cloud Build's service account, simplifying authentication.
Option A introduces complexity with a separate service account,
Option B adds manual steps, which is not efficient,
Option C suggests embedding the role, which may not be the best approach,
Option E doesn't address authentication effectively.

QUESTION 5

Answer - C) Utilize the Terraform templates from the Cloud Foundation Toolkit. Implement the templates with the necessary parameters to establish the Google Cloud department and requisite infrastructure.

Option C is the correct choice as it recommends leveraging Terraform templates from the Cloud Foundation Toolkit, ensuring scalability and dependability while automating department creation.
Option A introduces a manual script which is less scalable,
Option B suggests Terraform but without templates and lacks scalability,
Option D is highly manual and not scalable.

QUESTION 6

Answer - B) Circulate the Incident Summary Document to every stakeholder immediately.

Option B is the correct choice as it suggests circulating the Incident Summary Document to every stakeholder immediately, providing a concise overview of the incident.
Option A delays communication,
Option C is inefficient for a large number of stakeholders,
Option D is not the initial step and focuses on personal apologies rather than incident summary.

QUESTION 7

Answer - A and B

Option A - Authorizing developers to integrate updates autonomously while ensuring rollback capabilities can expedite the process without compromising safety.
Option B - Implementing a peer-review system with automated checks maintains code quality without hindering deployment efficiency.
Options C, D, and E are not the optimal steps to adjust the process.

QUESTION 8

Answer - B) Set up node pool autoscaling and a Horizontal Pod Autoscaler.

A) Incorrect - Vertical scaling alone may not provide the needed flexibility for unpredictable workloads.
B) Correct - This combination ensures efficient scaling both at the node and pod level, adapting to usage peaks.
C) Incorrect - Cron-based scaling may not accurately match unpredictable demand.
D) Incorrect - Default settings may not optimally handle the specific requirements of a large-scale data analytics service.
E) Incorrect - Manual scaling is less efficient and might not respond quickly enough to usage changes.

QUESTION 9

Answer - C) Confirm that your service's compute and storage demands are within the resource quotas for each intended region.

A) Incorrect - While selecting appropriate machine types is necessary, it's not the first consideration.

B) Incorrect - A pilot deployment is a later step, after ensuring resource availability.
C) Correct - Verifying that the service's resource needs fit within the regional quotas is crucial for a smooth deployment.
D) Incorrect - Monitoring setup comes after confirming the feasibility of the resource requirements.
E) Incorrect - Custom metrics for autoscaling are important but secondary to initial resource quota checks.

QUESTION 10

Answer - C) Implement Cloud Monitoring to track CPU and memory metrics and analyze the scalability of each service.

A) Incorrect - Cloud Debugger is mainly used for debugging applications, not for monitoring performance and resource usage.
B) Incorrect - Cloud Trace focuses on latency and request tracing, not on detailed resource metrics.
C) Correct - Cloud Monitoring provides comprehensive CPU and memory metrics, essential for cost optimization.
D) Incorrect - Cloud Logging provides logs but requires manual effort for detailed performance analysis.
E) Incorrect - Cloud Profiler is more suited for profiling applications rather than continuous monitoring for cost optimization.

QUESTION 11

Answer - B) Assign the roles/logging.viewer role to a Google Group that includes all relevant team members.

A) Incorrect - The compute.viewer role gives broader access than necessary for just viewing logs.
B) Correct - This grants the necessary access in an efficient way, adhering to the principle of least privilege.
C) Incorrect - Custom roles are an option, but a predefined role is sufficient in this case.
D) Incorrect - The compute.admin role provides excessive permissions for the requirement.
E) Incorrect - Assigning roles individually is less efficient than using a group.

QUESTION 12

Answer - C) Store the container images in Google Container Registry using a global hostname such as gcr.io.

A) Incorrect - Cloud Storage is not specialized for container image distribution and may not provide optimal efficiency.
B) Incorrect - Using region-specific hostnames can complicate image management for a multi-region deployment.
C) Correct - GCR with a global hostname is the most efficient and streamlined way to manage and distribute container images across multiple regions.
D) Incorrect - Using Compute Engine instances for image storage is inefficient and not scalable for this purpose.
E) Incorrect - Custom replication services are unnecessary and less efficient than using GCR's built-in capabilities.

QUESTION 13

Answer - B) Review the Cloud Monitoring metrics for the service to identify any anomalies since the update.

A) Incorrect - Rolling back without understanding the issue may not resolve the problem.
B) Correct - Reviewing monitoring metrics helps in identifying the root cause of the slowdown.
C) Incorrect - Adding more instances without diagnosing the problem could increase costs without resolving the issue.
D) Incorrect - Communicating with users is important, but it should not replace immediate investigative actions.
E) Incorrect - A code review is a longer process and may delay the resolution of the issue.

QUESTION 14

Answer - D) Configure an aggregated log sink at the folder level for all projects, directing Cloud Storage access logs to a single Pub/Sub topic.

A) Incorrect - Access Transparency logs provide visibility into Google's operations, not user access to Cloud Storage.
B) Incorrect - DLP scans are for identifying sensitive data, not for monitoring access logs.
C) Incorrect - Individual log sinks for each bucket complicate centralized analysis.
D) Correct - An aggregated log sink at the folder level provides a centralized and efficient way to collect and analyze access logs.
E) Incorrect - While Cloud Audit Logs are valuable, they need to be centralized for effective real-time analysis.

QUESTION 15

Answer - C) Implement the API service on Google Kubernetes Engine (GKE) with Anthos Service Mesh, setting up routing rules based on the API version in the request and managing version rollouts with traffic splitting.

A) Incorrect - Cloud Endpoints is primarily an API management tool and does not provide the same level of routing flexibility as GKE with Anthos Service Mesh.
B) Incorrect - While Cloud Run supports traffic splitting, it does not offer the same granular control for API version-based routing as GKE with Anthos Service Mesh.
C) Correct - GKE with Anthos Service Mesh provides advanced capabilities for routing based on API versions and supports gradual rollout of new versions with traffic splitting.
D) Incorrect - App Engine's routing capabilities are not as advanced as GKE with Anthos Service Mesh for this specific use case.
E) Incorrect - Compute Engine with a custom load balancer requires significant manual setup and does not offer the ease of version management found in GKE with Anthos Service Mesh.

QUESTION 16

Answer - C) Create a Managed Instance Group with a single instance and configure health checks to monitor its status.

Option C is the correct choice because it aligns with Site Reliability Engineering (SRE) principles by

automatically replacing the instance when it becomes unhealthy, ensuring high reliability.
 Option A - Option A is incorrect because notifying the application development team may introduce delays in response and doesn't provide automated failover.
 Option B - Option B is incorrect because while Load Balancers provide traffic distribution, they do not automatically replace instances in the event of failure.
 Option D - Option D is incorrect because manual monitoring and initiation of replacements do not provide automated failover capabilities as needed for high reliability.

QUESTION 17

Answer - B) Utilize Cloud Pub/Sub to trigger a Cloud Build workflow.

Option B is the correct choice because it allows you to trigger a Cloud Build workflow when new code versions are committed to Cloud Source Repositories, achieving automation with minimal setup complexity.
 Option A - Option A introduces an additional layer of complexity with App Engine and Cloud Functions, which may not be necessary.
 Option C - Option C suggests creating a custom orchestrator service, which may be more complex than needed for this task.
 Option D - Option D uses Cloud Scheduler, which is not the most suitable choice for triggering a build workflow when code changes occur.

QUESTION 18

Answer - B) Implement Google Cloud Artifact Registry and leverage its multi-cloud support with consistent access controls.

Option B is the correct choice because it recommends using Google Cloud Artifact Registry, which supports multi-cloud environments and offers consistent access controls for efficient container image management.
 Option A - Option A suggests using different registries for each cloud, which can lead to complexity and inconsistency.
 Option C - Option C involves developing custom scripts, which may not be as efficient as using a managed service.
 Option D - Option D relies on default controls, which may not provide the required security and consistency.

QUESTION 19

Answer - A) Temporarily relax the iam.disableServiceAccountKeyCreation policy constraint at the organization level, create the key, and then re-enforce the policy.

Option A is the correct choice.
 Option A - Temporarily relaxing the policy constraint at the organization level allows you to create the service account key securely, aligning with Google's recommended practices.
 Option B - Overriding the policy at the department level may not align with organizational policies and is not the recommended approach.
 Option C - Enabling the default service account key may not provide the necessary security for the analytics platform.

Option D - Adding a clause to the project's IAM policy to deactivate the constraint is not a recommended practice and may lead to unintended consequences.

QUESTION 20

Answer - B) Ensure the Maven Compute Engine instance is equipped with a linked service account that has the necessary Identity and Access Management (1AM) roles.

Option B is the correct choice.
Option B - Ensuring that the Maven Compute Engine instance is equipped with a linked service account containing the necessary IAM roles aligns with Google Cloud's recommended practices for Ansible authorization.
Option A - Implementing a Terraform module for Secret Manager is unrelated to Ansible authorization.
Option C - Adding the gcloud auth application-default login command to the Maven build process is not the recommended practice for Ansible authorization.
Option D - Creating a dedicated service account and setting GOOGLE_CREDENTIALS is a valid but more complex approach compared to Option B.

QUESTION 21

Answer - C) Conduct performance monitoring to identify bottlenecks and areas for optimization.

Explanation for Option C - Conducting performance monitoring is the first step to assess the current state of the platform and identify potential bottlenecks and areas that require optimization before the event. It helps in making informed decisions about resource allocation.
Explanation for Option A - Increasing server capacity without understanding the current performance and resource utilization may lead to unnecessary costs.
Explanation for Option B - Implementing auto-scaling is essential, but it should come after performance monitoring to determine the scaling strategy effectively.
Explanation for Option D - Developing a contingency plan is important but should not be the initial action. It's crucial to assess and optimize the platform's performance first.

QUESTION 22

Answer - B) Announce the update to all stakeholders, provide training on the new model, and gradually transition to the improved version while monitoring its performance.

Explanation for Option B - Announcing the update, providing training, and gradually transitioning to the new model with performance monitoring is a best practice to ensure a smooth transition and minimize disruptions.
Explanation for Option A - Implementing the new model without informing anyone can lead to resistance and confusion among users when changes are noticed. Communication is essential.
Explanation for Option C - Updating the model during off-peak hours is a good practice, but communication and training are crucial to ensure a smooth transition.
Explanation for Option D - Replacing the old model without prior communication can lead to confusion and resistance to change among users.

QUESTION 23

Answer - C) Google Cloud Build

Option A) Google Cloud Storage is for object storage, not CI/CD.
Option B) Google Cloud Functions is for event-driven serverless functions, not CI/CD.
Option D) Google Cloud Pub/Sub is a messaging service, not CI/CD.
Option C) Google Cloud Build is a fully managed CI/CD platform that automates building, testing, and deploying containerized applications to GKE, making it the most suitable choice for this scenario.

QUESTION 24

Answer - C) Apply canary testing by routing a portion of traffic to the new version.

A) This option minimizes downtime but doesn't facilitate immediate user feedback or performance analysis under real-world conditions.
 B) Ensures zero downtime but lacks the capability for real-time performance analysis and immediate rollback.
 C) This option is ideal for real-time performance analysis and immediate rollback if necessary, as it exposes the new version to a subset of real users under actual load conditions.
 D) Shadow testing is useful for performance analysis but doesn't expose the new version directly to real users.
 E) A/B testing is more focused on user behavior analysis rather than application performance under varied loads.

QUESTION 25

Answer - B) Count the number of documents opened within 300 ms, then divide by the total number of document open requests.

Option A - Average time could be skewed by outliers and does not accurately measure against the threshold.
 Option B - This is the correct method, as it directly assesses the proportion of requests meeting the performance target.
 Option C - Percentile calculations are insightful but do not focus on the specific threshold of 300 ms.
 Option D - User complaints are subjective and not a quantifiable metric for SLI.
 Option E - Server error frequency does not relate to the performance of document opening times.

QUESTION 26

Answer - C) Shared: Incident response and SLI/SLO development; SRE team: Infrastructure scaling; App Dev team: Code development.

Option A - Solely assigning SLI/SLO setting to the SRE team can lead to a disconnect between operational metrics and application capabilities.
 Option B - This distribution could lead to inefficiencies, as full stack development requires operational insights.
 Option C - This collaborative approach ensures a balance between operational excellence and innovative development.
 Option D - Exclusively burdening the SRE team with system maintenance and on-call duties can lead to

operational tunnel vision.
 Option E - While collaboration on performance metrics is beneficial, dividing responsibilities more distinctly can lead to better specialization and efficiency.

QUESTION 27

Answer - A) Estimate a 5% increase in revenue due to improved performance, justifying the investment.

Option A - A 5% revenue increase on a $2,000,000 revenue stream significantly outweighs the $10,000 investment.
 Option B - A 0.5% increase might not cover the cost of the upgrade.
 Option C - While user retention is important, it needs to translate into a substantial revenue increase to justify the cost.
 Option D - A $20,000 increase on a $2,000,000 revenue doesn't justify a $10,000 investment.
 Option E - New customer acquisition is beneficial but needs to result in a significant revenue increase to justify the cost.

QUESTION 28

Answer - A) and B)

Option A - More frequent and complex updates can help utilize the error budget for innovation while monitoring stability.
 Option B - Expanding SLI scope provides a more comprehensive understanding of the service's performance.
 Option C - Increasing the error budget may not be necessary and could lead to complacency.
 Option D - Tightening SLOs might risk setting overly stringent expectations.
 Option E - While user feedback is valuable, it's not directly related to adjusting SLOs or managing the error budget.

QUESTION 29

Answer - B) Use the gcloud CLI to set up an instance template that includes the installation of the Cloud Operations agent in the startup script.

Option A - While effective, custom images require maintenance and may not be as adaptable as other methods.
 Option B - Using an instance template with a startup script ensures consistent and automated deployment of the monitoring agent for all new VMs.
 Option C - Manual installation is time-consuming and prone to human error, especially in dynamic environments.
 Option D - Default GCE settings may not meet specific monitoring needs and may not include the Cloud Operations agent.
 Option E - Automating via a script is a potential solution but may not be as immediate or reliable as using an instance template.

QUESTION 30

Answer - B) Use the BigQuery Slot Recommender to automatically receive recommendations for optimal slot allocation.

Option A - Manual review is time-consuming and may not always lead to optimal decisions.
Option B - The BigQuery Slot Recommender provides data-driven recommendations, minimizing manual effort and optimizing resource usage.
Option C - A fixed number of slots may not efficiently handle varying query loads.
Option D - Custom scripting requires maintenance and may not adapt quickly to changing needs.
Option E - Default allocation may not be cost-efficient for all workloads and usage patterns.

QUESTION 31

Answer - A) Grant the Cloud Function service account the role of roles/pubsub.subscriber on the relevant Pub/Sub topic.

Option B, disabling the Cloud Function and reverting to the previous version, does not address the permissions issue and is not recommended.
Option C, reconfiguring the Cloud Function to use a different Pub/Sub topic, may not resolve the underlying permissions problem.
Option D, increasing resource allocation, does not directly address the permissions issue.

QUESTION 32

Answer - B) Use the curl -H "Authorization:Bearer $(gcloud auth print-identity-token)" command for authentication. Test the service at https://api-financialxy.z.run.app privately.

Option A, deploying with canary releases, is a deployment strategy but does not address authentication.
Option C, deploying with the dev tag, is related to deployment but not authentication.
Option D, updating traffic to the latest revision, does not address authentication for testing new revisions.

QUESTION 33

Answer - B) Enable automated image vulnerability scanning in Google Container Registry.

- Option A is manual and time-consuming for multiple clusters.
- Option C may not provide the level of security needed.
- Option D adds complexity with third-party tools.
Enabling automated image vulnerability scanning in Google Container Registry (Option B) ensures that container images are scanned for vulnerabilities automatically before deployment, providing effective security without manual efforts.

QUESTION 34

Answer - B) Implement Canary deployments to gradually roll out new microservices versions and monitor their performance before full deployment.

Explanation:
Option B is the correct choice because implementing Canary deployments allows you to gradually roll out new microservices versions, monitor their performance, and test them before full deployment, which is a best practice for microservices in a CI/CD pipeline.

Option A, GKE Autopilot, is focused on cluster management and doesn't address deployment strategies.
Option C, VPC peering, is about network isolation and doesn't directly relate to CI/CD or microservices deployment.
Option D, Helm charts, is useful for managing configurations but doesn't specifically address deployment strategies or testing.

QUESTION 35

Answer - D) Utilize Google Cloud's Secret Manager service to securely store and manage secrets, integrating them into your Cloud Build deployment script.

Explanation:
Option D is the correct choice as it leverages Google Cloud's Secret Manager to securely store and manage secrets, seamlessly integrating them into the Cloud Build deployment script with proper security.
Option A suggests using a secret management tool, which is vague and not specific to Google Cloud's services.
Option B proposes storing secrets in plaintext files, which is not secure.
Option C suggests using a Cloud Storage bucket but lacks the security and management features of Google Cloud's Secret Manager.

QUESTION 36

Answer - B) Implement a content delivery network (CDN) to cache and deliver frequently accessed documents closer to users.

Option B is the correct choice as it addresses the network capacity issue by implementing a CDN to cache and deliver frequently accessed documents, reducing the strain on the network.
Option A is incorrect as upgrading the instance type may not directly resolve the network capacity problem.
Option C is incorrect as optimizing database queries, while important, may not fully address the network capacity issue.
Option D is incorrect as deploying additional firewalls may not directly impact network performance and could potentially introduce more congestion.

QUESTION 37

Answer - D) Adopt a blue/green deployment strategy, and evaluate the new system once the deployment is finalized.

Option D is the correct choice as it aligns with the requirement to ensure the ability to revert by keeping the current system (blue) running alongside the new one (green) until the deployment is finalized.
Option A is incorrect as it focuses on monitoring without a clear rollback strategy.
Option B is incorrect as rolling updates may not provide the same level of safety in case of issues.
Option C is incorrect as it involves periodic assessments but may not facilitate an immediate rollback.

QUESTION 38

Answer - A) Revise the associated Service Level Objective (SLO) to incorporate these frequent restarts within the error budget.

Option A is the correct choice as it aligns with SRE principles by adjusting the SLO to account for frequent restarts, ensuring they fall within the error budget. This approach optimizes service reliability while maintaining stability.

Option B suggests creating detailed incident reports for every alert, which may be excessive for brief interruptions. Option C involves geographic distribution of alerts, which may not directly address the issue. Option D recommends automatic alert resolution, which may not optimize service reliability for this specific scenario.

QUESTION 39

Answer - C) Conduct stress testing on the website to evaluate its current performance and scalability.

Option A - Incorrect: While Cloud Run offers scaling, it's not the first step for preparation.
Option B - Incorrect: Ansible playbook helps in deployment but isn't the first step in scalability planning.
Option C - Correct: Stress testing is crucial to understand current capabilities and identify areas for improvement.
Option D - Incorrect: Pre-provisioning is vital but should follow an initial performance assessment.
Option E - Incorrect: Dynamic resource adjustment is helpful but not the primary step for handling traffic surges.

QUESTION 40

Answer - A) Deploy Cloud Profiler and integrate Node.js profiling capabilities within your application.

Option A - Correct: Cloud Profiler provides continuous, low-overhead performance monitoring suitable for pinpointing bottlenecks.
Option B - Incorrect: Using --inspect flag is more suited for debugging specific issues, not continuous monitoring.
Option C - Incorrect: A standalone profiling server introduces additional complexity and maintenance.
Option D - Incorrect: While helpful, Dataflow and IoT Core metrics do not specifically identify application-level bottlenecks.

QUESTION 41

Answer - C) Modify your alerting thresholds to only notify for prolonged or critical performance issues.

Option A - Incorrect: In-depth analysis for each minor issue is not practical and can increase fatigue.
Option B - Incorrect: Global rotation distributes the load but doesn't address the core issue of frequent alerts.
Option C - Correct: Adjusting alert thresholds to focus on significant issues helps reduce unnecessary notifications and team stress.
Option D - Incorrect: Redefining error budgets might affect service reliability perception without addressing alert frequency.

QUESTION 42

Answer - A) Analyze the region-specific GKE clusters using Cloud Logging to identify any error patterns or service disruptions.

Option A - Correct: Immediate log analysis helps identify the root cause of the issue, which is in line with SRE practices.

Option B - Incorrect: Adding resources without diagnosing the issue can be premature and may not solve the underlying problem.

Option C - Incorrect: Traffic redirection is a reactive measure and should be considered after understanding the issue.

Option D - Incorrect: While monitoring resource usage is important, it might not provide specific insights into application-level issues.

QUESTION 43

Answer - B) Designate a primary project for each division and configure their dashboards to scope metrics from these projects.

Option A - Incorrect: A master dashboard might not provide the required separation and clarity for division-specific metrics.

Option B - Correct: Assigning a primary project per division for dashboard scoping aligns with Google Cloud best practices and ensures clear data separation.

Option C - Incorrect: An overarching project might lead to complexities in monitoring and data segregation.

Option D - Incorrect: Creating separate dashboards for each project can be overly complex and not user-friendly.

QUESTION 44

Answer - A) Increase the minimum number of instances in App Engine's automatic scaling configuration.

Option A - Correct: Adjusting the App Engine scaling settings can directly address performance issues during traffic spikes.

Option B - Incorrect: Moving to Compute Engine involves significant changes and may not be necessary.

Option C - Incorrect: While caching can help, it doesn't directly address the observed sluggishness in the overall system.

Option D - Incorrect: Changing storage classes might not have a substantial impact on the overall system performance.

QUESTION 45

Answer - C) Configure Anthos Config Management with the GitHub repository to enforce policy updates.

Option A - Incorrect: Config Connector is not primarily used for policy enforcement from source code repositories.

Option B - Incorrect: While Cloud Functions can react to changes, they are not typically used for direct policy enforcement in GKE.

Option C - Correct: Anthos Config Management is designed for synchronizing and applying configurations and policies stored in repositories like GitHub.

Option D - Incorrect: Although feasible, GitHub Actions with Cloud Build is a more complex solution compared to Anthos Config Management.

QUESTION 46

Answer - A) Encrypt sensitive data at rest and in transit, using a robust encryption service like Cloud KMS.

Option A - Correct: Encryption both at rest and in transit, with a service like Cloud KMS, is crucial for protecting sensitive information.
Option B - Incorrect: Storing sensitive information in plaintext is highly insecure.
Option C - Incorrect: Embedding client data in application code is unsafe and not a best practice.
Option D - Incorrect: While third-party tools can be used, Cloud KMS offers integrated and secure key management within Google Cloud.

QUESTION 47

Answer - B) Use a liveness probe in the Kubernetes Deployment to restart the pod when it reaches a certain memory threshold.

Option A - Incorrect: Increasing memory allocation may postpone the issue but does not address the underlying problem.
Option B - Correct: Liveness probes can automatically restart pods when they hit memory thresholds, helping to manage memory leak issues temporarily.
Option C - Incorrect: Scheduled restarts may not coincide with when the memory leak becomes problematic.
Option D - Incorrect: Manual monitoring and intervention are not scalable or reliable for continuous operations.

QUESTION 48

Answer - D) Adjust the Dataflow job's memory allocation to a higher value.

Option A suggests enabling Cloud Debugger, but it doesn't directly address the memory allocation issue.
Option B increases worker nodes but doesn't tackle the memory spikes causing shutdowns.
Option C reduces parallelism, which may affect performance but doesn't directly resolve the memory problem.
Option D is the recommended approach to address the memory spikes and prevent worker shutdowns.

QUESTION 49

A) Create an incident analysis report detailing the underlying problems, insights gained, individual responsibilities, and remedial tasks assigned to specific team members. Share it exclusively with the requesting department head.

Option A is the correct choice as it provides a comprehensive incident analysis report with insights, individual responsibilities, and remedial tasks, exclusively shared with the requesting department head.
Option B summarizes the problems and insights but lacks individual responsibilities and corrective actions, and it has broader distribution.
Option C shares the report with the department head but lacks structured remedial tasks.
Option D is similar to Option B but lacks individual responsibilities and corrective actions, making Option A the most comprehensive choice.

QUESTION 50

Answer - B) Evaluate the canary alongside the latest stable production release.

Option B is the appropriate configuration for canary analysis in a containerized environment as it allows you to evaluate the canary alongside the latest stable production release, providing real-world performance insights.
Options A, C, and D do not offer the same real-world context for analysis, making option B the suitable choice.

PRACTICE TEST 5 - QUESTIONS ONLY

QUESTION 1

Your organization manages a large-scale e-commerce application on Google Cloud. To ensure optimal performance and minimize downtime, you want to implement rolling updates for your application's microservices. What should you consider for a successful implementation, following Google's recommended DevOps practices?

A) Use Google Cloud Deployment Manager to create and manage microservices resources, and configure auto-healing in Google Cloud Load Balancing.
 B) Implement Google Cloud Endpoints for API management and utilize Google Cloud CDN for content delivery to optimize performance.
 C) Leverage Google Cloud Pub/Sub for real-time event streaming of microservices updates, and employ Google Cloud Armor for DDoS protection.
 D) Set up Google Kubernetes Engine (GKE) for container orchestration, use RollingUpdate strategy in GKE, and monitor using Google Cloud Operations.

QUESTION 2

Your company is migrating a legacy application to Google Cloud. The application uses a relational database to store customer data, and data integrity is crucial. What approach should you follow to migrate the database while ensuring data consistency, following Google's recommended DevOps practices?

A) Perform a one-time data dump from the legacy database to Google Cloud Storage and then import the data into a Google Cloud SQL database.
 B) Set up a real-time data replication mechanism between the legacy database and a Google Cloud SQL database to ensure data consistency during migration.
 C) Create a new schema in Google Cloud SQL, export data from the legacy database, and import it into the new schema to minimize disruption.
 D) Migrate the application code to Google Cloud and configure it to access the legacy database until all data is migrated, then switch to a Google Cloud SQL database.

QUESTION 3

You are deploying a containerized application on Google Kubernetes Engine (GKE). The application consists of microservices that communicate internally using gRPC. You want to optimize network performance between these microservices. Which networking mode should you select for GKE nodes to achieve the best internal communication performance? 1. Bridge mode 2. Host mode 3. VPC-native mode 4. Legacy mode.

A) 1 and 3
B) 2 and 4
C) 3 and 4
D) 1 and 2

QUESTION 4

You're setting up Cloud Build to manage container deployments to GKE using kubectl. What's the most efficient authentication method?

A) Include the Kubernetes Engine Developer role in Cloud Build's configuration file.
B) Implement an additional Cloud Build step to manually fetch service account credentials.
C) Help the Cloud Build service account by granting it the Kubernetes Engine Developer role.
D) Create a dedicated service account with the Kubernetes Engine Developer role for Cloud Build.
E) Stick with the default Cloud Build service account.

QUESTION 5

As a Google Cloud professional overseeing the shift of your organization's operations, you need to establish an automated and scalable method for setting up new departments and infrastructure. What's the recommended approach?

A) Develop a script using the gcloud command-line tool to insert the required parameters from the submission. Archive the script in a version control system.
B) Construct a Terraform configuration and store it in your version control system. Duplicate and execute the terraform apply instruction to generate the new department.
C) Utilize the Terraform templates from the Cloud Foundation Toolkit. Implement the templates with the necessary parameters to establish the Google Cloud department and requisite infrastructure.
D) Manually configure each department through the Google Cloud console.

QUESTION 6

In the context of optimizing your media processing workflow in Google Cloud's Dataflow to reduce job execution time and repetitive tasks, what steps should you consider? (Choose two.)

A) Segment the automation procedures into finer-grained components.
B) Implement automatic progression confirmations transferring from the staging area to the production zone.
C) Run a script to facilitate the setup of the media processing workflow in Google Cloud Dataflow.
D) Set up an alert to inform the designated team to proceed with the next phase when human input is needed.

QUESTION 7

Your company has introduced a review committee to validate all modifications to the existing financial systems. What actions should you take to modify this process without negatively impacting the software deployment workflow? (Choose two.)

A) Permit developers to independently integrate their changes, while ensuring the application deployment environment can revert changes if problems arise.
B) Implement a peer-review mechanism for each modification submitted as part of the source code, reinforced by automated checks.
C) Replace the review committee with a high-ranking executive to maintain continuous oversight throughout the development and release cycle.
D) Guarantee the software development environment offers swift feedback to developers about the

consequences of their changes.

E) Group changes into more substantial, although less frequent, application updates.

QUESTION 8

Your team has deployed a machine learning model training service on a Regional GKE cluster. The service's workload involves processing large datasets and varies depending on the projects. You need to maintain high throughput during intense processing periods and reduce resource waste during idle times. What strategy should you adopt?

A) Utilize a Horizontal Pod Autoscaler based on network throughput.
B) Implement a Vertical Pod Autoscaler for dynamic resource allocation.
C) Configure node pool autoscaling based on CPU and memory demand.
D) Schedule manual scaling activities based on project timelines.
E) Set a fixed number of pods to handle the maximum anticipated workload.

QUESTION 9

Your company operates a multi-tenant environment on GKE, where different teams manage distinct applications. You need to set up development, testing, and production environments for each team while ensuring operational isolation and cost efficiency. What is the best approach to achieve this?

A) Create separate Google Cloud projects for each team, with dedicated GKE clusters for development, testing, and production.
B) Set up a single GKE cluster and use Kubernetes namespaces to separate each team's environment, applying RBAC for access control.
C) Implement separate GKE clusters within a single project, one for each environment, and use network policies for isolation.
D) Use a multi-cluster setup across different projects with shared VPCs, ensuring team-specific access via IAM roles.
E) Organize each team's environment within a single cluster using namespaces and enforce isolation through Identity Aware Proxy.

QUESTION 10

You manage a real-time data analysis system on Google Cloud using Dataflow. To effectively manage costs, you need to understand the resource utilization of your Dataflow jobs. What should you do?

A) Utilize Cloud Debugger to analyze the runtime efficiency of the Dataflow jobs.
B) Implement Cloud Monitoring to track the execution and resource metrics of the Dataflow jobs.
C) Use Cloud Trace for an in-depth analysis of the Dataflow jobs' processing times and resource usage.
D) Set up custom log-based metrics in Cloud Logging to monitor the performance of Dataflow jobs.
E) Apply Cloud Data Loss Prevention (DLP) to monitor and protect sensitive data processed by the Dataflow jobs.

QUESTION 11

The finance department needs to periodically review the cost management reports generated in Google Cloud Billing. They require view-only access to these reports. How should you set up their access in line with Google Cloud's best practices?

A) Assign the roles/billing.viewer role to each finance department member.
B) Provide the finance department with the roles/billing.admin role for complete access to billing reports.
C) Create a Google Group for the finance department and assign the roles/billing.viewer role to this group.
D) Grant each finance department member the roles/cloudPlatform.viewer role for access to all GCP resources.
E) Set up a custom role with specific permissions for billing report access and assign it to the finance department.

QUESTION 12

You are establishing an automated pipeline for a mobile application backend hosted on Google Cloud. The backend is developed using microservices, and each service has its own repository. You need to ensure that any new changes are thoroughly tested and deployed efficiently. What should be your approach?

A) Configure Cloud Build to automatically run unit and integration tests for each service upon a pull request. After successful testing, deploy each service to a production-like staging environment for further evaluation.
B) Set up individual Git hooks in each repository to enforce local testing pre-commit. Once committed, use Cloud Build to deploy services directly to production.
C) Implement a centralized Cloud Build process to build and test all microservices simultaneously post-merge. If tests pass, deploy to a canary environment before full production rollout.
D) Use manual triggers in Cloud Build for each microservice, requiring developers to initiate builds and tests. Upon successful completion, deploy to a shared test environment followed by production.
E) Establish Git pre-push hooks to run local tests and build containers. Upon successful completion, use Cloud Build for deployment to a dedicated integration environment and then to production.

QUESTION 13

Following a recent scaling configuration change on your Compute Engine-based web application, users are experiencing intermittent downtime. You suspect the issue might be related to the new scaling settings. What is the most effective first step to address this issue?

A) Immediately revert the scaling configuration changes to their previous state.
B) Analyze the Cloud Monitoring logs to understand the impact of the new scaling configuration.
C) Upgrade the machine types of your Compute Engine instances to higher-capacity models.
D) Send a notification to users apologizing for the inconvenience and assuring them that the issue is being investigated.
E) Perform load testing on the application to simulate user traffic and observe the system's behavior.

QUESTION 14

Your organization utilizes Google Cloud for hosting several applications, each in its own project. To strengthen security posture, there's a requirement to monitor and analyze VM instance logs for suspicious activities across all projects. How should you set up log collection for effective security monitoring?

A) Deploy a dedicated Security Information and Event Management (SIEM) system in each project to collect and analyze VM logs.
B) Use Cloud Audit Logs to track activities on VM instances and analyze them using third-party tools.
C) Create an aggregated log sink at the organization level, collecting logs from all VM instances into a centralized analysis tool.
D) Set up Stackdriver Logging agents on each VM instance to forward logs to a Cloud Logging bucket in each project.
E) Configure individual log sinks in each project to send VM logs to a shared BigQuery dataset for analysis.

QUESTION 15

Your organization is expanding its use of Terraform for managing cloud infrastructure. To maintain security and compliance, you need a system to manage both proprietary and community Terraform modules, ensuring they adhere to your security policies. What is the most effective approach to achieve this?

A) Utilize a private Terraform module registry hosted on Google Kubernetes Engine (GKE), with strict access controls and security scanning.
B) Store all Terraform modules in a secured version-controlled repository in Cloud Source Repositories, integrating with Cloud Build for module deployment.
C) Keep Terraform modules in a Cloud Storage bucket with VPC Service Controls, using Cloud IAM for access management.
D) Host both types of modules in Artifact Registry, implementing binary authorization and vulnerability scanning.
E) Use a third-party managed service for Terraform module management, ensuring it complies with your organization's security policies.

QUESTION 16

You're tasked with managing a critical application that relies on a single Google Cloud Compute Engine instance. To minimize downtime and align with Site Reliability Engineering (SRE) practices, what should you do?

A) Notify the software development team about instance failures for immediate investigation and resolution.
B) Deploy a Load Balancer to distribute traffic and provide redundancy for the Compute Engine instance.
C) Establish a Managed Instance Group with a single instance and configure health checks to automatically replace the instance if it becomes unhealthy.
D) Implement a Google Cloud Monitoring dashboard to manually monitor the instance's health and initiate replacements when needed.

QUESTION 17

In the context of setting up continuous deployment for your telemedicine application on Google Cloud, you want to ensure that only updates that pass stringent stress testing in a staging GKE cluster are deployed to the primary GKE cluster used by patients and healthcare providers. What configuration steps should you take with Binary Authorization?

A) Create an attestation for stress-tested updates and manually obtain a signature from the chief technical officer using their private key.

B) Configure an attestation for stress-tested updates using a private key stored in Cloud Key Management Service (Cloud KMS) along with a service account JSON key embedded as a Kubernetes Secret.

C) Generate an attestation for stress-tested updates and require the chief technical officer to provide a signature using a key stored in Cloud Key Management Service (Cloud KMS).

D) Set up an attestation for stress-tested updates using a private key secured in Cloud Key Management Service (Cloud KMS) with verification through Workload Identity.

QUESTION 18

Your company is expanding its containerized applications across various Google Cloud regions. You need a container registry solution that can efficiently distribute container images to multiple regions while ensuring low latency. What should you choose to meet this requirement?

A) Deploy a local container registry in each region to manage image distribution.

B) Utilize Google Cloud Artifact Registry with multi-region support to efficiently distribute container images.

C) Set up a separate Cloud Storage bucket in each region to store container images.

D) Implement third-party image distribution tools to manage image replication across regions.

QUESTION 19

Your organization needs to generate a service account key for a partner analytics platform, but you encounter an organization policy constraint error: 'iam.disableServiceAccountKeyCreation is enforced.' What is the most secure approach in line with Google's recommendations to resolve this issue?

A) Temporarily relax the iam.disableServiceAccountKeyCreation policy constraint at the organization level, create the key, and then re-enforce the policy.

B) Override the policy prohibiting service account key creation at the project level within the department and generate a key.

C) Activate the default service account key and retrieve it for the partner analytics platform.

D) Amend your project's IAM policy to disable the iam.disableServiceAccountKeyCreation constraint and proceed to create the required key.

QUESTION 20

Your company utilizes Apache Maven on Google Cloud Compute Engine instances for software build automation. You're tasked with incorporating configuration management automation through Ansible. It is imperative that the Ansible Maven instance possesses the authorization to manage Google Cloud assets. You aim to adhere to the prescribed practices by Google Cloud. What course of action should you take?

A) Implement the Terraform module so the Secret Manager is able to obtain credentials.

B) Ensure the Maven Compute Engine instance is equipped with a linked service account that has the necessary Identity and Access Management (1AM) roles.

C) Incorporate the gcloud auth application-default login command into the Maven build process prior to the execution of Ansible playbooks.
D) Establish a distinct service account exclusive to the Ansible host. Download and convey the service account key to the GOOGLE_CREDENTIALS environment variable within the Maven environment.

QUESTION 21

Your cloud-based gaming service is preparing for a major game launch with an expected surge in players. What should be your initial step to ensure the platform can handle the increased load?

A) Preemptively double the number of game servers to accommodate the expected players.
B) Implement automatic scaling to adjust server resources based on player traffic.
C) Conduct load testing to assess the platform's performance under expected player loads.
D) Prepare a disaster recovery plan in case of unexpected service disruptions.

QUESTION 22

Your organization relies on a machine learning model for fraud detection. You have developed an updated version of the model that performs better and want to deploy it without affecting ongoing fraud detection operations. What should you do?

A) Replace the old model with the new one immediately without informing anyone to prevent resistance to change. Notify users afterward.
B) Announce the update to the fraud detection team, provide training on the new model, and gradually transition to the improved version while monitoring its performance.
C) Update the model during peak fraud detection hours to ensure the most users are impacted. Notify users after the update is complete.
D) Deploy the new model without any prior communication to users to avoid resistance to change.

QUESTION 23

Your team is adopting a DevOps culture, and you want to emphasize the importance of continuous improvement through incident retrospectives. Which actions can help instill this mindset?

A) Assign blame during retrospectives to hold individuals accountable.
B) Encourage a blame-free environment during retrospectives.
C) Limit retrospectives to the engineering team only.
D) Conduct retrospectives sporadically, only after major incidents.

QUESTION 24

As a DevOps engineer, you're tasked with deploying a critical update to an existing application on Google Cloud. The update includes significant changes to the application's backend. Which deployment strategy should you adopt to ensure that the update is seamlessly integrated without impacting the current users, while also allowing for immediate feedback on system performance?

A) Utilize a rolling update strategy with gradual deployment.
B) Implement canary releases, initially exposing a small fraction of users.
C) Conduct comprehensive A/B testing with feature toggles.

D) Use blue/green deployment for instant switch-over.
E) Apply shadow testing to duplicate live traffic to the updated system.

QUESTION 25

You are in charge of monitoring a cloud-based messaging service, focusing on message delivery speed. The SLI targets a delivery time of less than 150 ms. Which method aligns with Google's recommendations for calculating this SLI?

A) Track the average message delivery time.
B) Count the messages delivered within 150 ms and divide this by the total number of messages sent.
C) Calculate the median and 95th percentile of message delivery times.
D) Record the number of messages not delivered within 150 ms and divide by total messages sent.
E) Monitor the number of messages queued for delivery and divide by the total messages sent.

QUESTION 26

You manage a cloud-based SaaS application on Google Cloud, providing real-time data analytics. The application's performance is critical, and you need to enhance monitoring beyond the existing SLI at the application level. Where should you measure additional SLIs to capture potential issues in service delivery? (Choose two)

A) Network latency metrics between your application and the database server.
B) User experience monitoring tools that simulate typical user interactions.
C) Application performance monitoring integrated into the analytics engine.
D) CPU and memory usage statistics on the application servers.
E) Google Cloud SQL query execution times.

QUESTION 27

Your organization is considering implementing an advanced security protocol for its cloud infrastructure, costing $15,000. The annual revenue is $10,000,000. The upgrade is expected to reduce the risk of costly data breaches. What approach should be taken to evaluate the investment?

A) Calculate the potential loss from a data breach, comparing it with the investment cost.
B) Estimate the cost of the investment as a percentage of annual revenue, deciding based on the percentage.
C) Consider only the direct cost savings from the investment, disregarding indirect benefits like enhanced security.
D) Evaluate the impact of the investment on operational efficiency, disregarding its cost.
E) Assess the investment based on the potential increase in customer trust and market reputation.

QUESTION 28

Managing a global cloud-based file storage service, you find that the service is significantly underutilizing its error budget. In aiming to use this budget more effectively without compromising service reliability, what two measures should you consider?

A) Implement a more aggressive rollout of new file management features.

B) Increase storage capacity in all regions to enhance performance.
C) Revise SLOs to reflect actual service performance and reliability.
D) Develop additional SLIs focused on file upload and download speeds.
E) Regularly schedule downtime for maintenance to align with the error budget.

QUESTION 29

Your organization utilizes multiple Google Cloud projects for its web application development lifecycle, including development, staging, and production environments. You are tasked with ensuring consistent network configurations across these environments. Which combination of Google Cloud tools and practices should you employ?

A) Deploy Cloud Build to apply network configurations and use Config Sync to maintain consistency across all projects.
 B) Implement Terraform for network configuration and leverage Cloud Monitoring to detect any configuration drifts.
 C) Use Cloud Deployment Manager to set network configurations and Policy Controller to enforce consistency.
 D) Configure Cloud Functions to apply network configurations and set up Cloud Monitoring to alert on discrepancies.
 E) Utilize Cloud Armor to manage network configurations and employ Cloud Logging for monitoring changes.

QUESTION 30

You manage a set of applications deployed on Google Kubernetes Engine (GKE) and are looking to optimize cluster resource usage. Your goal is to ensure the GKE nodes are appropriately sized based on historical usage data. Which approach aligns with Google Cloud's best practices?

A) Manually review Cloud Monitoring metrics for each GKE node and resize them based on average resource utilization.
 B) Utilize the GKE node auto-provisioning feature based on real-time and historical usage data.
 C) Implement a custom tool that periodically analyzes node utilization and resizes nodes accordingly.
 D) Set a static node size based on peak usage observed and adjust only when performance issues arise.
 E) Rely on default node sizes and manually intervene if specific applications require more resources.

QUESTION 31

You are managing a Cloud SQL database instance that is accessed by multiple applications. After a recent update, some applications are experiencing connectivity issues with the database. The error message suggests a permissions problem. To resolve this issue while following Google Cloud best practices, what should you prioritize?

A) Revert the database instance to a previous version that did not have connectivity issues.
B) Update the database instance's firewall rules to allow connections from the affected applications.
C) Create separate database instances for each application to isolate connectivity issues.
D) Increase the database instance's CPU and memory resources to handle more connections.

QUESTION 32

You are managing a Compute Engine instance hosting an application with an externally accessible IP address. The instance is associated with a custom service account. Despite installing the necessary agents, you are not seeing any log entries from this instance in Cloud Logging. What actions should you take to resolve this issue in accordance with Google's best practices?

A) Modify the service account permissions to include the Logs Writer role.
B) Switch the instance to operate with the Compute Engine's standard service account.
C) Ensure Private Google Access is enabled for the Compute Engine subnet.
D) Generate a service account key and configure the logging agents to authenticate using this key.

QUESTION 33

Your organization manages a complex microservices architecture on Google Kubernetes Engine (GKE). You need to ensure that each microservice can communicate securely with others while minimizing the attack surface. What should you implement to achieve this security goal?

A) Open all network ports between microservices for unrestricted communication.
B) Use Google Cloud Identity-Aware Proxy (IAP) to control access to microservices.
C) Implement a single shared API key for all microservices.
D) Restrict microservice communication to the same Kubernetes namespace.

QUESTION 34

Your organization is managing a Google Kubernetes Engine (GKE) cluster that hosts a mission-critical application. You want to ensure that the application can recover quickly from node failures. Which GKE feature should you leverage, and how should you configure it for optimal resilience?

A) Use Regional Clusters to span multiple zones within a region, ensuring that the application can continue running even if one zone experiences issues.
B) Deploy a separate standby cluster in a different region to serve as a failover option in case of regional outages.
C) Implement Vertical Pod Autoscaling to adjust the resource requests of pods dynamically, optimizing their performance during node failures.
D) Set up Node Pools with different instance types and distribution strategies to maximize the likelihood of a healthy node in the event of a failure.

QUESTION 35

You're tasked with optimizing deployment and testing strategies within Google Cloud for your CD workflow. Your objectives include streamlining production releases and minimizing the time required for deployment rollbacks. Additionally, you want to verify production traffic while gradually increasing its impact on users. What approach should you adopt?

A) Implement rolling updates for deployment along with dark launches
B) Utilize canary deployments combined with blue/green releases
C) Embrace a rebuild strategy for deployments and apply shadow releases
D) Choose rolling updates for deployment and implement A/B testing

QUESTION 36

Your role involves managing a cloud-based e-commerce platform on Google Cloud Platform (GCP). This platform relies on n2-highcpu-4 Compute Engine instances for processing customer orders. Recently, customers have experienced slow order processing times, and your Cloud Monitoring dashboard indicates that network capacity is consistently at its limit. What action should you take to optimize network performance for the e-commerce platform?

A) Upgrade the Compute Engine instances to n2-highcpu-16 for enhanced network capacity.
B) Implement a content caching mechanism to reduce the need for frequent network requests.
C) Optimize the database schema and queries used by the platform to reduce network traffic.
D) Install additional intrusion detection systems to monitor and secure network traffic.

QUESTION 37

You are responsible for deploying a cloud-based chat application on Google Kubernetes Engine (GKE). You need to guarantee the ability to quickly revert to the previous version in case of any problems with the update. Which deployment strategy should you employ?

A) Choose a dark launch strategy, and continuously monitor the new chat application's performance.
B) Opt for rolling updates, and evaluate the new application after the deployment stage concludes.
C) Implement a green/blue deployment approach, and assess the new application once the deployment process is finalized.
D) Utilize canary releases, and assess the new application periodically after its release.

QUESTION 38

Your organization manages a suite of microservices on Google Kubernetes Engine (GKE) for various workflows. The GKE clusters used in the testing workflows generate extensive logs that are primarily accessed through the kubectl logs utility. These logs have inconsistent formats. You aim to reduce logging-related costs while ensuring crucial operational logs are still captured. What action should you take?

A) Execute the gcloud container clusters update --logging=SYSTEM command on the GKE clusters used in the testing workflows.
B) Invoke the gcloud logging sinks update _Default --disabled command within the project related to the testing workflows.
C) Add the severity >= DEBUG resource.type = "k8s_container" exclusion filter to the _Default logging sink within the project tied to the testing workflows.
D) Execute the gcloud container clusters update --logging=WORKLOAD command on the GKE clusters used in the testing workflows.

QUESTION 39

As the lead cloud architect, you are tasked with optimizing a video streaming service on Google Cloud for an upcoming live event expected to attract a large audience. Which action should you prioritize to ensure the platform's readiness for high traffic, as per Google's recommended practices?

A) Transition the service to Kubernetes Engine to leverage its autoscaling features.
B) Create a Cloud Deployment Manager template for rapid scaling across multiple regions.

C) Initiate comprehensive load testing on the service to assess its current scalability and performance.
D) Arrange for increased server capacity based on historical viewership data, adding a buffer for projected audience growth.
E) Use Cloud Scheduler to automate scaling based on anticipated viewer numbers.

QUESTION 40

In your role managing a web application on Compute Engine, written in Go and interacting with Firestore, you observe occasional delays during high-demand periods. You aim to identify performance inefficiencies while maintaining a low-impact, maintenance-friendly monitoring setup. What is the best approach?

A) Implement Cloud Profiler with the Go profiler package integrated into your application.
B) Schedule regular execution of Go's built-in pprof tool on your Compute Engine instances, analyzing the results manually.
C) Create a custom performance analysis tool hosted on a separate Compute Engine instance to monitor the Go application.
D) Rely on Firestore and Compute Engine performance metrics in Cloud Monitoring to identify potential bottlenecks.

QUESTION 41

You are managing the DevOps practices for a globally distributed online education platform. The platform uses custom Virtual Machine instances on Google Cloud and integrates with services from other cloud providers. You need a flexible solution to manage and deploy these instances effectively. Which combination of tools should you choose?

A) Cloud Build with Terraform
B) Cloud Build with Google Cloud Deploy
C) Cloud Build with Ansible
D) Google Kubernetes Engine with Google Cloud Deploy

QUESTION 42

As an SRE, you manage a distributed API service on GKE. Users in one region are facing connectivity issues. What is the most effective first step to resolve this problem?

A) Immediately scale up the Kubernetes clusters in the problem region to handle potential overloads.
B) Use Cloud Monitoring to check for network-related issues in the affected region's GKE clusters.
C) Redirect API requests from the problematic region to clusters in other regions while investigating the issue.
D) Review Cloud Logging for the affected clusters to pinpoint any error logs or service disruption patterns.

QUESTION 43

As a cloud architect for a tech company with multiple development teams, each working on distinct Google Cloud projects, you need to set up Cloud Monitoring to track team-specific metrics accurately. How should you organize the Cloud Monitoring dashboards for optimal clarity and separation of metrics?

A) Aggregate all projects under a single comprehensive dashboard with filtering capabilities for each team.
B) Allocate one of the existing projects per team as the scoped project for their specific dashboard.
C) Create new scoped projects for each team and reorganize their respective Google Cloud projects under these.
D) Configure individual dashboards for each project and link them to team-specific summary dashboards for monitoring.

QUESTION 44

Your team is using Cloud Build for the CI/CD pipeline of a Node.js application, hosted in a GitHub repository. The policy dictates that deployments to production must only occur from the 'release' branch, post review by a technical committee. How should you configure the pipeline for compliance?

A) Set up branch protection rules on the 'release' branch in GitHub.
B) Add a 'cloudbuild.yaml' file in the repository's root with a condition to trigger only on 'release' branch updates.
C) Configure Cloud Build to trigger on 'Push to a branch' events targeting the 'release' branch.
D) Implement an approval step in the Cloud Build trigger settings for the 'release' branch.

QUESTION 45

In a multi-cluster GKE environment, you're required to implement network policies that are version-controlled in a GitLab repository. These network policies should be enforced across all clusters automatically upon any update. What is the most efficient method to achieve this?

A) Set up a GitLab CI/CD pipeline to deploy changes to GKE clusters using kubectl commands.
B) Configure Anthos Service Mesh to monitor the GitLab repository and apply network policy changes.
C) Utilize Anthos Config Management linked to the GitLab repository for automatic policy synchronization and enforcement.
D) Implement Config Connector to track the GitLab repository and apply network policy updates in GKE clusters.

QUESTION 46

You are developing a cloud-based system for a government agency that will handle classified information. What are the best practices to ensure the highest level of security for this sensitive data?

A) Encrypt the data using Cloud KMS and enforce strict IAM policies for access control.
B) Utilize public key infrastructure (PKI) for data encryption and store keys on-premises for added security.
C) Rely on Google Cloud's default security settings for data storage and encryption.
D) Regularly change database passwords and distribute them via email to authorized personnel.

QUESTION 47

You are managing a series of GKE clusters for an e-commerce platform. To maintain security, you need to ensure that only container images approved through your CI/CD pipeline are used in your deployments. What steps should you take to enforce this policy?

A) Set up the clusters as private clusters in GKE.
B) Implement Binary Authorization in the GKE clusters to enforce the deployment of only approved images.
C) Enable Cloud Web Security Scanner on the GKE clusters.
D) Activate Vulnerability Scanning in the Artifact Registry for all container images.

QUESTION 48

You're responsible for a Python-based streaming application on Google Cloud's Dataflow service. Lately, the workers are shutting down every 20 minutes due to memory spikes. What corrective action should you take?

A) Implement a Cloud Monitoring alert to notify you when memory spikes occur.
B) Adjust the Dataflow job's parallelism to reduce memory usage.
C) Increase the number of worker nodes in the Dataflow job.
D) Modify the Dataflow job's memory allocation to a higher value.

QUESTION 49

Your organization is transitioning to a DevOps culture, and your software application encountered intermittent performance issues recently. A department head has requested a formal incident analysis for preventive measures. What should you do?

A) Draft an incident analysis report detailing the underlying problems, solution strategies, insights gained, individual accountability, and remedial tasks assigned to specific team members. Distribute it exclusively to the requesting department head.
B) Draft an incident analysis report detailing the underlying problems, solution strategies, insights gained, individual accountability, and remedial tasks assigned to specific team members. Circulate it across the organization's technical documentation repository.
C) Draft an incident analysis report detailing the underlying problems, solution strategies, insights gained, and a structured set of remedial tasks. Distribute it exclusively to the requesting department head.
D) Draft an incident analysis report detailing the underlying problems, solution strategies, insights gained, and a structured set of remedial tasks. Circulate it across the organization's technical documentation repository.

QUESTION 50

Your company is looking to automate the deployment of its cloud-native applications on Google Cloud. What CI/CD approach should you consider to achieve this efficiently while safeguarding sensitive data and adhering to best practices?

A) Set up Jenkins on Compute Engine instances for versatile CI/CD pipelines.
B) Implement GitHub Actions integrated with Google Cloud Key Management Service (KMS) for enhanced data security.
C) Utilize a self-managed Jenkins server located in your data center for full control over CI/CD processes.
D) Leverage Google Cloud Build with Cloud Functions to streamline CI/CD and enhance scalability.
E) Explore CI/CD options with Azure DevOps for cross-cloud compatibility.
F) Set up Travis CI with AWS for flexible CI/CD workflows.

PRACTICE TEST 5 - ANSWERS ONLY

QUESTION 1

Answer - D) Set up Google Kubernetes Engine (GKE) for container orchestration, use RollingUpdate strategy in GKE, and monitor using Google Cloud Operations.

Option D aligns with Google's recommended DevOps practices by utilizing GKE's RollingUpdate strategy, which allows for controlled and smooth updates of microservices. Monitoring with Google Cloud Operations ensures optimal performance.
Option A mentions Deployment Manager but lacks details on rolling updates.
Option B focuses on API management and content delivery but not on updating strategies.
Option C mentions Pub/Sub and DDoS protection but is not directly related to rolling updates.

QUESTION 2

Answer - B) Set up a real-time data replication mechanism between the legacy database and a Google Cloud SQL database to ensure data consistency during migration.

Option B is the recommended approach for migrating a database while ensuring data consistency. Setting up real-time data replication minimizes the risk of data loss or inconsistency during migration, aligning with Google's recommended DevOps practices for data integrity.
Option A suggests a one-time data dump, which may lead to data inconsistency.
Option C involves creating a new schema but does not address real-time data replication.
Option D suggests accessing the legacy database until all data is migrated, which may not ensure data consistency.

QUESTION 3

Answer - B) 2 and 4

Options 2 and 4 are the recommended choices to optimize network performance between microservices in a containerized application on Google Kubernetes Engine (GKE). Using Host mode allows containers to share the host's network namespace, reducing network overhead. Selecting Legacy mode is preferable for gRPC communication within the cluster.
Option 1, Bridge mode, does not provide the same level of performance optimization.
Option 3, VPC-native mode, may be suitable for other scenarios but is not specifically focused on internal communication performance.

QUESTION 4

Answer - C) Help the Cloud Build service account by granting it the Kubernetes Engine Developer role.

Option C is the correct choice as it assists the Cloud Build service account by granting the necessary role, simplifying the authentication process.
Option A suggests embedding the role, which may not be the most efficient method,
Option B adds manual steps, which is not optimal,
Option D introduces additional complexity with a separate service account,

Option E doesn't effectively address authentication.

QUESTION 5

Answer - C) Utilize the Terraform templates from the Cloud Foundation Toolkit. Implement the templates with the necessary parameters to establish the Google Cloud department and requisite infrastructure.

Option C is the correct choice as it recommends leveraging Terraform templates from the Cloud Foundation Toolkit, ensuring scalability and dependability while automating department creation.
Option A introduces a manual script which is less scalable,
Option B suggests Terraform but without templates and lacks scalability,
Option D is highly manual and not scalable.

QUESTION 6

Answer - A and B

Options A and B are the correct choices. Segmenting automation procedures into finer-grained components (A) reduces redundancy and streamlines the workflow. Implementing automatic progression confirmations (B) helps in achieving smoother transitions between stages, reducing manual interventions.
Options C and D are not directly related to optimizing the workflow.

QUESTION 7

Answer - A and B

Option A - Allowing developers to integrate changes independently with rollback capabilities can streamline the process without compromising safety.
Option B - Implementing a peer-review mechanism with automated checks maintains code quality while not hindering deployment efficiency.
Options C, D, and E are not the most effective actions to adjust the process.

QUESTION 8

Answer - C) Configure node pool autoscaling based on CPU and memory demand.

A) Incorrect - Scaling based solely on network throughput may not address the CPU/memory-intensive nature of the workloads.
B) Incorrect - Vertical scaling might not be sufficient for the variable, intensive demands of model training.
C) Correct - Node pool autoscaling based on CPU and memory demand ensures efficient scaling for varying workloads.
D) Incorrect - Manual scaling cannot adapt quickly to unpredictable workloads and may lead to inefficiencies.
E) Incorrect - A fixed pod count does not allow for flexibility and can lead to resource wastage or inadequate processing power.

QUESTION 9

Answer - A) Create separate Google Cloud projects for each team, with dedicated GKE clusters for development, testing, and production.

A) Correct - This approach ensures operational isolation and optimal resource management across different teams.
B) Incorrect - Namespaces provide logical separation but might not offer the required isolation for different teams.
C) Incorrect - Separate clusters in a single project may not provide sufficient isolation between the teams.
D) Incorrect - Multi-cluster setups are complex and may not be the most cost-effective solution for this scenario.
E) Incorrect - Identity Aware Proxy is more suited for controlling user access, not for operational isolation between teams.

QUESTION 10

Answer - B) Implement Cloud Monitoring to track the execution and resource metrics of the Dataflow jobs.

A) Incorrect - Cloud Debugger is not designed for performance monitoring of Dataflow jobs.
B) Correct - Cloud Monitoring provides detailed insights into the resource usage and performance of Dataflow jobs.
C) Incorrect - Cloud Trace is more focused on tracing requests and latency, not resource utilization.
D) Incorrect - While Cloud Logging is valuable, it does not provide the comprehensive resource metrics that Cloud Monitoring does.
E) Incorrect - Cloud DLP is focused on data security, not on monitoring resource usage of Dataflow jobs.

QUESTION 11

Answer - C) Create a Google Group for the finance department and assign the roles/billing.viewer role to this group.

A) Incorrect - Assigning roles to individuals is less efficient than assigning to a group.
B) Incorrect - The billing.admin role provides more permissions than necessary for viewing reports.
C) Correct - This method is efficient and adheres to the principle of least privilege.
D) Incorrect - The cloudPlatform.viewer role gives broader access than necessary for the requirement.
E) Incorrect - Creating a custom role is unnecessary when a predefined role meets the needs.

QUESTION 12

Answer - A) Configure Cloud Build to automatically run unit and integration tests for each service upon a pull request. After successful testing, deploy each service to a production-like staging environment for further evaluation.

A) Correct - This approach ensures automated, isolated testing of each microservice and staged deployments for thorough evaluation.
B) Incorrect - Direct deployment to production post-commit risks introducing untested changes.
C) Incorrect - Testing post-merge may delay the identification of issues. Canary deployments are efficient

but require prior staging tests.
D) Incorrect - Manual triggers reduce the efficiency and consistency of the CI/CD pipeline.
E) Incorrect - Pre-push hooks are less reliable and comprehensive compared to automated testing in a CI/CD pipeline.

QUESTION 13

Answer - B) Analyze the Cloud Monitoring logs to understand the impact of the new scaling configuration.

A) Incorrect - Immediate reversion without analysis might not solve the problem and could lead to further issues.
B) Correct - Analyzing monitoring logs helps in pinpointing the issue caused by the scaling changes.
C) Incorrect - Upgrading machine types is a more reactive approach and may not address the root cause.
D) Incorrect - While communication with users is important, it should come after understanding the issue.
E) Incorrect - Load testing is useful, but it's more important to first analyze the impact of the recent changes.

QUESTION 14

Answer - C) Create an aggregated log sink at the organization level, collecting logs from all VM instances into a centralized analysis tool.

A) Incorrect - Deploying a SIEM system in each project is not scalable and leads to fragmented monitoring.
B) Incorrect - While Cloud Audit Logs are useful, they do not provide comprehensive VM instance log collection.
C) Correct - An organization-level aggregated log sink offers a unified and scalable approach for collecting and analyzing VM logs.
D) Incorrect - Forwarding logs to individual project buckets complicates centralized analysis.
E) Incorrect - Individual project log sinks do not provide the centralized approach needed for effective security monitoring.

QUESTION 15

Answer - D) Host both types of modules in Artifact Registry, implementing binary authorization and vulnerability scanning.

A) Incorrect - While GKE can host a registry, it may not provide the integrated security scanning needed for compliance.
B) Incorrect - Cloud Source Repositories are suitable for version control but lack direct integration for module management.
C) Incorrect - Cloud Storage provides storage capabilities but lacks the features needed for managing Terraform modules effectively.
D) Correct - Artifact Registry offers a secure way to store and manage modules, with features like binary authorization and vulnerability scanning for compliance.
E) Incorrect - Relying on a third-party service may introduce compliance risks and lacks the tight integration with Google Cloud services.

QUESTION 16

Answer - C) Establish a Managed Instance Group with a single instance and configure health checks to automatically replace the instance if it becomes unhealthy.

Option C is the correct choice because it aligns with Site Reliability Engineering (SRE) practices by automatically replacing the instance if it becomes unhealthy, minimizing downtime, and ensuring reliability.
Option A - Option A is incorrect because notifying the software development team may introduce delays in response and doesn't provide automated failover.
Option B - Option B is incorrect because while Load Balancers provide traffic distribution, they do not automatically replace instances in the event of failure.
Option D - Option D is incorrect because manual monitoring and initiation of replacements do not provide automated failover capabilities as needed for high reliability.

QUESTION 17

Answer - B) Configure an attestation for stress-tested updates using a private key stored in Cloud Key Management Service (Cloud KMS) along with a service account JSON key embedded as a Kubernetes Secret.

Option B is the correct choice because it ensures that only stress-tested updates are deployed to the primary GKE cluster by configuring an attestation with a private key stored in Cloud KMS and a service account JSON key as a Kubernetes Secret for verification.
Option A - Option A involves manual signing by the chief technical officer, which is not an automated process.
Option C - Option C mandates manual signature by the chief technical officer, introducing manual steps and complexity.
Option D - Option D mentions verification via Workload Identity, which is not the most direct approach for this use case.

QUESTION 18

Answer - B) Utilize Google Cloud Artifact Registry with multi-region support to efficiently distribute container images.

Option B is the correct choice because Google Cloud Artifact Registry supports multi-region distribution, ensuring efficient image distribution across various regions.
Option A - Option A suggests deploying separate registries, which can lead to complexity and management overhead.
Option C - Option C involves using Cloud Storage, which is not optimized for container image distribution.
Option D - Option D introduces third-party tools, which may not provide the same level of integration and support as Google Cloud services.

QUESTION 19

Answer - A) Temporarily relax the iam.disableServiceAccountKeyCreation policy constraint at the organization level, create the key, and then re-enforce the policy.

Option A is the correct choice.
 Option A - Temporarily relaxing the policy constraint at the organization level allows you to securely create the service account key while following Google's recommended practices.
 Option B - Overriding the policy at the project level may not align with organizational policies and is not the recommended approach.
 Option C - Activating the default service account key may not provide the necessary security for the analytics platform.
 Option D - Amending the project's IAM policy to disable the constraint is not a recommended practice and can have unintended consequences.

QUESTION 20

B) Ensure the Maven Compute Engine instance is equipped with a linked service account that has the necessary Identity and Access Management (1AM) roles.

To ensure that the Ansible Maven instance has the authorization to manage Google Cloud assets, you should ensure that the Maven Compute Engine instance is equipped with a linked service account that has the necessary Identity and Access Management (IAM) roles. This approach aligns with Google Cloud's recommended practices for granting permissions to resources. The other options involve different methods or tools and do not directly address the requirement for authorization within the Google Cloud environment.

QUESTION 21

Answer - C) Conduct load testing to assess the platform's performance under expected player loads.

Explanation for Option C - Conducting load testing is the first step to evaluate how the platform performs under the expected player loads. It helps identify performance bottlenecks and allows for optimization and capacity planning.
Explanation for Option A - Doubling the number of game servers without assessing the platform's actual performance through load testing may result in unnecessary costs.
Explanation for Option B - Implementing automatic scaling is important, but it should come after conducting load testing to determine the appropriate scaling strategy.
Explanation for Option D - Preparing a disaster recovery plan is essential but should not be the initial action. First, assess and optimize the platform's performance under load.

QUESTION 22

Answer - B) Announce the update to the fraud detection team, provide training on the new model, and gradually transition to the improved version while monitoring its performance.

Explanation for Option B - Announcing the update, providing training, and gradually transitioning to the new model with performance monitoring is a best practice to ensure a smooth transition and minimize disruptions in critical operations like fraud detection.
Explanation for Option A - Replacing the old model without informing anyone can lead to resistance and confusion among users when changes are noticed. Communication is essential.
Explanation for Option C - Updating the model during peak hours of fraud detection is generally not recommended, as it can disrupt operations.
Explanation for Option D - Deploying the new model without prior communication can lead to confusion

and resistance to change among users in a critical operation like fraud detection.

QUESTION 23

Answer - B) Encourage a blame-free environment during retrospectives.

Option A) Assigning blame during retrospectives can discourage open discussions and hinder a blame-free environment.
Option C) Limiting retrospectives to the engineering team only can exclude valuable insights from other stakeholders.
Option D) Conducting retrospectives sporadically, only after major incidents, doesn't promote a continuous improvement mindset.
Option B encourages a blame-free environment, which is crucial for fostering open discussions and continuous improvement during retrospectives.

QUESTION 24

Answer - B) Implement canary releases, initially exposing a small fraction of users.

A) While minimizing user impact, this approach doesn't provide immediate feedback on the new backend's performance.
B) This strategy allows for monitoring the new backend's performance with actual user traffic, facilitating immediate action if issues arise.
C) A/B testing focuses on user behavior and feature acceptance rather than backend performance.
D) Provides quick rollback but lacks the ability for real-time performance monitoring with live user traffic.
E) Useful for performance testing but does not involve direct user interaction with the new system.

QUESTION 25

Answer - B) Count the messages delivered within 150 ms and divide this by the total number of messages sent.

Option A - The average delivery time may not provide a true measure of performance against the specific threshold.
Option B - This approach is the most effective as it measures the proportion of messages meeting the set target.
Option C - Percentile metrics are informative but do not concentrate on the specific 150 ms threshold.
Option D - Focusing on non-compliant messages doesn't provide a positive measure of SLI.
Option E - The queue size is not directly relevant to the speed of message delivery.

QUESTION 26

Answer - B) and C)

Option A - While important, network latency is more of a symptom than a direct measure of application performance.
Option B - This provides insights into real user interactions and potential issues in application flow.
Option C - Direct integration into the analytics engine offers precise insights into the application's

performance and potential bottlenecks.
 Option D - CPU and memory usage are important but do not directly reflect the user experience or application efficiency.
 Option E - Query execution times are critical but only cover the database aspect, not the entire application performance.

QUESTION 27

Answer - A) Calculate the potential loss from a data breach, comparing it with the investment cost.

Option A - Comparing the cost of a potential data breach with the investment amount is a direct way to assess the value of the upgrade.
 Option B - While helpful, percentage of revenue does not directly relate to the risk of data breaches.
 Option C - Direct cost savings are important, but the main benefit here is risk reduction.
 Option D - Operational efficiency is important, but the primary concern is security.
 Option E - Customer trust and reputation are vital, but the financial assessment should also consider direct risk reduction.

QUESTION 28

Answer - A) and D)

Option A - Aggressive rollouts can maximize the error budget's potential while spurring innovation.
 Option B - Increasing capacity is a general improvement, not necessarily linked to error budget optimization.
 Option C - Revising SLOs may not be advisable if the current SLOs are already well-calibrated.
 Option D - Developing targeted SLIs can give more insight into specific aspects of service performance.
 Option E - Scheduling downtime may not be the best use of the error budget and can impact user perception negatively.

QUESTION 29

Answer - A) Deploy Cloud Build to apply network configurations and use Config Sync to maintain consistency across all projects.

Option A - Cloud Build can automate the application of configurations, while Config Sync ensures consistency across multiple environments.
 Option B - Terraform is a powerful tool, but it's not a Google-recommended practice for configuration consistency.
 Option C - Deployment Manager is effective for configuration, but Policy Controller is more focused on Kubernetes environments.
 Option D - Cloud Functions are not typically used for applying network configurations.
 Option E - Cloud Armor is specific to security, not general network configuration management.

QUESTION 30

Answer - B) Utilize the GKE node auto-provisioning feature based on real-time and historical usage data.

Option A - Manual reviews can be time-consuming and may not respond quickly to changes in demand.

Option B - GKE node auto-provisioning dynamically adjusts the cluster size based on workload needs, ensuring efficient resource utilization.
Option C - Custom tools require ongoing maintenance and might not be as effective as built-in GKE features.
Option D - Static sizing could lead to overprovisioning or resource shortages.
Option E - Relying on default sizes without auto-scaling might not adequately meet the needs of all applications.

QUESTION 31

Answer - B) Update the database instance's firewall rules to allow connections from the affected applications.

Option A, reverting to a previous database version, may not be a viable solution and does not address the underlying permissions issue.
Option C, creating separate database instances for each application, can be complex and expensive.
Option D, increasing resource allocation, may not directly resolve the permissions problem and could be unnecessary.

QUESTION 32

Answer - A) Modify the service account permissions to include the Logs Writer role.

Option B, switching to the standard service account, may not be necessary and can lead to other issues.
Option C, enabling Private Google Access, is related to network connectivity and does not directly affect Cloud Logging.
Option D, generating a service account key, is not typically required for configuring Cloud Logging.

QUESTION 33

Answer - B) Use Google Cloud Identity-Aware Proxy (IAP) to control access to microservices.

- Option A is a security risk with unrestricted communication.
- Option C is not a recommended practice for secure microservices.
- Option D may limit scalability and flexibility.
Using Google Cloud Identity-Aware Proxy (IAP) (Option B) allows you to control access to microservices securely while minimizing the attack surface, ensuring secure communication between microservices.

QUESTION 34

Answer - A) Use Regional Clusters to span multiple zones within a region, ensuring that the application can continue running even if one zone experiences issues.

Explanation:
Option A is the correct choice because it suggests using Regional Clusters in GKE, which spans multiple zones within a region, ensuring that the application can continue running even if one zone experiences issues. This enhances resilience and availability.
Option B, deploying a separate standby cluster in a different region, is a valid high-availability strategy but may introduce additional complexity and cost.

Option C, Vertical Pod Autoscaling, is focused on optimizing pod resource requests and doesn't directly address node failures.

Option D, Node Pools with different instance types, is a good practice but may not guarantee quick recovery from node failures as effectively as Regional Clusters.

QUESTION 35

Answer - B) Utilize canary deployments combined with blue/green releases

Option B is the correct choice because canary deployments allow gradual validation of production traffic, while blue/green releases simplify production releases, meeting the specified goals.

Option A is incorrect as dark launches are not typically used with rolling updates. Option C is incorrect because a rebuild strategy may not align with the goal of minimizing rollback times. Option D is incorrect because A/B testing doesn't directly address the goal of verifying production traffic while gradually increasing user impact.

QUESTION 36

Answer - B) Implement a content caching mechanism to reduce the need for frequent network requests.

Option B is the correct choice as it addresses the network capacity issue by implementing content caching to reduce the volume of network requests.

Option A is incorrect as upgrading the instance type may not directly resolve the network capacity problem.

Option C is incorrect as optimizing the database schema and queries, while important, may not fully address the network capacity issue.

Option D is incorrect as installing additional intrusion detection systems may not directly impact network performance and could introduce more complexity.

QUESTION 37

Answer - C) Implement a green/blue deployment approach, and assess the new application once the deployment process is finalized.

Option C is the correct choice as it aligns with the requirement to ensure a quick rollback by keeping the current version (green) running alongside the new one (blue) until the deployment is finalized.

Option A is incorrect as it focuses on monitoring without a clear rollback strategy.

Option B is incorrect as rolling updates may not provide the same level of safety in case of issues.

Option D is incorrect as it involves periodic assessments but may not facilitate an immediate rollback.

QUESTION 38

Answer - D) Execute the gcloud container clusters update --logging=WORKLOAD command on the GKE clusters used in the testing workflows.

Option D is the correct choice as it aligns with optimizing logging costs for testing workflows by configuring GKE clusters to capture workload-specific logs. This approach reduces unnecessary logs, thus minimizing costs. Option A suggests updating GKE clusters to system logging, which may not align with cost optimization. Option B recommends disabling the default logging sink, which may not effectively reduce costs. Option C adds an exclusion filter that might not reduce logging costs as intended for testing workflows.

QUESTION 39

Answer - C) Initiate comprehensive load testing on the service to assess its current scalability and performance.

Option A - Incorrect: Moving to Kubernetes is beneficial but not the first step in preparation.
Option B - Incorrect: Deployment Manager aids in scalability but is secondary to performance assessment.
Option C - Correct: Load testing is essential to gauge the platform's readiness for increased demand.
Option D - Incorrect: Advanced provisioning is important but follows the initial performance evaluation.
Option E - Incorrect: Automated scaling is useful, yet understanding current performance is priority.

QUESTION 40

Answer - A) Implement Cloud Profiler with the Go profiler package integrated into your application.

Option A - Correct: Cloud Profiler with Go integration offers a low-overhead way to continuously monitor and identify inefficiencies.
Option B - Incorrect: Regular use of pprof requires more active maintenance and is less suited for continuous monitoring.
Option C - Incorrect: A custom tool increases complexity and maintenance demands.
Option D - Incorrect: General Firestore and Compute Engine metrics do not directly address application-level performance issues.

QUESTION 41

Answer - A) Cloud Build with Terraform

Option A - Correct: Terraform allows for infrastructure as code, which is essential for a distributed system across multiple clouds, and Cloud Build can automate the build and deployment process.
Option B - Incorrect: While Cloud Deploy is useful for continuous delivery, it lacks the cross-cloud infrastructure management that Terraform offers.
Option C - Incorrect: Ansible is great for configuration management but does not provide the same level of infrastructure provisioning as Terraform.
Option D - Incorrect: GKE is specifically for containerized applications and may not be suitable for managing VM instances across multiple clouds.

QUESTION 42

Answer - D) Review Cloud Logging for the affected clusters to pinpoint any error logs or service disruption patterns.

Option A - Incorrect: Scaling up without diagnosing the root cause might not address connectivity issues.
Option B - Incorrect: While monitoring network issues is important, initial focus should be on identifying errors and service disruptions.
Option C - Incorrect: Redirecting traffic is a temporary workaround and should not be the first action.

Option D - Correct: Examining logs is a crucial first step in diagnosing the issue in line with SRE best practices.

QUESTION 43

Answer - B) Allocate one of the existing projects per team as the scoped project for their specific dashboard.

Option A - Incorrect: A single dashboard for all teams may lead to confusion and difficulty in metric segregation.
Option B - Correct: Using an existing project as a scoped project for each team ensures clarity and separation of metrics, following Google Cloud best practices.
Option C - Incorrect: Creating new scoped projects can be unnecessary and may complicate the existing setup.
Option D - Incorrect: While this provides detail, it may be too granular and challenging to manage at a higher level.

QUESTION 44

Answer - A) Set up branch protection rules on the 'release' branch in GitHub. and C) Configure Cloud Build to trigger on 'Push to a branch' events targeting the 'release' branch.

Option A - Correct: Branch protection ensures that changes to the 'release' branch are reviewed, aligning with policy.
Option B - Incorrect: The 'cloudbuild.yaml' file controls build steps, not branch-specific triggers.
Option C - Correct: Configuring triggers for specific branches in Cloud Build aligns with the controlled deployment process.
Option D - Incorrect: Cloud Build does not have a built-in approval step feature in its trigger settings.

QUESTION 45

Answer - C) Utilize Anthos Config Management linked to the GitLab repository for automatic policy synchronization and enforcement.

Option A - Incorrect: GitLab CI/CD with kubectl is less automated and requires more manual intervention.
Option B - Incorrect: Anthos Service Mesh is not the primary tool for policy synchronization from a repository.
Option C - Correct: Anthos Config Management is ideal for syncing and enforcing policies from version-controlled repositories like GitLab.
Option D - Incorrect: Config Connector is not primarily focused on enforcing network policies from repositories.

QUESTION 46

Answer - A) Encrypt the data using Cloud KMS and enforce strict IAM policies for access control.

Option A - Correct: Using Cloud KMS for encryption and strict IAM policies ensures robust security for classified information.

Option B - Incorrect: While PKI is secure, on-premises key storage may not leverage the full benefits of cloud security.

Option C - Incorrect: Default settings may not meet the specific security requirements for classified data.

Option D - Incorrect: Distributing passwords via email is insecure, and regular changes can be operationally challenging.

QUESTION 47

Answer - B) Implement Binary Authorization in the GKE clusters to enforce the deployment of only approved images.

Option A - Incorrect: While private clusters increase network security, they don't address container image validation.

Option B - Correct: Binary Authorization ensures that only containers verified by your CI/CD pipeline are deployed.

Option C - Incorrect: Cloud Web Security Scanner is used for finding security vulnerabilities in web apps, not for container image validation.

Option D - Incorrect: Vulnerability Scanning checks for known vulnerabilities in images but doesn't enforce CI/CD pipeline approval.

QUESTION 48

Answer - D) Modify the Dataflow job's memory allocation to a higher value.

Option A suggests monitoring alerts but doesn't directly address the memory issue causing worker shutdowns.

Option B, changing parallelism, may affect performance but doesn't directly resolve the memory spikes.

Option C increases worker nodes but doesn't tackle the memory problem.

Option D is the recommended approach to address the memory spikes and prevent worker shutdowns.

QUESTION 49

A) Draft an incident analysis report detailing the underlying problems, solution strategies, insights gained, individual accountability, and remedial tasks assigned to specific team members. Distribute it exclusively to the requesting department head.

Option A is the correct choice because it provides a comprehensive incident analysis report with details, individual accountability, and remedial tasks, exclusively shared with the requesting department head. Option B summarizes the information but lacks individual accountability and has broader distribution. Option C provides a detailed report but lacks structured remedial tasks and has limited distribution. Option D is similar to Option B but lacks individual accountability and has broader distribution, making Option A the most suitable choice.

QUESTION 50

Answer - B) Implement GitHub Actions integrated with Google Cloud Key Management Service (KMS) for enhanced data security.

Options A, C, D, E, and F - Incorrect. These options may not provide the best security measures for safeguarding sensitive data.
 Option B is the correct choice as it suggests implementing GitHub Actions integrated with Google Cloud KMS to enhance data security while maintaining efficient CI/CD processes.

PRACTICE TEST 6 - QUESTIONS ONLY

QUESTION 1

Your organization is managing a large-scale application on Google Cloud. You want to improve security by ensuring that all Compute Engine instances use authorized and verified container images. Which approach should you take to achieve this goal while minimizing manual efforts and ensuring compliance with company policies?

A) Manually inspect and validate each container image before deployment, and update instances accordingly.

B) Use Google Cloud IAM to restrict access to container images and enforce strict permissions.

C) Implement Google Cloud Security Command Center to scan and verify container images, then use deployment manager to update instances.

D) Configure a Binary Authorization policy that enforces image verification for Compute Engine instances.

QUESTION 2

Your organization is managing a large-scale e-commerce application on Google Cloud. You want to ensure high availability and disaster recovery for your application. Which combination of Google Cloud services and strategies should you consider for achieving these objectives, following Google's recommended DevOps practices?

A) Implement Google Cloud Endpoints to create APIs for microservices and utilize Google Cloud Pub/Sub for asynchronous communication between services.

B) Utilize Google Cloud VPN for secure communication between microservices and implement Google Cloud Scheduler for task automation.

C) Set up a global load balancer with health checks and configure multi-region replication for your data storage.

D) Implement a CI/CD pipeline with Google Cloud Build and Google Kubernetes Engine (GKE) for automated deployment and scaling.

QUESTION 3

You are managing a Google Cloud project with multiple services, and you need to establish secure communication between them. The services are deployed in different Google Cloud regions and VPCs. Which Google Cloud networking product or feature should you choose to enable secure and private communication between these services? 1. Cloud VPN 2. Cloud Interconnect 3. VPC Peering 4. Cloud Router.

A) 1 and 2
B) 2 and 3
C) 3 and 4
D) 1 and 4

QUESTION 4

In your Cloud Build setup for deploying containers to GKE using kubectl, what's the recommended authentication approach?

A) Embed the Kubernetes Engine Developer role in Cloud Build's configuration.
B) Add an extra Cloud Build step to manually obtain service account credentials for kubectl.
C) Assist the Cloud Build service account by giving it the Kubernetes Engine Developer role.
D) Create a dedicated service account with the Kubernetes Engine Developer role for Cloud Build.
E) Continue using the default Cloud Build service account.

QUESTION 5

As you assess the risk associated with a new storage solution for an online gaming service, you have the following figures for the new solution: MTTD: 3 minutes, MTTR: 15 minutes, MTBF: 60 days, User Impact: 33%. What should be the risk assessment figures for the new storage solution failover?

A) MTTD: 3 MTTR: 15 MTBF: 60 Impact: 50%
B) MTTD: 3 MTTR: 15 MTBF: 60 Impact: 33%
C) MTTD: 3 MTTR: 45 MTBF: 60 Impact: 50%
D) MTTD: 3 MTTR: 45 MTBF: 60 Impact: 33%

QUESTION 6

You are tasked with improving your media processing workflow in Google Cloud's Dataflow to minimize repetitive tasks and decrease job execution time. What steps should you take? (Choose two.)

A) Segment the automation procedures into finer-grained components.
B) Implement automatic progression confirmations transferring from the staging area to the production zone.
C) Run a script to facilitate the setup of the media processing workflow in Google Cloud Dataflow.
D) Set up an alert to inform the designated team to proceed with the next phase when human input is needed.

QUESTION 7

Your organization employs a review committee to validate all alterations to the existing financial systems. What should you do to modify this process while ensuring it does not disrupt the software deployment workflow? (Choose two.)

A) Enable developers to independently integrate their changes, with safeguards in place for reverting changes if issues arise.
B) Introduce a peer-review process for each modification submitted as part of the source code, backed by automated validations.
C) Substitute the review committee with a high-ranking executive to provide continuous supervision throughout the development and release cycle.
D) Certify that the software development environment delivers prompt feedback to developers regarding the consequences of their changes.
E) Group changes into more substantial, albeit less frequent, application updates.

QUESTION 8

You are managing a cloud-based application on Google Cloud using Terraform for orchestration. The application relies on an autoscaled group of Compute Engine instances. During an update via a CI/CD pipeline, you encounter an error while trying to increase the memory capacity in the instance template. The error indicates that the current instance template is in use. How would you resolve this issue while ensuring minimal disruption?

A) Temporarily remove the instance group from Terraform's state, modify the instance template, then re-import the instance group.

B) Apply the create_before_destroy lifecycle rule in the instance template to ensure the new template is created before the old one is destroyed.

C) Manually delete the existing instance group, then recreate it with the updated instance template.

D) Create a new instance template with increased memory and associate it with the instance group, then delete the old template.

E) Update the instance template directly in the GCP console, bypassing Terraform.

QUESTION 9

In your organization, each department requires its own set of data processing applications hosted on GKE. You need to set up separate environments for development and production while maintaining strict access control and budget efficiency. How should you structure the GKE environment?

A) Establish individual Google Cloud projects for each department, with a GKE cluster for development and another for production, using IAM for access control.

B) Create a multi-cluster environment within a single Google Cloud project, segregating departments by clusters and using VPC peering for network isolation.

C) Deploy a centralized GKE cluster and divide it into namespaces for each department, implementing RBAC to restrict access.

D) Construct separate GKE clusters for each department in a shared project, using network security policies to ensure isolation.

E) Opt for a single GKE cluster and allocate different node pools for each department, controlling access through service accounts.

QUESTION 10

Your team is using BigQuery for large-scale data analysis and wishes to optimize query costs. You need to track and analyze resource usage to manage expenses effectively. What is the most suitable approach to achieve this?

A) Deploy Cloud Data Loss Prevention (DLP) to monitor the BigQuery usage and optimize costs.

B) Use Cloud Trace to analyze the execution paths of BigQuery queries and their resource consumption.

C) Implement Cloud Monitoring to track BigQuery's query execution times and data processed.

D) Set up detailed logging in Cloud Logging for each query to manually assess resource consumption.

E) Utilize Cloud Profiler to profile BigQuery queries and identify areas for cost reduction.

QUESTION 11

After a recent update, your cloud-based document collaboration service on Google Cloud has been experiencing random crashes. You need to identify and fix the underlying issues. What actions should you take?

A) Use Cloud Logging to examine log files for error patterns related to the crashes.
B) Implement Cloud Profiler to analyze the performance of your service and identify bottlenecks.
C) Deploy Cloud Trace to track the request flow and pinpoint where failures are occurring.
D) Set up Google Cloud Managed Service for Prometheus to monitor system metrics and alert on anomalies.
E) Integrate Error Reporting to automatically detect and report errors occurring in the service.

QUESTION 12

You need to design a CI/CD pipeline for a Google Cloud-based API service that requires extensive security testing due to handling sensitive data. The pipeline should ensure that every update undergoes rigorous security checks before deployment. How should you proceed?

A) Integrate automated security testing tools within Cloud Build, running them post-merge into the master branch. If tests pass, deploy the API service to a secured staging environment, followed by production.
B) Mandate developers to perform security testing on their local environments before committing to the repository. After commits, use Cloud Build for deployment to a testing environment and then to production.
C) Set up a pre-commit hook in the Git repository to enforce security tests locally. Post-commit, automate deployment to a staging environment, bypassing additional security tests.
D) Utilize Cloud Build to deploy the API service to a staging environment first, where all security tests are conducted. Upon successful testing, proceed with production deployment.
E) Implement a manual review process for all commits, followed by automated security tests in Cloud Build. Successful tests trigger deployments to a pre-production environment and then to production.

QUESTION 13

You manage a Compute Engine-based analytics platform. After deploying a new data analysis tool, you notice an increase in error rates and slower query responses. Your priority is to resolve these issues promptly. What initial step should you take?

A) Immediately downgrade the data analysis tool to the previous version to eliminate errors.
B) Examine the Cloud Monitoring metrics for any anomalies or performance issues related to the new tool.
C) Scale up the Compute Engine resources to handle the increased load from the new tool.
D) Inform the users about the issues and provide a timeline for when they can expect a resolution.
E) Conduct an in-depth performance analysis of the new data analysis tool to identify bottlenecks.

QUESTION 14

Your organization is deploying a series of new applications on GKE and needs to ensure that all container images comply with internal security standards. You are responsible for enforcing a policy where only approved images are used in GKE deployments. What is the most effective approach to meet this requirement?

A) Implement Binary Authorization in GKE to enforce deployment of only signed and verified images.
B) Use Cloud Security Command Center to continuously monitor and assess GKE deployments for compliance.
C) Configure IAM roles and permissions for developers to restrict their ability to deploy non-compliant images.
D) Enable Vulnerability Scanning in Container Registry to scan images and prevent the deployment of those with known vulnerabilities.
E) Set up a custom script in the CI/CD pipeline to check image compliance against a list of approved images before deployment.

QUESTION 15

As part of a shift to a more secure and compliant infrastructure management practice, your company decides to enhance the management of its Terraform modules used for Google Cloud deployments. There's a mix of in-house developed and third-party modules. You need a solution that ensures only approved modules are used while maintaining easy access for your development teams. What should you do?

A) Implement a self-hosted Terraform module registry on a Compute Engine instance, with Cloud IAM policies to control access.
B) Set up a dedicated Artifact Registry for Terraform modules, enabling IAM-based access control and audit logging for compliance.
C) Use a version-controlled Cloud Source Repository to store all Terraform modules, integrating with Cloud Build for testing and validation.
D) Host Terraform modules on a Cloud Storage bucket with Object Lifecycle Management to ensure module versioning and compliance.
E) Deploy a managed Terraform Enterprise server within your VPC, integrating with VPC Service Controls for enhanced security.

QUESTION 16

Your organization operates multiple Google Cloud projects, and you need to centralize logs for compliance purposes. Project teams should only access their own logs, while the compliance oversight team should have access to all logs. What's the best approach to meet these requirements?

A) Create separate centralized logging projects for each team and grant project-level IAM roles accordingly. Provide the compliance oversight team with viewer rights in all projects.
 B) Consolidate logs into a single centralized Cloud Logging project, and assign IAM roles to project teams to limit their access to their own logs. Give the compliance oversight team logging.viewer permissions in the central project.
 C) Streamline logs into separate Google Cloud Storage buckets for each team, allowing access control at the bucket level. Provide the compliance oversight team with object writer rights in all buckets.
 D) Establish BigQuery datasets for each project team within a unified logging project. Assign dataset-level IAM roles for access control, and grant the compliance oversight team BigQuery admin privileges in the central project.

QUESTION 17

While establishing continuous deployment for your telemedicine application on Google Cloud, you want to ensure that only updates passing rigorous stress testing in a staging GKE cluster are deployed to the primary GKE cluster used by patients and healthcare providers. What Binary Authorization configuration steps should you take to achieve this?

A) Create an attestation for stress-tested updates and manually obtain a signature from the chief technical officer using their private key.

B) Configure an attestation for stress-tested updates using a private key stored in Cloud Key Management Service (Cloud KMS) along with a service account JSON key embedded as a Kubernetes Secret.

C) Generate an attestation for stress-tested updates and require the chief technical officer to provide a signature using a key stored in Cloud Key Management Service (Cloud KMS).

D) Set up an attestation for stress-tested updates using a private key secured in Cloud Key Management Service (Cloud KMS) with verification through Workload Identity.

QUESTION 18

Your team is responsible for managing containerized applications in a secure and compliant manner on Google Cloud. You want to enforce access controls and auditing for container images and Helm charts. What should you do to achieve this goal effectively?

A) Use a generic object storage service for container image storage, implementing custom IAM policies for access control.

B) Implement Google Cloud Artifact Registry with integrated IAM controls and audit logging for container image and Helm chart management.

C) Rely on third-party container image registries that offer advanced security features.

D) Set up separate IAM roles for each team member and manage access manually.

QUESTION 19

Your automated data transformation workflows need to securely access database credentials and support credential rotation in case of suspected compromise. What should you do to achieve this while following best practices?

A) Instruct data engineers to manually input credentials during job setup and avoid storing them in persistent storage.

B) Store credentials in Secret Manager, encrypting them with a key from Cloud Key Management Service. Grant the automated workflow access to Secret Manager using Identity and Access Management.

C) Encrypt credentials and embed them in the workflow's codebase. Store an encryption key in a separate repository and provide workflow access to this key.

D) Store credentials in a dedicated configuration file within Cloud Source Repositories and grant specific data engineers access to the configuration file.

QUESTION 20

Your data transformation jobs are being executed and monitored through an automated workflow. You want the workflow to securely retrieve database credentials. You also want to facilitate credential rotation in the event of a suspected compromise. What should you do?

A) Require data engineers to input credentials during job setup. Advise engineers to avoid storing credentials in persistent storage.
B) Store credentials in Secret Manager encrypted with a key from Cloud Key Management Service. Grant the automated workflow access to Secret Manager via Identity and Access Management.
C) Encrypt credentials and include them in the workflow's codebase. Save an encryption key in a distinct repository and provide your workflow with access to this key.
D) Keep credentials in a dedicated configuration file on Cloud Source Repositories. Grant a few data engineers access to this configuration file.

QUESTION 21

Your online streaming platform is gearing up for a live event that is expected to attract a large audience. What should be your initial step to ensure the platform's stability during the event?

A) Upgrade the content delivery network (CDN) to handle increased traffic.
B) Enable real-time monitoring of server resources for quick adjustments.
C) Perform load testing to evaluate the platform's performance under the expected surge in viewers.
D) Develop a communication plan for addressing customer inquiries during the event.

QUESTION 22

You are responsible for a critical e-commerce platform with a well-defined Service Level Objective (SLO). Updates are deployed frequently by the engineering team. In case of a severe issue leading to an SLO breach, you want the team to prioritize platform stability over introducing new features. What proactive measure can you take to ensure this prioritization before a critical incident occurs?

A) Set a rule that the engineering team must halt all updates until the SLO breach is resolved.
B) Establish a policy where any breach of the SLO triggers an immediate freeze on feature development.
C) Schedule regular meetings with the engineering team to discuss the importance of platform stability.
D) Collaborate with product managers to ensure that new feature requests are put on hold when the SLO is at risk of being breached.

QUESTION 23

Your organization is striving to make incident retrospectives a routine practice to improve incident response and prevent recurrences. Which approach is most aligned with this goal?

A) Perform retrospectives only when a major incident occurs.
B) Conduct retrospectives only with the teams directly involved in an incident.
C) Establish a schedule to conduct retrospectives on a regular basis, involving cross-functional teams.
D) Limit retrospectives to a post-mortem analysis without action items.

QUESTION 24

You need to implement a deployment strategy for a large-scale, user-centric application in Google Cloud. The application requires frequent updates with minimal user disruption. The strategy must allow for testing in a production-like environment to evaluate new features under realistic loads. What deployment approach should you choose?

A) Deploy using a green/blue strategy with manual cutover.
B) Implement phased rollouts with feature flags.
C) Utilize canary testing, gradually increasing user exposure.
D) Conduct A/B testing segmented by user location.
E) Apply rolling updates during low-traffic periods.

QUESTION 25

Your software development team is working on a multi-component web application using Kubernetes. You need a strategy for managing source code and configuration files while ensuring efficient collaboration. What approach aligns best with Google Cloud DevOps practices?

A) Utilize a shared Google Cloud Storage bucket for storing all code and configuration files, with access provided to all team members.
B) Implement a distributed version control system like Git, with a repository hosting service for centralized access to the codebase.
C) Store code and configuration files on an internal file server, with a manual logging system for tracking changes.
D) Use individual Google Drive folders for each developer, with periodic manual merges to synchronize changes.
E) Employ a centralized version control system with developers checking out and committing changes directly to the main server.

QUESTION 26

Your company hosts a multi-tier web application on Google Cloud, including a frontend interface and backend APIs. You currently monitor backend API performance. To fully understand the service's reliability, where else should you measure SLIs? (Choose two)

A) End-to-end response time from the user's perspective, including frontend and backend processing.
B) Google Cloud Load Balancer's request handling and routing efficiency.
C) Disk I/O operations on backend servers.
D) Availability and latency of external services integrated with your backend APIs.
E) Google Cloud Firewall efficiency in filtering and passing traffic.

QUESTION 27

A cloud-based service is considering an upgrade to its network infrastructure to improve speed, at a cost of $8,000. The service's annual revenue is $1,000,000. The expected benefit is a reduction in latency that could lead to better customer satisfaction. How should the company determine if the investment is worthwhile?

A) Evaluate the increase in customer satisfaction and its potential impact on revenue.
B) Calculate the percentage of the investment against the annual revenue to decide.
C) Assess the upgrade based solely on the expected reduction in latency.
D) Consider the upgrade cost relative to potential savings in operational expenses.

E) Analyze the upgrade's impact on service reliability and consequent customer retention.

QUESTION 28

Following a major service disruption in your cloud-based messaging system, you are conducting a postmortem analysis. The issue was traced back to an overlooked configuration change. What actions should you take to improve future responses?

A) Develop a more rigorous configuration change review and testing process.
B) Hold individual team members accountable for the oversight.
C) Require executive approval for all future configuration changes.
D) Increase the frequency of team meetings to discuss potential risks in system changes.
E) Automate the rollback process for configuration changes when service disruptions are detected.

QUESTION 29

As part of a cloud infrastructure team, you manage several GKE clusters across different stages of the software development lifecycle. You need to ensure Kubernetes configurations, including network policies and resource quotas, are consistent and adhere to organizational standards. What approach should you adopt?

A) Configure Cloud Build to deploy Kubernetes configurations and use Config Connector for consistency across clusters.
B) Apply Kubernetes configurations manually in each cluster and use Cloud Monitoring to verify adherence to standards.
C) Utilize Terraform to manage Kubernetes resources and set up Cloud Logging to track configuration changes.
D) Implement Config Sync for Kubernetes configuration management and Policy Controller for policy enforcement.
E) Leverage Cloud Functions to apply configurations and employ Cloud IAM for policy management.

QUESTION 30

Your team operates several Compute Engine instances for various applications and seeks to optimize the instances' disk storage based on usage patterns. What is the most efficient way to achieve this following Google Cloud recommendations?

A) Periodically review the disk utilization metrics in Cloud Monitoring and manually resize disks based on trends.
B) Implement a custom script that adjusts disk size based on daily utilization logs.
C) Use the Persistent Disk Recommender to automatically get recommendations for optimal disk size.
D) Maintain a constant disk size that accommodates potential peak usage scenarios.
E) Manually monitor disk usage reports each month and resize disks as needed.

QUESTION 31

You are responsible for a set of Compute Engine instances running a critical application. These instances are configured to send their logs to Stackdriver Logging. However, you notice that logs from one of the instances are missing in the Stackdriver Logs Viewer. What should you do first to troubleshoot this issue?

A) SSH into the affected Compute Engine instance and check if the Stackdriver agent is running.
B) Check the Stackdriver agent's test log message in the Logs Viewer.
C) Upgrade the Stackdriver agent on all Compute Engine instances to the latest version.
D) Ensure the service account for the affected instance has the monitoring.write access scope enabled.

QUESTION 32

You have recently deployed an application on a Compute Engine instance with an externally accessible IP address. This instance is associated with a custom service account. However, you have noticed that no log entries are appearing in Cloud Logging, even though you have confirmed that the necessary agents are installed. To address this issue following Google's recommended best practices, what steps should you take?

A) Modify the service account permissions to include the Logs Writer role.
B) Switch the instance to operate with the Compute Engine's standard service account.
C) Ensure Private Google Access is enabled for the Compute Engine subnet.
D) Generate a service account key and configure the logging agents to authenticate using this key.

QUESTION 33

Your team manages a Google Kubernetes Engine (GKE) cluster for a critical application. You want to ensure high availability and fault tolerance. What should you configure to achieve this objective?

A) Use a single node pool with a single node in the cluster for simplicity.
B) Implement auto-scaling for the node pool to handle traffic spikes.
C) Distribute the cluster across multiple zones for redundancy.
D) Disable automatic node repairs to prevent disruptions.

QUESTION 34

You manage a Google Kubernetes Engine (GKE) cluster for a critical e-commerce application. The application has multiple microservices deployed as separate Deployments in the cluster. One of the microservices, named "checkout-service," is experiencing high CPU utilization, affecting the overall application performance. What action should you take to address this issue effectively?

A) Scale up the number of Pods in the "checkout-service" Deployment to handle increased traffic.
B) Implement Horizontal Pod Autoscaling for the "checkout-service" based on CPU utilization.
C) Update the GKE cluster's machine type to a higher CPU capacity.
D) Modify the Ingress controller configuration to direct traffic away from the "checkout-service" temporarily.

QUESTION 35

You are in charge of devising deployment and validation strategies for your CD workflow in Google Cloud. Your key objectives are to streamline production releases and minimize deployment rollback times. You also want to verify production traffic while gradually increasing user impact. Which method should you select?

A) Implement blue/green deployments and employ shadow releases

B) Utilize rolling updates for deployment along with dark launches

C) Adopt a recreate strategy for deployments and integrate canary releases

D) Employ rolling updates for deployment and conduct A/B testing

QUESTION 36

You are administering a cloud-based customer support platform on Google Cloud Platform (GCP) that relies on n2-highcpu-4 Compute Engine instances for handling customer inquiries. Lately, customers have reported slow response times, and your Cloud Monitoring dashboard shows that network capacity is consistently at its limit. What should you do to enhance network performance for the customer support platform?

A) Upgrade the Compute Engine instances to n2-highcpu-16 for improved network performance.

B) Implement a load balancer to distribute incoming customer inquiries more evenly across the existing Compute Engine instances.

C) Optimize the platform's application code to minimize network traffic.

D) Deploy additional network security measures to safeguard customer data and mitigate traffic congestion.

QUESTION 37

You oversee a financial services platform hosted on Google Compute Engine. You suspect irregular network activities and wish to monitor and record network traffic for investigative purposes. What action should you take?

A) Enable VPC Flow Logs on the relevant subnets within the development and production VPCs, with a sample volume scale of 1.0. Start by enabling it in development and then in production.

B) Enable VPC Flow Logs on the relevant subnets within the development and production VPCs, with a sample volume scale of 0.5. Start by enabling it in development and then in production.

C) Enable VPC Flow Logs only on the production VPC subnets with a sample volume scale of 1.0.

QUESTION 38

Your organization manages a suite of microservices on Google Kubernetes Engine (GKE) for various workflows. The GKE clusters used in the production workflows generate extensive logs that are primarily accessed through the kubectl logs utility. These logs have inconsistent formats. You aim to reduce logging-related costs while ensuring crucial operational logs are still captured. What action should you take?

A) Execute the gcloud container clusters update --logging=SYSTEM command on the GKE clusters used in the production workflows.

B) Invoke the gcloud logging sinks update _Default --disabled command within the project related to the production workflows.

C) Add the severity >= DEBUG resource.type = "k8s_container" exclusion filter to the _Default logging sink within the project tied to the production workflows.

D) Execute the gcloud container clusters update --logging=WORKLOAD command on the GKE clusters used in the production workflows.

QUESTION 39

Your organization's data analytics platform on Google Cloud is anticipating a substantial increase in usage due to an upcoming marketing campaign. What should be your first course of action to prepare the platform for this surge, in line with Google Cloud best practices?

A) Convert the platform to utilize Google Cloud Functions for scalable processing power.
B) Design a CloudFormation template to quickly deploy additional resources as needed.
C) Execute thorough performance testing to determine the platform's scalability under increased load.
D) Proactively scale up BigQuery resources based on projected data processing needs and past usage patterns.
E) Implement an automatic scaling policy using Cloud Composer based on expected usage metrics.

QUESTION 40

In your GKE environment, certain data analysis tasks are underperforming, and you suspect memory pressure issues on the nodes. Without direct command execution access, how can you identify the Pods that may be causing these memory issues?

A) Utilize Metrics Explorer to monitor the node/memory/used_bytes metric for insights into memory usage.
B) Find Pods using in-memory data structures, and use the top command to check memory utilization.
C) Investigate the container/memory/used_bytes metric in Metrics Explorer to identify high memory usage at the container level.
D) Locate Pods with large memory requests and use the free -m command to gauge their memory consumption.

QUESTION 41

Your company's cloud-based retail analytics platform is expanding, requiring an adaptable DevOps setup for managing a mix of Google Cloud resources and third-party cloud services. What toolset should you implement to support dynamic and efficient deployment of resources?

A) Cloud Build with Chef
B) Cloud Build with Spinnaker
C) Google Kubernetes Engine with Terraform
D) Cloud Build with Google Cloud Deploy

QUESTION 42

Your team is responsible for a multi-regional e-commerce platform on GKE. Suddenly, one region experiences a severe service degradation. As per SRE guidelines, how should you initially respond to this situation?

A) Begin by scaling the affected region's GKE clusters to increase their handling capacity.
B) First, inspect Cloud Logging for the specific regional clusters to uncover any anomalies or errors.
C) Immediately reroute e-commerce traffic from the troubled region to stable regions.
D) Use Cloud Monitoring to assess if there's a spike in resource demand, like CPU or memory, in the affected region.

QUESTION 43

Your organization experienced a significant outage in its cloud-based streaming service. As part of your SRE practices, you need to determine when a post-mortem analysis is necessary. Which two triggers should prompt an in-depth review?

A) A key stakeholder demands a detailed report.
B) Monitoring systems detect a critical service failure.
C) A developer suggests investigating the incident further.
D) Automated rollback occurs due to a detected error in a new deployment.
E) Sensitive data exposure was identified during the outage.

QUESTION 44

You are managing a Python web application's CI/CD pipeline on Cloud Build, with the source code in a GitLab repository. The organization requires that any production deployment is triggered from a 'main' branch after passing a peer review. Which steps should you take to ensure this process is followed?

A) Apply merge request approval settings in GitLab for the 'main' branch.
B) Include a script in the 'cloudbuild.yaml' that checks the branch name before deployment.
C) Set Cloud Build to trigger on 'Pull request' events for the 'main' branch.
D) Create a Cloud Build trigger that activates on 'Push to a branch' events, specifically for the 'main' branch.

QUESTION 45

You're responsible for ensuring compliance with security standards across multiple GKE clusters. The security policies are maintained in a SVN repository. You need a solution to automatically apply these policy updates to the clusters. What approach should you adopt?

A) Link the SVN repository with Cloud Build to trigger builds that apply policy updates using gcloud commands.
B) Use Anthos Config Management connected to the SVN repository for automatic enforcement of policy changes.
C) Configure a Cloud Scheduler job to periodically pull updates from the SVN repository and apply them using kubectl.
D) Implement Anthos Service Mesh integrated with the SVN repository for real-time policy application.

QUESTION 46

You're managing a web application deployment on Google Cloud with Terraform and notice that your CI/CD pipeline creates new instances without terminating old ones, leading to inflated costs. How should you reconfigure your pipeline to ensure only the latest instance is running after each deployment?

A) Configure the pipeline to store and retrieve Terraform state files from a secure Cloud Storage bucket to maintain consistent infrastructure state.
B) Implement a script in the CI/CD pipeline to manually terminate old instances before deploying new ones.
C) Store Terraform state files in the same version control system as your application code for easy pipeline access.

D) Add a pre-deployment step in your pipeline that uses Terraform to destroy existing infrastructure before deploying the latest changes.

QUESTION 47

As a DevOps engineer, you're tasked with enhancing the security of a cloud-based application deployed on GKE. Your goal is to prevent unauthorized or untested container images from being deployed. Which combination of tools and configurations should you employ to achieve this?

A) Configure GKE to use private clusters and restrict network access.
B) Use Binary Authorization in GKE to ensure only images that pass specific checks are deployed.
C) Implement Cloud Security Command Center to monitor and control image deployments in GKE.
D) Enable continuous vulnerability scanning in Artifact Registry and configure policy checks in the CI/CD pipeline.

QUESTION 48

You oversee a Python-based streaming application on Google Cloud's Dataflow service, and you've noticed that the workers shut down every 20 minutes due to memory spikes. What action should you take to resolve this issue?

A) Implement Cloud Profiler to identify memory usage patterns and apply optimizations.
B) Decrease the number of worker nodes in the Dataflow job's configuration to alleviate memory pressure.
C) Enable additional logging to monitor memory consumption and worker shutdowns.
D) Adjust the Dataflow job's memory allocation to a higher value.

QUESTION 49

You are responsible for managing a containerized application on Google Kubernetes Engine (GKE). The application requires periodic scaling to accommodate variable workloads. What strategies can you employ to automate the scaling process efficiently? (Choose two.)

A) Implement Horizontal Pod Autoscaling in your GKE cluster based on CPU utilization metrics.
B) Use Google Cloud Scheduler to manually trigger scaling events based on anticipated load changes.
C) Set a fixed number of replicas for your application pods to ensure consistent performance.
D) Utilize Google Cloud Pub/Sub to receive real-time alerts and manually adjust the pod count.
E) Implement Vertical Pod Autoscaling to automatically adjust resource requests and limits.

QUESTION 50

Your team is tasked with automating the deployment of microservices-based applications on Google Cloud. What CI/CD approach should you adopt to minimize manual oversight, ensure scalability, and align with best practices?

A) Utilize Jenkins on your local development environment for simplified CI/CD workflows.
B) Set up Jenkins on Compute Engine instances to manage microservices deployments effectively.
C) Leverage Google Cloud Build with Cloud Functions to streamline CI/CD processes and enhance scalability for microservices.

D) Employ Travis CI integrated with Google Kubernetes Engine (GKE) for versatile microservices deployments.

E) Explore CI/CD options with Azure DevOps for cross-cloud compatibility.

F) Set up CircleCI with AWS for comprehensive CI/CD pipelines.

PRACTICE TEST 6 - ANSWERS ONLY

QUESTION 1

Answer - D) Configure a Binary Authorization policy that enforces image verification for Compute Engine instances.

Option D is the recommended approach. Binary Authorization allows you to enforce policies on container images, ensuring that only authorized and verified images can be used for Compute Engine instances, thus improving security and compliance while minimizing manual efforts.
 Option A involves manual inspection, which can be time-consuming and error-prone.
 Option B focuses on access control but does not enforce image verification.
 Option C includes security scanning but lacks the direct enforcement of image policies during instance updates.

QUESTION 2

Answer - C) Set up a global load balancer with health checks and configure multi-region replication for your data storage.

Option C aligns with the objectives of ensuring high availability and disaster recovery for a large-scale application by setting up a global load balancer and configuring multi-region replication for data storage.
 Options A, B, and D mention various services but do not directly address high availability and disaster recovery.

QUESTION 3

Answer - B) 2 and 3

Options 2 and 3 are the recommended choices for enabling secure and private communication between services deployed in different Google Cloud regions and VPCs. Using Cloud Interconnect provides dedicated and reliable network connections, while VPC Peering allows for private communication between VPCs.
 Option 1, Cloud VPN, is more suitable for secure communication over the public internet.
 Option 4, Cloud Router, is used for dynamic routing within a VPC but does not directly address inter-VPC communication.

QUESTION 4

Answer - D) Create a dedicated service account with the Kubernetes Engine Developer role.

Option D is the correct choice as it recommends creating a dedicated service account with the necessary role for Cloud Build, ensuring efficient authentication.
 Option A suggests embedding the role, which may not be the best approach,
 Option B introduces manual steps, which is not efficient,
 Option C helps the service account but might not be the optimal method,
 Option E doesn't effectively address authentication.

QUESTION 5

Answer - B) MTTD: 3 MTTR: 15 MTBF: 60 Impact: 33%

Option B represents the risk assessment figures for the new storage solution failover, matching the provided MTTD, MTTR, MTBF, and a 33% user impact.
 Option A has incorrect user impact,
 Option C has incorrect MTTR,
 Option D has incorrect MTTR and user impact.

QUESTION 6

Answer - A and B

Options A and B are the correct choices. Segmenting automation procedures into finer-grained components (A) reduces redundancy and streamlines the workflow. Implementing automatic progression confirmations (B) helps in achieving smoother transitions between stages, reducing manual interventions.
 Options C and D are not directly related to optimizing the workflow.

QUESTION 7

Answer - A and B

Option A - Allowing developers to integrate changes independently with rollback capabilities can expedite the process without compromising safety.
 Option B - Implementing a peer-review process with automated validations maintains code quality without hindering deployment efficiency.
 Options C, D, and E are not the optimal actions to adjust the process.

QUESTION 8

Answer - D) Create a new instance template with increased memory and associate it with the instance group, then delete the old template.

A) Incorrect - Temporarily removing the instance group can lead to state inconsistencies.
B) Incorrect - create_before_destroy is helpful but does not address the issue of the template being in use.
C) Incorrect - Manually deleting the instance group can cause significant disruption.
D) Correct - This ensures a smooth transition with minimal disruption by first creating a new template.
E) Incorrect - Bypassing Terraform breaks the automation and consistency of the infrastructure as code approach.

QUESTION 9

Answer - A) Establish individual Google Cloud projects for each department, with a GKE cluster for development and another for production, using IAM for access control.

A) Correct - This method provides clear operational and access segregation while maintaining cost-effectiveness.

B) Incorrect - A multi-cluster environment in a single project can lead to access control complexities.
C) Incorrect - Namespaces offer logical separation but may not be sufficient for strict departmental isolation.
D) Incorrect - Using separate clusters in a shared project could lead to access and resource allocation conflicts.
E) Incorrect - Different node pools in a single cluster do not provide the required level of isolation for departments.

QUESTION 10

Answer - C) Implement Cloud Monitoring to track BigQuery's query execution times and data processed.

A) Incorrect - Cloud DLP is for data security, not for monitoring resource usage in BigQuery.
B) Incorrect - Cloud Trace is more suitable for latency and request tracing, not for query cost analysis.
C) Correct - Cloud Monitoring can track query performance metrics in BigQuery, aiding in cost management.
D) Incorrect - While Cloud Logging provides logs, it requires manual effort for performance analysis.
E) Incorrect - Cloud Profiler is not typically used for querying and cost optimization in BigQuery.

QUESTION 11

Answer - C) Deploy Cloud Trace to track the request flow and pinpoint where failures are occurring.

A) Incorrect - Cloud Logging is useful for logs but may not provide in-depth insights into crash causes.
B) Incorrect - Cloud Profiler is more focused on performance analysis, not on identifying crash causes.
C) Correct - Cloud Trace can track request flows and help identify where and why crashes are occurring.
D) Incorrect - Prometheus is great for monitoring, but it's more suited for general system metrics than for tracking specific crashes.
E) Incorrect - Error Reporting helps with error detection but lacks the depth needed to diagnose crash causes.

QUESTION 12

Answer - A) Integrate automated security testing tools within Cloud Build, running them post-merge into the master branch. If tests pass, deploy the API service to a secured staging environment, followed by production.

A) Correct - Integrating automated security testing in Cloud Build ensures consistent and thorough security validation before production deployment.
B) Incorrect - Relying solely on local security testing is not sufficient for sensitive data handling applications.
C) Incorrect - Skipping additional security tests in the staging environment could miss crucial vulnerabilities.
D) Incorrect - Conducting all security tests only in the staging environment delays the identification of potential issues.
E) Incorrect - While manual reviews are valuable, they should complement, not replace, automated security testing.

QUESTION 13

Answer - B) Examine the Cloud Monitoring metrics for any anomalies or performance issues related to the new tool.

A) Incorrect - Downgrading without understanding the specific cause might not resolve the problem.
B) Correct - Monitoring metrics can provide insights into how the new tool is affecting performance.
C) Incorrect - Scaling up resources without diagnosing the issue can be costly and ineffective.
D) Incorrect - Communicating with users is important but secondary to diagnosing the problem.
E) Incorrect - A comprehensive performance analysis is time-consuming and should follow initial diagnostic steps.

QUESTION 14

Answer - A) Implement Binary Authorization in GKE to enforce deployment of only signed and verified images.

A) Correct - Binary Authorization ensures that only approved and verified container images are deployed, aligning with the security requirement.
B) Incorrect - While Cloud Security Command Center is useful for monitoring, it does not prevent the deployment of non-compliant images.
C) Incorrect - IAM roles control access but do not enforce image compliance standards at deployment.
D) Incorrect - Vulnerability Scanning identifies vulnerabilities but does not enforce a policy of using only approved images.
E) Incorrect - Custom scripts in the CI/CD pipeline are less reliable and scalable compared to Binary Authorization.

QUESTION 15

Answer - B) Set up a dedicated Artifact Registry for Terraform modules, enabling IAM-based access control and audit logging for compliance.

A) Incorrect - Self-hosting on Compute Engine requires additional management and may not provide the desired level of security and compliance.
B) Correct - Artifact Registry with IAM access control and audit logging offers a secure and compliant way to manage Terraform modules.
C) Incorrect - While Cloud Source Repositories are good for version control, they lack specific features for Terraform module management.
D) Incorrect - Cloud Storage offers storage but does not provide the specialized features for managing Terraform modules effectively.
E) Incorrect - Managed Terraform Enterprise is a robust solution, but integrating with VPC Service Controls may add complexity and cost.

QUESTION 16

Answer - D) Establish BigQuery datasets for each project team within a unified logging project. Assign dataset-level IAM roles for access control, and grant the compliance oversight team BigQuery admin privileges in the central project.

Option D is the correct choice because it allows for granular access control with BigQuery datasets for

each project team within a unified logging project. The compliance oversight team has admin privileges for centralized access.
 Option A - Option A is incorrect because creating separate centralized logging projects may introduce unnecessary complexity and doesn't ensure central access.
 Option B - Option B is incorrect because it suggests consolidating logs into a single project without considering the compliance requirement for separate team access.
 Option C - Option C is incorrect because using Google Cloud Storage buckets may not provide the necessary granularity for log access control within a project.

QUESTION 17

Answer - B) Configure an attestation for stress-tested updates using a private key stored in Cloud Key Management Service (Cloud KMS) along with a service account JSON key embedded as a Kubernetes Secret.

Option B is the correct choice because it ensures that only stress-tested updates are deployed to the primary GKE cluster by configuring an attestation with a private key stored in Cloud KMS and a service account JSON key as a Kubernetes Secret for verification.
 Option A - Option A involves manual signing by the chief technical officer, which is not an automated process.
 Option C - Option C mandates manual signature by the chief technical officer, introducing manual steps and complexity.
 Option D - Option D mentions verification via Workload Identity, which is not the most direct approach for this use case.

QUESTION 18

Answer - B) Implement Google Cloud Artifact Registry with integrated IAM controls and audit logging for container image and Helm chart management.

Option B is the correct choice because Google Cloud Artifact Registry provides integrated IAM controls and audit logging for secure and compliant container image and Helm chart management.
 Option A - Option A suggests using generic object storage, which may lack specific features for container images.
 Option C - Option C mentions third-party registries, which may not have the same level of integration with Google Cloud.
 Option D - Option D proposes manual access management, which is not as efficient and auditable as using a managed service.

QUESTION 19

Answer - B) Store credentials in Secret Manager, encrypting them with a key from Cloud Key Management Service. Grant the automated workflow access to Secret Manager using Identity and Access Management.

Option B is the correct choice.
 Option B - Storing credentials in Secret Manager, encrypted with a key from Cloud Key Management Service, and granting workflow access via Identity and Access Management aligns with best practices for secure credential management and rotation.

Option A - Instructing data engineers to manually input credentials is error-prone and less secure.
Option C - Embedding credentials in the workflow's codebase is not recommended as it exposes sensitive information.
Option D - Storing credentials in a dedicated configuration file may not provide adequate security and access control.

QUESTION 20

B) Store credentials in Secret Manager encrypted with a key from Cloud Key Management Service. Grant the automated workflow access to Secret Manager via Identity and Access Management.

To securely retrieve database credentials and facilitate credential rotation, you should store the credentials in Secret Manager, encrypt them with a key from Cloud Key Management Service (Cloud KMS), and grant the automated workflow access to Secret Manager via Identity and Access Management (IAM). This approach ensures secure storage of credentials and allows for easy rotation in case of compromise. The other options involve less secure practices, such as storing credentials in code or configuration files or requiring manual input, which can pose security risks.

QUESTION 21

Answer - C) Perform load testing to evaluate the platform's performance under the expected surge in viewers.

Explanation for Option C - Performing load testing is the first step to assess how the platform performs under the expected surge in viewers. It helps identify performance bottlenecks and informs capacity planning.
Explanation for Option A - Upgrading the CDN is important but should be based on the results of load testing to determine the actual requirements.
Explanation for Option B - Enabling real-time monitoring is valuable, but it should complement load testing to make informed adjustments during the event.
Explanation for Option D - Developing a communication plan is essential but should not be the initial action. First, assess and optimize the platform's performance under load.

QUESTION 22

Answer - B) Establish a policy where any breach of the SLO triggers an immediate freeze on feature development.

Explanation for Option B - Establishing a policy that freezes feature development in the event of an SLO breach is a proactive measure to ensure the prioritization of stability during critical incidents. It provides clear guidelines.
Explanation for Option A - Halting all updates until an SLO breach is resolved may not be efficient and may lead to delays without clear guidelines.
Explanation for Option C - Regular meetings to discuss platform stability are valuable, but they may not ensure immediate action during critical incidents.
Explanation for Option D - Collaborating with product managers is important, but it may not provide an immediate response to SLO breaches without a predefined policy.

QUESTION 23

Answer - C) Establish a schedule to conduct retrospectives on a regular basis, involving cross-functional teams.

Option A) Performing retrospectives only after major incidents limits the opportunity for continuous improvement and prevention of smaller incidents.
Option B) Conducting retrospectives only with directly involved teams can exclude valuable perspectives from other teams who can contribute to improvements.
Option D) Limiting retrospectives to post-mortem analysis without action items doesn't drive the necessary changes for improvement.
Option C aligns with the goal by establishing a routine schedule that involves cross-functional teams, promoting continuous improvement and proactive incident prevention.

QUESTION 24

Answer - C) Utilize canary testing, gradually increasing user exposure.

A) Ensures zero downtime but doesn't facilitate testing under realistic user loads.
B) Allows for controlled feature release but lacks the ability to test under actual load conditions.
C) Ideal for evaluating new features under realistic loads with the ability to quickly rollback if issues are detected.
D) More suited for user experience testing rather than performance under load.
E) Minimizes user disruption but does not allow for testing in a production-like environment with real user traffic.

QUESTION 25

Answer - B) Implement a distributed version control system like Git, with a repository hosting service for centralized access to the codebase.

Option A - While Google Cloud Storage is scalable, it lacks version control features essential for collaborative development.
Option B - This is the recommended approach as it combines the benefits of distributed version control with centralized access and collaboration.
Option C - An internal file server does not provide robust version control or collaboration features.
Option D - Google Drive lacks necessary version control mechanisms and makes integrating changes cumbersome.
Option E - Centralized systems are less flexible than distributed version control systems like Git.

QUESTION 26

Answer - A) and D)

Option A - This gives a complete picture of the user experience, covering both frontend and backend services.
Option B - While important, this does not fully represent the end-user experience.
Option C - Disk I/O is a part of server performance but not directly tied to user-perceived service reliability.
Option D - External services' performance can significantly impact the overall service quality

experienced by users.
 Option E - Firewall efficiency is crucial for security but not a direct indicator of application performance or reliability.

QUESTION 27

Answer - A) Evaluate the increase in customer satisfaction and its potential impact on revenue.

Option A - Understanding how enhanced customer satisfaction can translate into increased revenue is key to justifying the cost.
 Option B - The investment's percentage of annual revenue is a factor but doesn't provide the full picture.
 Option C - While latency reduction is important, its direct impact on financials should be assessed.
 Option D - Operational savings are important, but the main benefit here is improved customer experience.
 Option E - Service reliability is crucial, but the financial justification should also consider direct revenue impact.

QUESTION 28

Answer - A) Develop a more rigorous configuration change review and testing process.

Option A - Implementing a thorough review and testing process can prevent similar issues in the future.
 Option B - Focusing on individual blame does not contribute to a solution-oriented, collaborative environment.
 Option C - Requiring executive approval for all changes can slow down the process and isn't scalable.
 Option D - While communication is important, it doesn't directly address the need for a systematic review process.
 Option E - Automation can be helpful, but it's more important to prevent errors than to rely on rollbacks.

QUESTION 29

Answer - D) Implement Config Sync for Kubernetes configuration management and Policy Controller for policy enforcement.

Option A - Config Connector is used for managing Google Cloud resources through Kubernetes, not for configuration consistency.
 Option B - Manual application of configurations is error-prone and not scalable.
 Option C - Terraform is a powerful tool, but it's not focused on Google's Kubernetes configuration practices.
 Option D - Config Sync and Policy Controller are Google-recommended tools for maintaining consistency and enforcing policies in GKE environments.
 Option E - Cloud Functions are not typically used for applying Kubernetes configurations, and Cloud IAM manages access control, not resource configurations.

QUESTION 30

Answer - C) Use the Persistent Disk Recommender to automatically get recommendations for optimal disk size.

Option A - While effective, manual review is less efficient than automated recommendations.
 Option B - Custom scripting can be complex and may not adapt quickly to changing storage needs.
 Option C - The Persistent Disk Recommender provides data-driven, automated recommendations for efficient disk sizing.
 Option D - Constant disk sizing may lead to underutilization or constraints during unexpected usage spikes.
 Option E - Monthly manual monitoring is less responsive and efficient compared to automated tools.

QUESTION 31

Answer - A) SSH into the affected Compute Engine instance and check if the Stackdriver agent is running.

Option B, checking the Stackdriver agent's test log message, may not directly address the issue of missing logs from a specific instance.
Option C, upgrading the Stackdriver agent, is a valid action but not necessarily the first step in troubleshooting.
Option D, ensuring the service account access scope, may not be the initial step to diagnose the problem.

QUESTION 32

Answer - A) Modify the service account permissions to include the Logs Writer role.

Option B, switching to the standard service account, may not be necessary and can lead to other issues.
Option C, enabling Private Google Access, is related to network connectivity and does not directly affect Cloud Logging.
Option D, generating a service account key, is not typically required for configuring Cloud Logging.

QUESTION 33

Answer - C) Distribute the cluster across multiple zones for redundancy.

- Option A is not fault-tolerant and lacks redundancy.
- Option B helps with scalability but doesn't provide fault tolerance alone.
- Option D may lead to extended downtime during hardware failures.
Distributing the GKE cluster across multiple zones (Option C) provides redundancy and enhances fault tolerance, ensuring high availability for the critical application.

QUESTION 34

Answer - B) Implement Horizontal Pod Autoscaling for the "checkout-service" based on CPU utilization.

Explanation:
 Option B is the correct choice because implementing Horizontal Pod Autoscaling based on CPU utilization allows the "checkout-service" to dynamically adjust its Pod count to handle increased load, effectively addressing the high CPU utilization issue.
 Option A suggests manually scaling up Pods, which is not efficient for handling variable loads.
 Option C involves updating the cluster's machine type, which may not be necessary if only one

microservice is experiencing high CPU utilization.
Option D, modifying the Ingress controller, is a drastic measure that may disrupt service unnecessarily.

QUESTION 35

Answer - A) Implement blue/green deployments and employ shadow releases

Option A is the correct choice because blue/green deployments simplify production releases, and shadow releases enable gradual validation of production traffic, aligning with the specified goals.
Option B is incorrect as dark launches are not typically used with rolling updates. Option C is incorrect because a recreate strategy may not align with the goal of minimizing rollback times. Option D is incorrect because A/B testing doesn't directly address the goal of verifying production traffic while gradually increasing user impact.

QUESTION 36

Answer - B) Implement a load balancer to distribute incoming customer inquiries more evenly across the existing Compute Engine instances.

Option B is the correct choice as it addresses the network capacity issue by implementing a load balancer to evenly distribute customer inquiries.
Option A is incorrect as upgrading the instance type may not directly resolve the network capacity problem.
Option C is incorrect as optimizing application code, while important, may not fully address the network capacity issue.
Option D is incorrect as deploying additional network security measures may not directly impact network performance and could introduce more congestion.

QUESTION 37

Answer - A) Enable VPC Flow Logs on the relevant subnets within the development and production VPCs, with a sample volume scale of 1.0. Start by enabling it in development and then in production.

Option A is the correct choice as it enables VPC Flow Logs with a sample volume scale of 1.0 in both development and production environments, ensuring comprehensive network traffic monitoring for investigation.
Option B is incorrect as it reduces the sample volume scale, potentially missing important data.
Option C is incorrect as it only enables VPC Flow Logs in the production environment, overlooking the development environment's insights.

QUESTION 38

Answer - A) Execute the gcloud container clusters update --logging=SYSTEM command on the GKE clusters used in the production workflows.

Option A is the correct choice as it aligns with optimizing logging costs for production workflows by configuring GKE clusters to capture system logs. This approach reduces unnecessary logs and minimizes costs. Option B suggests disabling the default logging sink, which may not effectively reduce costs. Option C adds an exclusion filter that might not reduce logging costs as intended for production workflows. Option D recommends updating GKE clusters to capture workload-specific logs, which may not align with cost optimization for production workflows.

QUESTION 39

Answer - C) Execute thorough performance testing to determine the platform's scalability under increased load.

Option A - Incorrect: While Cloud Functions offer scalability, assessing current capability is the first step.
Option B - Incorrect: CloudFormation assists in resource deployment but isn't the initial action for scalability.
Option C - Correct: Performance testing is the key initial step to understand scalability needs and limitations.
Option D - Incorrect: Scaling BigQuery resources is crucial but should come after understanding current performance.
Option E - Incorrect: Automatic scaling is effective, but first, the platform's existing performance must be evaluated.

QUESTION 40

Answer - C) Investigate the container/memory/used_bytes metric in Metrics Explorer to identify high memory usage at the container level.

Option A - Incorrect: Node-level metrics provide overall usage but lack pod-specific details.
Option B - Incorrect: Without direct access, running top is not feasible.
Option C - Correct: Container-specific memory metrics can pinpoint which Pods are consuming excessive memory.
Option D - Incorrect: Without command execution access, free -m cannot be utilized.

QUESTION 41

Answer - B) Cloud Build with Spinnaker

Option A - Incorrect: Chef focuses on configuration management and does not provide a comprehensive deployment solution.
Option B - Correct: Spinnaker supports multi-cloud deployment strategies, and Cloud Build can be integrated for continuous integration and delivery.
Option C - Incorrect: While Terraform and GKE are powerful, they may not cover the specific needs of a retail analytics platform requiring integration with third-party services.
Option D - Incorrect: Google Cloud Deploy is useful but may not offer the same level of multi-cloud orchestration as Spinnaker.

QUESTION 42

Answer - B) First, inspect Cloud Logging for the specific regional clusters to uncover any anomalies or errors.

Option A - Incorrect: Adding resources without identifying the cause might not resolve the issue effectively.

Option B - Correct: Investigating logs to identify the cause of the degradation is in accordance with SRE principles for problem-solving.
Option C - Incorrect: Traffic rerouting is a mitigation step, not an initial diagnostic action.
Option D - Incorrect: While resource spikes can be indicative, they may not provide immediate insights into the cause of service degradation.

QUESTION 43

Answer - B) Monitoring systems detect a critical service failure. and E) Sensitive data exposure was identified during the outage.

Option A - Incorrect: External demands alone should not dictate review policy.
Option B - Correct: Critical service failures are a primary indicator for in-depth reviews.
Option C - Incorrect: While valuable, internal suggestions alone aren't definitive triggers.
Option D - Incorrect: Automated rollbacks indicate functioning error detection, not necessarily needing an in-depth review.
Option E - Correct: Data exposure incidents are critical and warrant thorough investigation.

QUESTION 44

Answer - A) Apply merge request approval settings in GitLab for the 'main' branch. and D) Create a Cloud Build trigger that activates on 'Push to a branch' events, specifically for the 'main' branch.

Option A - Correct: Merge request approvals in GitLab ensure that changes to the 'main' branch undergo peer review.
Option B - Incorrect: Scripts in 'cloudbuild.yaml' are for defining build steps, not for enforcing branch policies.
Option C - Incorrect: 'Pull request' events are for pre-merge checks, not for post-merge deployment triggers.
Option D - Correct: A Cloud Build trigger for 'Push to a branch' events on 'main' ensures deployment occurs post-review.

QUESTION 45

Answer - B) Use Anthos Config Management connected to the SVN repository for automatic enforcement of policy changes.

Option A - Incorrect: While Cloud Build can be used, it's not as streamlined for policy synchronization as Anthos Config Management.
Option B - Correct: Anthos Config Management is designed for such scenarios, offering an automated way to enforce policies from a version-controlled repository.
Option C - Incorrect: Cloud Scheduler with periodic updates is less efficient and real-time compared to Anthos Config Management.
Option D - Incorrect: Anthos Service Mesh is not the ideal tool for direct integration with version control systems for policy enforcement.

QUESTION 46

Answer - A) Configure the pipeline to store and retrieve Terraform state files from a secure Cloud Storage bucket to maintain consistent infrastructure state.

Option A - Correct: Using a Cloud Storage backend for Terraform ensures that the state is consistently managed and prevents duplicate environments.
Option B - Incorrect: Manual termination scripts can be error-prone and are not a best practice.
Option C - Incorrect: Storing state files in version control is not recommended due to potential conflicts and security concerns.
Option D - Incorrect: Destroying existing infrastructure as a routine step can lead to service downtime and is not efficient.

QUESTION 47

Answer - B) Use Binary Authorization in GKE to ensure only images that pass specific checks are deployed.

Option A - Incorrect: Private clusters limit network access but don't control image deployment based on CI/CD validation.
Option B - Correct: Binary Authorization allows you to enforce deployment policies for container images, ensuring security compliance.
Option C - Incorrect: Cloud Security Command Center provides broad security monitoring but doesn't enforce deployment policies for specific images.
Option D - Incorrect: While vulnerability scanning is important, it needs to be combined with deployment policies for full enforcement.

QUESTION 48

Answer - D) Adjust the Dataflow job's memory allocation to a higher value.

Option A suggests profiling, but it doesn't directly address the memory allocation issue.
Option B, reducing worker nodes, may not resolve the memory spikes causing shutdowns.
Option C adds more logging, which may not prevent memory spikes.
Option D is the recommended approach to address the memory spikes and prevent worker shutdowns.

QUESTION 49

Answer - A) Implement Horizontal Pod Autoscaling in your GKE cluster based on CPU utilization metrics.
E) Implement Vertical Pod Autoscaling to automatically adjust resource requests and limits.

Option A is correct because it enables automated scaling based on CPU utilization, which efficiently accommodates variable workloads.
Option E is also correct as Vertical Pod Autoscaling adjusts resource requests automatically to optimize resource usage.
Options B, C, and D involve manual intervention and are not as efficient for automated scaling.

QUESTION 50

Answer - C) Leverage Google Cloud Build with Cloud Functions to streamline CI/CD processes and enhance scalability for microservices.

Options A, B, D, E, and F - Incorrect. These options may not provide the optimal scalability and automation required for microservices-based applications.
 Option C is the correct choice as it suggests leveraging Google Cloud Build with Cloud Functions to streamline CI/CD processes and enhance scalability for microservices deployments on Google Cloud.

PRACTICE TEST 7 - QUESTIONS ONLY

QUESTION 1

Your microservices-based application on Google Kubernetes Engine (GKE) is experiencing instability after a recent container image update. You want to revert to the previous version of the container image to restore stability. What is the recommended approach for rolling back to the previous container image version in GKE while minimizing downtime and ensuring consistency?

A) Reassign the 'latest' tag to the previous container image version and update the deployment.
 B) Modify the deployment to use the sha256 digest of the previous container image.
 C) Rebuild the container image with the previous version and deploy it as a new service in parallel.
 D) Introduce a new label 'stable' for the previous container image version and update the deployment to use this label.

QUESTION 2

Your company has adopted a microservices architecture for its cloud-based application. You want to ensure efficient communication between microservices while maintaining security and observability. Which Google Cloud services and practices should you consider to achieve this, following Google's recommended DevOps guidelines?

A) Use Google Cloud Identity-Aware Proxy (IAP) for secure access to microservices and implement Google Cloud Trace for performance monitoring.
 B) Implement Google Cloud Endpoints to create APIs for microservices and utilize Google Cloud Pub/Sub for asynchronous communication between services.
 C) Set up Google Cloud Memorystore for caching between microservices and use Google Cloud Functions for serverless processing.
 D) Utilize Google Cloud VPN for secure communication between microservices and implement Google Cloud Scheduler for task automation.

QUESTION 3

You are responsible for managing a complex microservices architecture on Google Kubernetes Engine (GKE). You need to ensure high availability and reliability for your application. Which two Kubernetes concepts or techniques should you consider for achieving this goal? I. Implement PodDisruptionBudgets to control disruptions during maintenance. 2. Use Horizontal Pod Autoscaling (HPA) to adjust resources dynamically. 3. Deploy multi-cluster clusters across different regions for redundancy. 4. Set up Network Policies for fine-grained network control between microservices.

A) 1 and 2 B) 2 and 3 C) 3 and 4 D) 1 and 4

QUESTION 4

In your role overseeing a web service streaming metrics into Cloud Monitoring, how should you authorize a subset of the operations team to set up dashboards efficiently?

A) Implement a Service Perimeter in Cloud IAM to manage access.

B) Leverage VPC Service Controls to limit who can configure dashboards.
C) Delegate a custom IAM role with specific permissions.
D) Assign the IAM role of monitoring.dashboardEditor to the operations team.

QUESTION 5

You're conducting a risk assessment for a new storage solution for an online gaming service. The new solution has the following figures: MTTD: 3 minutes, MTTR: 45 minutes, MTBF: 60 days, User Impact: 50%. What should be the risk assessment figures for the new storage solution failover?

A) MTTD: 3 MTTR: 15 MTBF: 60 Impact: 50%
B) MTTD: 3 MTTR: 15 MTBF: 60 Impact: 33%
C) MTTD: 3 MTTR: 45 MTBF: 60 Impact: 50%
D) MTTD: 3 MTTR: 45 MTBF: 60 Impact: 33%

QUESTION 6

You're examining your media processing workflow in Google Cloud's Dataflow with the goal of reducing repetitive tasks and shortening job execution times. What actions should you consider? (Choose two.)

A) Segment the automation procedures into finer-grained components.
B) Implement automatic progression confirmations transferring from the staging area to the production zone.
C) Run a script to facilitate the setup of the media processing workflow in Google Cloud Dataflow.
D) Set up an alert to inform the designated team to proceed with the next phase when human input is needed.

QUESTION 7

Your organization's critical CRM system, hosted on GKE in Google Cloud, anticipates a 15% quarterly workload increase for the next year. With the system currently utilizing 40% of available CPU resources, how should you address this growth?

A) Rely on the GKE cluster autoscaler to automatically scale resources as needed, eliminating the need for manual intervention.
B) The existing 40% CPU utilization provides a sufficient buffer to handle the workload increase without requiring additional capacity.
C) Increase node capacity by 90% in anticipation of the quarterly workload growth and conduct load testing to validate resource adequacy.
D) Assess node pool size limits, implement a horizontal pod autoscaler for workloads, and perform load testing to determine the necessary resources to manage the expected demand increase.

QUESTION 8

In a Google Cloud environment, you're using Terraform to manage a set of Compute Engine instances for a database cluster. When updating the machine type in the instance template, your CI/CD pipeline fails, showing that the instance template is currently in use. What is the best practice to update the instance template without causing service disruption?

A) Exclude the current instance template from Terraform's state, update it, and then re-import it.
B) Implement a phased rollout by creating a new instance template and gradually shifting instances to it.
C) Directly modify the instance template in the Google Cloud console, and then synchronize the changes with Terraform.
D) Use Terraform's replace_triggered_by attribute to replace the instance template automatically.
E) Decommission the database cluster and recreate it using the new instance template.

QUESTION 9

As the lead DevOps engineer, you are tasked with configuring a GKE environment for multiple business units within your enterprise, each managing distinct sets of applications. You must ensure that each unit operates independently with regard to their resources while maintaining overall cost-efficiency. What setup would you choose?

A) Designate a separate Google Cloud project for each business unit, with individual GKE clusters for their respective applications, using IAM to manage access rights.
B) Configure a single GKE cluster and allocate dedicated node pools to each business unit, using network policies to separate traffic.
C) Construct individual namespaces within a unified GKE cluster for each business unit, applying RBAC for secure access management.
D) Implement a multi-cluster GKE setup across various projects, with inter-cluster communication enabled through shared VPCs.
E) Create a singular GKE cluster for all units, using Kubernetes service accounts for access management and resource control.

QUESTION 10

You manage a video streaming service hosted on GKE, which requires significant data transfer for its content. To reduce network-related costs, what action should you take?

A) Implement a content delivery network (CDN) to cache and deliver streaming content closer to users.
B) Convert your GKE cluster to use preemptible VM instances to lower compute costs.
C) Redesign your application architecture to use serverless Cloud Functions to reduce data transfer needs.
D) Migrate your GKE cluster to a region closer to the majority of your user base.
E) Use Network Service Tiers to select a pricing model that matches your data transfer patterns.

QUESTION 11

Your e-commerce platform hosted on Google Kubernetes Engine (GKE) has started to exhibit increased response times. You need to quickly identify and address any performance bottlenecks. Which steps should you follow?

A) Analyze the GKE cluster logs using Cloud Logging for insights into the performance issues.
B) Employ Cloud Monitoring to track the resource usage and load patterns of the GKE cluster.
C) Use Cloud Trace to analyze the request flows within the platform and identify slow components.
D) Implement Cloud SQL Insights to monitor the performance of the database used by the platform.
E) Integrate Cloud Profiler to identify and optimize inefficient code in the platform's services.

QUESTION 12

You are configuring a CI/CD pipeline for a complex web application on Google Cloud, which includes several interconnected components. You need to ensure the pipeline supports comprehensive testing and reliable deployment of the entire application stack. What is the best setup for this scenario?

A) Set up Cloud Build to run unit tests for each component upon pull requests. After passing, aggregate components in a staging environment for integration testing, then deploy to production.
B) Implement Git hooks for pre-push testing in local environments. Successful local tests trigger Cloud Build for containerization and direct deployment to production.
C) Configure a multi-stage Cloud Build pipeline, where each stage represents a component. Each stage runs specific tests, and upon overall success, the application is deployed to a test environment before production.
D) Create separate pipelines for each component, using Cloud Build for testing and deployment to individual staging environments. Upon success, manually trigger production deployment.
E) Use Cloud Build for initial unit testing of individual components. Merge components into a single repository for integration testing, followed by deployment to a canary environment and then production.

QUESTION 13

You oversee a cloud-based e-commerce platform with a microservices architecture. The platform's performance is critical during high-traffic events like sales. You want to set an SLO that ensures user satisfaction during these peak times. What SLI should you monitor?

A) Transaction completion SLI: the percentage of successfully completed transactions out of all attempted transactions.
B) Page load time SLI: the average time taken for product pages to load.
C) Shopping cart uptime SLI: the availability of the shopping cart service during peak hours.
D) Server response time SLI: the average response time of the backend servers during high-traffic periods.
E) Checkout process efficiency SLI: the ratio of successful checkouts to the total number of checkout attempts.

QUESTION 14

As part of enhancing security for your cloud-native applications, you need to ensure that any containers running on your GKE clusters are based on secure and trusted base images. How can you automate the process of validating and enforcing the use of these base images?

A) Set up a CI/CD pipeline with a step to validate container images against a list of trusted base images before deployment.
B) Implement Binary Authorization with a policy that allows deployments only if containers are based on trusted base images.
C) Regularly run vulnerability scans on deployed containers in GKE and manually update any that do not use trusted base images.
D) Use IAM policies to restrict developers from deploying containers that are not based on trusted base images.
E) Configure Cloud Monitoring alerts to notify when a container not based on a trusted base image is

deployed.

QUESTION 15

Your company uses Terraform to manage infrastructure as code for deploying serverless solutions. You have modules that depend on both open-source and proprietary code. Your compliance department has raised concerns over using un-vetted open-source Terraform modules. You need to ensure consistent management of all modules, while enforcing access controls and maintaining compliance with VPC Service Con- trols. What action should you take?

A) Manage both open-source and proprietary modules using a self-hosted GitLab server integrated with Google Workspace for identity management.
 B) Set up a Terraform module registry service within a Google Kubernetes Engine (GKE) cluster, using a Cloud Storage bucket for storing the modules.
 C) Store both open-source and proprietary Terraform modules in OCI format using Artifact Registry.
 D) Keep both types of Terraform modules in a version—con- trolled repository, and use Cloud Build to periodically copy the modules to a Cloud Storage bucket. Use the Cloud Storage bucket as a module source, specifying the URL format https://[bucket].storage-googleapis.com/[module].
 E) None of the above.

QUESTION 16

Your organization needs to manage logs from various Google Cloud projects for compliance purposes. Each project team should access their own logs, and the compliance oversight team should have access to logs from all projects. What approach should you take to meet these requirements?

A) Assign IAM roles to each project team, allowing access only to their own logs in a centralized logging project. Grant the compliance oversight team viewer permissions in the central project.
 B) Establish separate centralized logging projects for each team and grant project-level IAM roles accordingly. Provide the compliance oversight team with admin rights in all projects.
 C) Streamline logs into distinct Google Cloud Storage buckets designated for each project team. Apply bucket-level access controls and grant the compliance oversight team object viewer rights in all buckets.
 D) Create custom log sinks for each project team and configure them to export logs to a central logging project. Assign IAM roles for log access control and grant the compliance oversight team log writer privileges in the central project.

QUESTION 17

In the process of setting up continuous deployment for your telemedicine application on Google Cloud, you want to ensure that only updates that pass rigorous stress testing in a staging GKE cluster are deployed to the primary GKE cluster used by patients and healthcare providers. What steps should you take with Binary Authorization for this purpose?

A) Create an attestation for stress-tested updates and manually obtain a signature from the chief technical officer using their private key.
 B) Configure an attestation for stress-tested updates using a private key stored in Cloud Key Management Service (Cloud KMS) along with a service account JSON key embedded as a Kubernetes Secret.
 C) Generate an attestation for stress-tested updates and require the chief technical officer to provide a

signature using a key stored in Cloud Key Management Service (Cloud KMS).

D) Set up an attestation for stress-tested updates using a private key secured in Cloud Key Management Service (Cloud KMS) with verification through Workload Identity.

QUESTION 18

Your team manages a popular file-sharing platform on Google Cloud. You need to assess the platform's reliability from the user's standpoint without making any software alterations. What steps should you take to achieve this effectively? (Select two.)

A) Examine the existing telemetry data and introduce additional metrics as required.

B) Modify the application's source code to gather more detailed user activity data.

C) Analyze both historical and real-time file access logs to understand user interactions with the platform.

D) Create virtual user accounts capable of emulating typical user actions on the platform.

E) Focus exclusively on analyzing server error logs to determine system performance.

QUESTION 19

Your automated data transformation workflows require secure access to database credentials and the ability to facilitate credential rotation if needed. What is the recommended approach to accomplish this, following Google's best practices?

A) Ensure data engineers input credentials manually during job setup and avoid persistent storage.

B) Store credentials in Secret Manager, encrypt them with a key from Cloud Key Management Service, and grant the automated workflow access through Identity and Access Management.

C) Encrypt credentials and include them in the workflow's codebase. Save an encryption key in a separate repository and provide workflow access to this key.

D) Store credentials in a dedicated configuration file on Cloud Source Repositories and grant specific data engineers access to this file.

QUESTION 20

You are consulting for a financial institution that has a legal requirement to retain transaction records for a decade. You need to set up a logging solution with Cloud Logging to export and preserve the records while keeping storage costs as low as possible. What should you do?

A) Construct a Cloud Run service that retrieves the records from Cloud Logging and stores them into BigQuery for long-term retention.

B) Provision a Cloud Storage bucket and adjust your transaction processing system to write records directly to this bucket.

C) Set up a Cloud Logging sink and direct it to Cloud Pub/Sub with a subscription that retains messages containing the transaction records for a period of ten years.

D) Configure a sink in Cloud Logging, assign it a unique name, create a Cloud Storage archive class bucket for storing the transaction records, and designate this bucket as the destination for the exported logs.

QUESTION 21

Your CI/CD pipeline uses Cloud Build to compile and deploy your application to Google Kubernetes

Engine (GKE). After a recent change in the build configuration, the pipeline fails to deploy the application. What should be your initial step to troubleshoot this issue?

A) Disable the CI/CD pipeline temporarily to avoid further failures.
B) Check the build logs in Cloud Build to identify the specific error or failure message.
C) Revert to a previous version of the build configuration that was known to work.
D) Create a new GKE cluster to deploy the application.

QUESTION 22

You manage a critical financial platform with a defined Service Level Objective (SLO). Your engineering team frequently deploys updates. To ensure that platform stability is prioritized over new feature development in the event of an SLO breach, what proactive step should you take before such an incident occurs?

A) Implement a rule that restricts any updates when the SLO is at risk of being breached.
B) Create a policy that enforces a freeze on feature development immediately upon an SLO breach.
C) Hold regular discussions with the engineering team to emphasize the importance of platform stability.
D) Collaborate with product managers to delay new feature releases when the SLO is at risk.

QUESTION 23

Your organization is transitioning to a culture of learning from incidents through retrospectives. What key elements should be part of this cultural shift?

A) Blame allocation and punitive measures for incidents.
B) A focus on individual accountability during retrospectives.
C) Open and blame-free discussions during retrospectives.
D) Limited participation in retrospectives to only the technical teams involved.
E) Regular retrospectives with actionable items for continuous improvement.

QUESTION 24

You are overseeing the deployment of a new feature in your mobile banking application hosted on Google Cloud. Post-deployment, you observe a significant increase in transaction failures and slower loading times for the feature. This impacts customer experience and could potentially lead to a loss of trust. What should be your immediate course of action to address these issues effectively?

A) Increase the compute resources allocated to the application servers.
B) Roll back the feature to its previous stable version.
C) Analyze the application logs and metrics to pinpoint the cause of failures and delays.
D) Conduct an immediate user survey to gather feedback on the new feature.
E) Implement a canary release strategy for more controlled future deployments.

QUESTION 25

As a lead DevOps engineer, you're overseeing a project that involves frequent updates to a set of Docker container images used in a Kubernetes environment. You need a systematic approach to track and manage these updates. What is the most effective method?

A) Save the Docker images in a common network directory with a naming convention to indicate different versions.
 B) Utilize a container registry with tagging for different versions of the Docker images.
 C) Keep the Docker image files in a shared Google Drive folder, updating the file names for each new version.
 D) Store Docker image files on individual developers' machines and manually synchronize changes.
 E) Use an FTP server for storing Docker images, with a separate folder for each version.

QUESTION 26

You oversee a global content delivery network (CDN) service in Google Cloud, focusing on delivering high-definition media content. You currently monitor the cache hit ratio as an SLI. To ensure comprehensive service monitoring, which additional metrics should you track? (Choose two)

A) Latency and throughput measurements at edge locations.
 B) Internal network latency between your origin servers and the CDN nodes.
 C) Real-time bandwidth usage statistics of the CDN.
 D) Google Cloud Load Balancer's session persistence and connection draining capabilities.
 E) Storage I/O performance for media files on Google Cloud Storage.

QUESTION 27

As an SRE for a cloud-based financial transaction platform, you receive an alert indicating a major service outage affecting transaction processing. As the Incident Commander, what is your first course of action after assembling your team?

A) Begin a root cause analysis to identify the source of the outage.
 B) Initiate a conference call with all clients to inform them of the outage.
 C) Set up a real-time incident response communication channel for the team.
 D) Immediately start working on a hotfix to restore transaction processing.
 E) Send a preliminary incident report to the company's management and stakeholders.

QUESTION 28

You are analyzing a recent incident where a cloud-based application experienced downtime due to an overloaded API gateway. The postmortem revealed inadequate load testing. What measures should you take to mitigate similar future incidents?

A) Implement comprehensive load and stress testing for all critical system components.
 B) Create a policy for immediate disciplinary action against the team responsible for the API gateway.
 C) Mandate that all future updates require managerial sign-off.
 D) Schedule regular meetings to discuss potential scalability issues with the development team.
 E) Restrict the number of changes that can be made to the API gateway each month.

QUESTION 29

Your company's data analytics team uses BigQuery across various Google Cloud projects for different environments like development, testing, and production. You need to ensure that BigQuery dataset access policies are uniformly applied and managed across all these projects. What is the best combination of tools and practices to achieve this?

A) Use Cloud Deployment Manager to set BigQuery policies and Config Sync to maintain uniformity across environments.
 B) Implement custom scripts to apply BigQuery policies in each project and use Cloud Monitoring for compliance checks.
 C) Leverage Cloud Build to apply BigQuery dataset policies and utilize Policy Controller for enforcing uniform access controls.
 D) Configure Cloud IAM roles and permissions for BigQuery access and rely on Cloud Audit Logs to track policy adherence.
 E) Apply BigQuery policies manually in each project and schedule regular audits with Cloud Security Command Center.

QUESTION 30

When configuring a DevOps process for automating infrastructure provisioning with Terraform on Google Cloud, what is the recommended approach for securing authentication credentials when using Terraform within a managed GKE cluster?

A) Share a single JSON key for a Google service account among all components of the CI/CD platform.
B) Embed the JSON key for a Google service account directly within the Terraform configuration files.
C) Utilize a separate JSON key for each infrastructure component and store them in a publicly accessible Git repository.
D) Secure the JSON key for a Google service account within your CI/CD platform's secrets management and configure Terraform to use it for authentication.
E) Leverage the GKE cluster's default service account for Terraform authentication.

QUESTION 31

You are managing a Cloud Function that processes data from Google Cloud Storage and logs events using the Stackdriver Logging agent. However, you notice that some of the Cloud Function's logs are not appearing in the Stackdriver Logs Viewer. What action should you take first to investigate this issue?

A) SSH into the Cloud Function instance and check the Stackdriver agent's status.
B) Check the Stackdriver agent's test log message in the Logs Viewer.
C) Upgrade the Stackdriver agent for Cloud Functions to the latest version.
D) Ensure the Cloud Function's service account has the monitoring.write access scope enabled.

QUESTION 32

You are responsible for a Compute Engine instance hosting a recently deployed application with an externally accessible IP address. The instance is associated with a custom service account. Despite the presence of the required agents, you are not observing any log entries in Cloud Logging. What should be your course of action in line with Google's recommended best practices?

A) Modify the service account permissions to include the Logs Writer role.
B) Switch the instance to operate with the Compute Engine's standard service account.
C) Ensure Private Google Access is enabled for the Compute Engine subnet.
D) Generate a service account key and configure the logging agents to authenticate using this key.

QUESTION 33

You are implementing a CI/CD pipeline for a Google Kubernetes Engine (GKE) application. As part of the deployment process, you want to ensure that you can quickly revert to the previous state in case of issues with a new deployment. What should you include in your CI/CD pipeline to enable this rollback capability?

A) Create a new GKE cluster for every deployment and switch traffic to the old cluster in case of issues.
B) Implement manual rollback by manually reconfiguring the deployment in case of issues.
C) Use Kubernetes Helm charts to manage deployments and use Helm rollback commands for quick reverts.
D) Keep multiple versions of container images and use kubectl commands to switch between them.

QUESTION 34

Your organization runs a multi-tier web application on Google Kubernetes Engine (GKE). The application consists of frontend, backend, and database services, each deployed in separate Pods. Recently, there has been a surge in traffic to the frontend service, leading to performance issues. What GKE feature or practice should you implement to address this problem efficiently?

A) Implement Horizontal Pod Autoscaling for the frontend service to dynamically adjust the number of Pods based on traffic.
B) Increase the CPU and memory resources allocated to the frontend Pods.
C) Deploy a second frontend service in a separate cluster to distribute the traffic load.
D) Scale up the GKE cluster to accommodate the increased traffic load.

QUESTION 35

Your responsibility involves designing deployment and validation strategies within Google Cloud for your CD workflow. Your primary objectives are to simplify production releases and decrease the time needed for deployment rollbacks. You also aim to verify production traffic while gradually increasing the user impact. Which approach should you choose?

A) Implement red/black deployments and use A/B testing
B) Utilize blue/green deployments combined with canary releases
C) Embrace a rebuild strategy for deployments and apply shadow releases
D) Choose rolling updates for deployment and conduct dark launches

QUESTION 36

You are overseeing the operation of a cloud-based gaming platform, and you've noticed that the error budget for server uptime has been exhausted during the current observation period. The development team is preparing to launch a major game update. What action should you take to align with SRE principles and ensure a successful game update release?

A) Analyze additional performance metrics related to the gaming platform's operation and identify SLOs with available error budget. Reallocate error budget from these SLOs to support the game update release.
 B) Alert the development team about the depleted error budget and request comprehensive testing to minimize errors during the game update release.

C) Initiate a formal request process to secure an increase in the error budget specifically for the game update release.

D) Inform the development team about the exhausted error budget and discuss the option of postponing the game update or accepting potential performance issues during the release.

QUESTION 37

You are responsible for a media streaming application hosted on Google Cloud Compute Engine. You suspect unauthorized data transfers and want to establish a monitoring solution to record network traffic for future analysis. What should you do?

A) Enable VPC Flow Logs on the relevant subnets in both the development and production VPCs, with a sample volume scale of 1.0, starting with development and then production.

B) Enable VPC Flow Logs on the relevant subnets in both the development and production VPCs, with a sample volume scale of 0.5, starting with development and then production.

C) Enable VPC Flow Logs only on the production VPC subnets with a sample volume scale of 1.0.

QUESTION 38

Your organization manages a suite of microservices on Google Kubernetes Engine (GKE) for various workflows. The GKE clusters used in the staging workflows generate extensive logs that are primarily accessed through the kubectl logs utility. These logs have inconsistent formats. You aim to reduce logging-related costs while ensuring crucial operational logs are still captured. What action should you take?

A) Execute the gcloud container clusters update --logging=WORKLOAD command on the GKE clusters used in the staging workflows.

B) Invoke the gcloud logging sinks update _Default --disabled command within the project related to the staging workflows.

C) Add the severity >= DEBUG resource.type = "k8s_container" exclusion filter to the _Default logging sink within the project tied to the staging workflows.

D) Execute the gcloud container clusters update --logging=SYSTEM command on the GKE clusters used in the staging workflows.

QUESTION 39

You are overseeing a Cloud Dataflow service on Google Cloud, and you notice an unusual number of requests from a specific IP address. You need to monitor these requests efficiently with minimal maintenance. What is the most effective approach to achieve this using Google Cloud best practices?

A) Implement a Dataflow metric in Cloud Monitoring for the specific IP address.

B) Use the Dataflow template to create a log-based metric in Cloud Monitoring for the IP address. Develop a script to filter these requests from the Dataflow logs.

C) Adjust the Dataflow job code to send metrics of the specific IP address directly to Cloud Monitoring.

D) Write a script that analyzes the Dataflow logs and sends the particular IP address metrics to Cloud Monitoring.

QUESTION 40

You manage a GKE cluster running various machine learning workloads. You've noticed sporadic CPU performance issues and need to identify potential causes. With no direct node access, what's the best way to identify Pods that could be contributing to CPU pressure?

A) Monitor the node/cpu/usage_rate metric using Metrics Explorer to determine overall CPU load.
B) Examine Pods with high CPU request values and use the htop command to assess their CPU usage.
C) Utilize Metrics Explorer to analyze the container/cpu/used_cores metric for CPU usage insights at the container level.
D) Identify Pods with high CPU requests and execute vmstat to understand their CPU impact.

QUESTION 41

As the DevOps leader for a multinational streaming service, you need to streamline the deployment of a complex environment that includes Google Cloud services and various external cloud resources. Which tool combination would best suit the deployment and management of such a diverse infrastructure?

A) Cloud Build with Google Cloud Deploy
B) Cloud Build with Jenkins
C) Google Kubernetes Engine with Cloud Deploy
D) Cloud Build with Kubernetes and Helm

QUESTION 42

You are overseeing a distributed application on Google App Engine, which experiences high traffic. To manage its performance effectively, you need to monitor request rates. Which Stackdriver metric should you use to track this aspect of your App Engine service?

A) appengine/http/server/response_count
B) appengine/system/network/sent_bytes_count
C) appengine/http/server/request_latencies
D) appengine/http/server/request_count

QUESTION 43

Following a disruption in your cloud-based customer support platform, you are revising incident review protocols. What two scenarios should mandate a comprehensive incident analysis in accordance with SRE best practices?

A) The incident caused a significant increase in customer support tickets.
B) An automated system halted a deployment due to performance regressions.
C) A service-level objective (SLO) breach occurred for a critical customer-facing service.
D) The development team recommends a review for educational purposes.
E) There was a temporary performance degradation, but no service outage.

QUESTION 44

As part of a DevOps team, you are configuring a CI/CD process in Cloud Build for a Java application. The source code is stored in a Mercurial repository on Bitbucket. Your organization's protocol is that deployments to production should be done from the 'prod' branch after approval from senior developers. What configurations are necessary?

A) Implement branch-level restrictions in Bitbucket for the 'prod' branch.
B) Configure a 'cloudbuild.yaml' file to check the source branch in the build script.
C) Set up a Cloud Build trigger on 'Pull request' events linked to the 'prod' branch.
D) Create a Cloud Build trigger to react to 'Push to a branch' events, specifically for the 'prod' branch.

QUESTION 45

You are managing a cloud-based SQL database service and encounter an issue with one of the instances experiencing high latency. This is affecting user transactions. How should you handle this situation to ensure minimal disruption to users while adhering to best practices?

A) Inform the incident response team, assess if other instances can handle additional load, then reroute traffic from the problematic instance and isolate it for troubleshooting.
B) Directly reroute traffic away from the affected instance and disconnect it, then monitor the traffic patterns to ensure stability in the remaining cluster.
C) Increase the resources for the remaining instances, reroute the traffic, and then disconnect the problematic instance for analysis.
D) Add a new database instance to the cluster, wait for it to be operational, then shift traffic from the failing instance and investigate the issue.

QUESTION 46

Your team uses Terraform for managing a series of compute resources on Google Cloud. Recently, you've observed redundant resources being created with each update via your CI/CD pipeline, resulting in increased costs. What strategy should you employ to address this issue?

A) Ensure the CI/CD pipeline properly utilizes a Terraform backend like Cloud SQL to manage state and avoid duplication.
B) Set the pipeline to automatically remove all existing resources before each deployment cycle using Terraform commands.
C) Keep Terraform state files in a version-controlled repository and fetch them at each deployment to maintain infrastructure consistency.
D) Configure the pipeline to use a dedicated Terraform state file stored in Cloud Storage, ensuring accurate tracking of deployed resources.

QUESTION 47

In your role overseeing GKE cluster deployments for a healthcare application, you must ensure the highest level of security for container images. What measures should you implement to maintain strict control over the container images deployed in production?

A) Establish the clusters as private clusters within GKE for enhanced network security.
B) Implement a policy with Binary Authorization to allow only verified container images in production deployments.
C) Activate real-time threat detection in the clusters using Cloud Security Command Center.
D) Continuously scan all container images for vulnerabilities in Artifact Registry and flag any issues in the

CI/CD pipeline.

QUESTION 48

You are responsible for a platform that has maintained a high level of user satisfaction for the past 9 months, consistently meeting its Service Level Objective (SLO). To align with Site Reliability Engineering (SRE) principles, what actions should you take? (Choose two.)

A) Tighten the SLO to be more demanding.
B) Redirect engineering efforts to improve reliability in other areas.
C) Give higher priority to introducing new features over reliability improvements.
D) Accelerate the platform's deployment frequency and risk tolerance.
E) Broaden the scope of Service Level Indicators (SLIs).

QUESTION 49

You are managing a multi-cloud environment, including Google Cloud and another cloud provider. Your organization is looking to improve cost optimization and wants to identify underutilized resources in both clouds. What approach should you take to achieve this goal? (Choose two.)

A) Use Google Cloud Cost Management tools to analyze Google Cloud resource usage.
B) Implement third-party cost optimization solutions for the other cloud provider.
C) Create custom scripts to periodically check resource utilization in both clouds.
D) Migrate all workloads to a single cloud provider to simplify cost optimization.
E) Leverage Google Cloud's multi-cloud management capabilities to gain insights into resource utilization across clouds.

QUESTION 50

Your organization is looking to automate the deployment of its data analytics pipelines on Google Cloud while ensuring the highest level of security and compliance. What CI/CD approach should you consider for this purpose?

A) Implement Jenkins on a self-managed Kubernetes cluster hosted in your data center.
B) Utilize GitLab CI/CD pipelines integrated with Google Cloud Data Loss Prevention (DLP) for enhanced data security and compliance.
C) Set up Jenkins on Compute Engine instances to manage data analytics pipeline deployments.
D) Employ GitHub Actions integrated with Google Cloud Security Command Center (SCC) for comprehensive security and compliance checks.
E) Explore CI/CD options with Azure DevOps for cross-cloud deployments.
F) Set up Travis CI with AWS for flexible CI/CD workflows.

PRACTICE TEST 7 - ANSWERS ONLY

QUESTION 1

Answer - B) Modify the deployment to use the sha256 digest of the previous container image.

Option B is the recommended approach. By modifying the deployment to use the sha256 digest of the previous container image, you ensure a precise rollback to a known version, minimizing downtime and ensuring consistency.
 Option A suggests reassigning the 'latest' tag, which may not be as precise and can lead to potential issues.
 Option C involves creating a new service, which may introduce complexity and additional resource consumption.
 Option D introduces a new label, which may not be necessary for a simple rollback scenario.

QUESTION 2

Answer - B) Implement Google Cloud Endpoints to create APIs for microservices and utilize Google Cloud Pub/Sub for asynchronous communication between services.

Option B aligns with the microservices architecture and practices, providing efficient communication between microservices through APIs created with Google Cloud Endpoints and asynchronous communication using Google Cloud Pub/Sub.
 Option A mentions security and monitoring but does not focus on communication.
 Option C involves caching and serverless processing, which may not be directly related to microservices communication.
 Option D suggests VPN and task automation, which are not specific to microservices communication.

QUESTION 3

Answer - A) 1 and 2

Options 1 and 2 are the recommended choices to ensure high availability and reliability for a complex microservices architecture on Google Kubernetes Engine (GKE). Implementing PodDisruptionBudgets helps control disruptions during maintenance, and using Horizontal Pod Autoscaling (HPA) ensures dynamic resource adjustment for high availability.
 Option 3, deploying multi-cluster clusters across different regions, is relevant for disaster recovery but may not address day-to-day high availability concerns.
 Option 4, setting up Network Policies, is important for network security but not directly related to availability and reliability.

QUESTION 4

Answer - B) Leverage VPC Service Controls to limit who can configure dashboards.

Option B is the correct choice as it efficiently restricts access to dashboard configuration using VPC Service Controls.
 Option A introduces complexity with Service Perimeter,

Option C suggests custom roles which may not be necessary,
Option D grants a broad role without specific control.

QUESTION 5

Answer - C) MTTD: 3 MTTR: 45 MTBF: 60 Impact: 50%

Option C represents the risk assessment figures for the new storage solution failover, accounting for the longer MTTR and the same MTBF, along with a 50% user impact.
Option A has incorrect MTTR,
Option B has incorrect MTTR and user impact,
Option D has incorrect MTTR and user impact.

QUESTION 6

Answer - A and B

Options A and B are the correct choices. Segmenting automation procedures into finer-grained components (A) reduces redundancy and streamlines the workflow. Implementing automatic progression confirmations (B) helps in achieving smoother transitions between stages, reducing manual interventions.
Options C and D are not directly related to optimizing the workflow.

QUESTION 7

Answer - B and D

Option B - The current 40% CPU utilization allows for workload growth without additional capacity.
Option D - Implementing a horizontal pod autoscaler and conducting load testing is a proactive approach to handle the expected increase in demand.
Options A and C are not the most suitable actions.

QUESTION 8

Answer - B) Implement a phased rollout by creating a new instance template and gradually shifting instances to it.

A) Incorrect - Removing and re-importing the template can disrupt the existing configuration management.
B) Correct - A phased rollout minimizes disruption and allows for gradual migration to the new configuration.
C) Incorrect - Modifying directly in the console can cause inconsistencies with Terraform's state.
D) Incorrect - The replace_triggered_by attribute does not exist in Terraform and does not solve the issue.
E) Incorrect - Decommissioning the entire cluster is an extreme step that causes significant disruption.

QUESTION 9

Answer - A) Designate a separate Google Cloud project for each business unit, with individual GKE clusters for their respective applications, using IAM to manage access rights.

A) Correct - This setup ensures the independence of each business unit with optimal resource utilization and security.
B) Incorrect - Dedicated node pools offer resource segregation but not the necessary operational independence.
C) Incorrect - While namespaces provide logical isolation, they may not offer the level of separation required.
D) Incorrect - Multi-cluster setups might be over-complex for this scenario and could lead to higher costs.
E) Incorrect - A single cluster approach does not adequately separate the business units' operations.

QUESTION 10

Answer - A) Implement a content delivery network (CDN) to cache and deliver streaming content closer to users.

A) Correct - A CDN can significantly reduce data transfer costs by caching content closer to users.
B) Incorrect - Preemptible VM instances reduce compute costs, not data transfer costs.
C) Incorrect - Using Cloud Functions might not significantly impact data transfer costs for a video streaming service.
D) Incorrect - While important, merely changing regions may not be the most effective way to reduce data transfer costs.
E) Incorrect - Network Service Tiers can optimize costs but are less effective than a CDN for a streaming service.

QUESTION 11

Answer - B) Employ Cloud Monitoring to track the resource usage and load patterns of the GKE cluster.

A) Incorrect - While Cloud Logging provides valuable logs, it may not give the complete picture of performance bottlenecks.
B) Correct - Cloud Monitoring provides comprehensive insights into resource usage, which is crucial for addressing response time issues.
C) Incorrect - Cloud Trace is more focused on tracking request flows, not on resource usage and load patterns.
D) Incorrect - Cloud SQL Insights is specific to Cloud SQL performance and may not address overall platform issues.
E) Incorrect - Cloud Profiler is focused on code efficiency, which is only one aspect of performance bottlenecks.

QUESTION 12

Answer - A) Set up Cloud Build to run unit tests for each component upon pull requests. After passing, aggregate components in a staging environment for integration testing, then deploy to production.

A) Correct - This approach ensures both isolated component testing and comprehensive integration testing in a staged environment.
B) Incorrect - Local pre-push testing is insufficient for a complex web application requiring integration testing.
C) Incorrect - While multi-stage pipelines are effective, they should culminate in a combined staging test, not separate tests per component.

D) Incorrect - Separate pipelines for each component can lead to integration issues. A unified approach is more effective.

E) Incorrect - Merging components into a single repository post-unit testing complicates version control and continuous integration.

QUESTION 13

Answer - A) Transaction completion SLI: the percentage of successfully completed transactions out of all attempted transactions.

A) Correct - This SLI directly reflects the user's ability to complete purchases, which is critical for user satisfaction during sales events.

B) Incorrect - While important, page load time does not directly reflect the critical transaction process.

C) Incorrect - Shopping cart uptime is important but is only one part of the overall transaction process.

D) Incorrect - Server response time is a broader metric that may not specifically address user transactions.

E) Incorrect - Checkout process efficiency is similar to transaction completion but focuses on a narrower part of the user experience.

QUESTION 14

Answer - B) Implement Binary Authorization with a policy that allows deployments only if containers are based on trusted base images.

A) Incorrect - While CI/CD validation is important, it does not provide the enforcement mechanism at the deployment stage.

B) Correct - Binary Authorization enforces deployment policies at the cluster level, ensuring containers are based on trusted images.

C) Incorrect - Manual updates post-deployment are reactive and not efficient for ensuring compliance.

D) Incorrect - IAM policies control access but do not enforce container base image compliance.

E) Incorrect - Monitoring alerts are reactive and do not prevent the deployment of non-compliant containers.

QUESTION 15

Answer - B) Set up a Terraform module registry service within a Google Kubernetes Engine (GKE) cluster, using a Cloud Storage bucket for storing the modules.

Option B is incorrect because it suggests using GKE and Cloud Storage, but it doesn't address the compliance and access control concerns raised by the compliance department.

Option C - Option C is incorrect because it suggests using Artifact Registry for storage, but it doesn't provide a clear solution for addressing the specific concerns raised by the compliance department regarding open-source modules and access control.

Option D - Option D is incorrect because it lacks a clear solution for access control and compliance with VPC Service Controls, which are crucial in this scenario.

Option E - Option E is incorrect because there is a suitable solution among the provided options (Option A) that addresses the compliance and access control concerns.

QUESTION 16

Answer - B) Establish separate centralized logging projects for each team and grant project-level IAM roles accordingly. Provide the compliance oversight team with admin rights in all projects.

Option B is the correct choice because it aligns with the requirement for each project team to access their own logs in separate centralized logging projects. The compliance oversight team has admin rights in all projects for centralized access.
 Option A - Option A is incorrect because it suggests consolidating logs into a single project without considering the compliance requirement for separate team access.
 Option C - Option C is incorrect because using Google Cloud Storage buckets may not provide the necessary granularity for log access control within a project.
 Option D - Option D is incorrect because creating custom log sinks may not be the most efficient way to meet the requirements and could lead to complexity.

QUESTION 17

Answer - B) Configure an attestation for stress-tested updates using a private key stored in Cloud Key Management Service (Cloud KMS) along with a service account JSON key embedded as a Kubernetes Secret.

Option B is the correct choice because it ensures that only stress-tested updates are deployed to the primary GKE cluster by configuring an attestation with a private key stored in Cloud KMS and a service account JSON key as a Kubernetes Secret for verification.
 Option A - Option A involves manual signing by the chief technical officer, which is not an automated process.
 Option C - Option C mandates manual signature by the chief technical officer, introducing manual steps and complexity.
 Option D - Option D mentions verification via Workload Identity, which is not the most direct approach for this use case.

QUESTION 18

Answer - A) Examine the existing telemetry data and introduce additional metrics as required.
 Answer - C) Analyze both historical and real-time file access logs to understand user interactions with the platform.

Option A and Option C are the correct choices.
 Option A - Reviewing existing telemetry data and adding more metrics, if needed, helps evaluate reliability without software changes.
 Option B - Modifying the application's source code contradicts the requirement to avoid software alterations.
 Option D - Creating virtual user accounts for emulation is not aligned with evaluating reliability from the user's perspective.
 Option E - Focusing solely on server error logs may not provide a comprehensive user viewpoint.

QUESTION 19

Answer - B) Store credentials in Secret Manager, encrypt them with a key from Cloud Key Management

Service, and grant the automated workflow access through Identity and Access Management.

Option B is the correct choice.
 Option B - Storing credentials in Secret Manager, encrypting them with a key from Cloud Key Management Service, and granting workflow access via Identity and Access Management aligns with Google's best practices for secure credential management and rotation.
 Option A - Ensuring manual input of credentials is less secure and may lead to errors.
 Option C - Embedding credentials in the workflow's codebase is not recommended for security reasons.
 Option D - Storing credentials in a dedicated configuration file may not provide sufficient access control and security.

QUESTION 20

D) Configure a sink in Cloud Logging, assign it a unique name, create a Cloud Storage archive class bucket for storing the transaction records, and designate this bucket as the destination for the exported logs.

To meet the legal requirement of retaining transaction records for a decade while minimizing storage costs, you should configure a sink in Cloud Logging to export the records to Cloud Storage. Specifically, you should create a Cloud Storage archive class bucket for long-term storage and designate this bucket as the destination for the exported logs. This approach ensures compliance with the retention policy and cost-effectively stores the records. The other options do not align with the requirement of retaining records for ten years or may not be the most cost-effective solution.

QUESTION 21

Answer - B) Check the build logs in Cloud Build to identify the specific error or failure message.

Explanation for Option B - Checking the build logs in Cloud Build is the first step to identify the specific error or failure message that caused the pipeline to fail. It provides valuable information for debugging and resolving the issue.
Explanation for Option A - Temporarily disabling the CI/CD pipeline may prevent further deployments, but it doesn't address the root cause of the issue.
Explanation for Option C - Reverting to a previous version of the build configuration should be considered after identifying the cause of the failure. It may not be necessary if the issue can be resolved in the current configuration.
Explanation for Option D - Creating a new GKE cluster is a significant action and is not a troubleshooting step for CI/CD pipeline issues. It doesn't address the issue in the build configuration.

QUESTION 22

Answer - B) Create a policy that enforces a freeze on feature development immediately upon an SLO breach.

Explanation for Option B - Creating a policy that enforces a feature development freeze immediately upon an SLO breach is a proactive measure to ensure stability is prioritized during critical incidents with clear guidelines.
Explanation for Option A - Implementing a rule that restricts updates when the SLO is at risk is a good practice, but it may not ensure immediate action.
Explanation for Option C - Holding discussions with the engineering team emphasizes stability but may

not guarantee an immediate response during critical incidents.
Explanation for Option D - Collaborating with product managers is important, but it may not provide immediate action without a predefined policy.

QUESTION 23

Answer - C) Open and blame-free discussions during retrospectives.
E) Regular retrospectives with actionable items for continuous improvement.

Option A) Blame allocation and punitive measures discourage open discussions and hinder a learning culture.
Option B) Focusing on individual accountability can lead to a blame culture and is not conducive to learning.
Option D) Limiting participation to only technical teams can exclude valuable perspectives from other stakeholders.
Options C and E promote open and blame-free discussions and regular retrospectives with actionable items, which are essential for a cultural shift towards learning from incidents.

QUESTION 24

Answer - C) Analyze the application logs and metrics to pinpoint the cause of failures and delays.

A) While increasing resources might help, it's a reactive measure that doesn't address the root cause of the issue.
 B) Rolling back is a viable option but should be considered after understanding the problem, as it may not be necessary if the issue can be quickly resolved.
 C) This is the most effective first action, as it helps in identifying the exact issue, which is crucial for a targeted and efficient solution.
 D) Gathering user feedback is useful but not an immediate priority when dealing with system failures and performance issues.
 E) Canary releases are beneficial for future deployments but do not address the current problem.

QUESTION 25

Answer - B) Utilize a container registry with tagging for different versions of the Docker images.

Option A - A common network directory lacks the organization and versioning capabilities required for efficient management.
 Option B - Container registries with version tagging provide an organized, scalable, and accessible method for managing Docker images.
 Option C - Google Drive is not suited for Docker image version control and does not support continuous integration and delivery pipelines.
 Option D - Storing on individual machines hinders collaboration and does not provide a single source of truth.
 Option E - FTP servers are outdated and do not offer the streamlined version control and integration capabilities of container registries.

QUESTION 26

Answer - A) and C)

Option A - Measuring performance at edge locations directly correlates with user experience and content delivery efficiency.
 Option B - Internal network latency is important but does not directly impact the end-user experience.
 Option C - Bandwidth usage stats provide insights into service scalability and potential bottlenecks in content delivery.
 Option D - While important for overall operation, session persistence and connection draining are more relevant to specific scenarios rather than general CDN performance.
 Option E - Storage I/O is crucial for origin server performance but less so for the CDN delivery aspect.

QUESTION 27

Answer - C) Set up a real-time incident response communication channel for the team.

Option A - Root cause analysis is crucial but not the immediate first step before ensuring effective team communication.
 Option B - Communicating with clients is important but should be managed after internal coordination is established.
 Option C - Establishing a dedicated communication channel is essential for coordinating the response efficiently.
 Option D - Implementing a fix is important but should follow an initial assessment and coordination.
 Option E - Preliminary reporting is premature at this stage; focus should be on managing the incident first.

QUESTION 28

Answer - A) Implement comprehensive load and stress testing for all critical system components.

Option A - Comprehensive testing can identify potential scalability and performance issues before they impact production.
 Option B - Punitive measures do not foster a constructive approach to problem-solving.
 Option C - Managerial sign-offs can create bottlenecks and may not effectively address the core issue.
 Option D - Regular discussions are beneficial but do not replace the need for systematic testing.
 Option E - Restricting changes might hinder innovation and agility and doesn't directly address testing inadequacies.

QUESTION 29

Answer - C) Leverage Cloud Build to apply BigQuery dataset policies and utilize Policy Controller for enforcing uniform access controls.

Option A - Deployment Manager is effective for deployment but does not specifically manage policy uniformity.
 Option B - Custom scripts are not an efficient way to ensure policy uniformity and compliance.
 Option C - Cloud Build automates policy application, and Policy Controller ensures these policies are enforced consistently.
 Option D - While Cloud IAM is crucial for access control, it doesn't automate policy application across

multiple projects.
 Option E - Manual application of policies is time-consuming and prone to human error, and regular audits are reactive rather than proactive.

QUESTION 30

Answer - D) Secure the JSON key for a Google service account within your CI/CD platform's secrets management and configure Terraform to use it for authentication.

The most secure and recommended method is to store the JSON key within the CI/CD platform's secrets management and configure Terraform to use it. Other options introduce security risks or poor credential management practices.
 Option A - Sharing a single JSON key among all components lacks security and isolation. Option B - Embedding the JSON key directly in Terraform files is insecure. Option C - Storing separate JSON keys in a public Git repository is a security risk. Option E - Leveraging the GKE cluster's default service account lacks control and security.

QUESTION 31

Answer - A) SSH into the Cloud Function instance and check the Stackdriver agent's status.

Option B, checking the Stackdriver agent's test log message, may not directly address the issue of missing logs from the Cloud Function.
Option C, upgrading the Stackdriver agent, is a valid action but not necessarily the first step to investigate.
Option D, ensuring the service account access scope, may not be the initial step in diagnosing the problem.

QUESTION 32

Answer - A) Modify the service account permissions to include the Logs Writer role.

Option B, switching to the standard service account, may not be necessary and can lead to other issues.
Option C, enabling Private Google Access, is related to network connectivity and does not directly affect Cloud Logging.
Option D, generating a service account key, is not typically required for configuring Cloud Logging.

QUESTION 33

Answer - C) Use Kubernetes Helm charts to manage deployments and use Helm rollback commands for quick reverts.

- Option A is resource-intensive and not practical for quick rollbacks.
- Option B relies on manual intervention and is not efficient for rapid reverts.
- Option D involves managing container images and may not be as streamlined as Helm charts for rollbacks.
Using Kubernetes Helm charts (Option C) allows you to manage deployments and use Helm rollback commands to quickly revert to a previous state in a controlled and efficient manner.

QUESTION 34

Answer - A) Implement Horizontal Pod Autoscaling for the frontend service to dynamically adjust the number of Pods based on traffic.

Explanation:
 Option A is the correct choice because implementing Horizontal Pod Autoscaling for the frontend service allows it to dynamically adjust the number of Pods based on traffic, effectively addressing performance issues during traffic surges.
 Option B, increasing resource allocation, may not be sufficient to handle sudden traffic spikes.
 Option C suggests deploying a separate cluster, which adds complexity and may not be necessary.
 Option D, scaling up the entire cluster, is a less efficient solution compared to Pod autoscaling, as it affects all services, not just the frontend.

QUESTION 35

Answer - B) Utilize blue/green deployments combined with canary releases

Option B is the correct choice because blue/green deployments simplify production releases, and canary releases enable gradual validation of production traffic, aligning with the specified objectives.
 Option A is incorrect as red/black deployments are not typically used with A/B testing. Option C is incorrect because a rebuild strategy may not align with the goal of minimizing rollback times. Option D is incorrect because dark launches are not typically used with rolling updates.

QUESTION 36

Answer - A) Analyze additional performance metrics related to the gaming platform's operation and identify SLOs with available error budget. Reallocate error budget from these SLOs to support the game update release.

Option A is the correct choice as it adheres to SRE principles by reallocating error budget from other SLOs to ensure a successful game update release.
 Option B is incorrect as it focuses on testing but does not directly address the error budget issue.
 Option C is incorrect as increasing the error budget may not be the best approach for managing errors.
 Option D is incorrect as it suggests delaying the release or accepting potential performance issues without exploring other solutions.

QUESTION 37

Answer - A) Enable VPC Flow Logs on the relevant subnets in both the development and production VPCs, with a sample volume scale of 1.0, starting with development and then production.

Option A is the correct choice as it enables VPC Flow Logs with a sample volume scale of 1.0 in both development and production environments, allowing comprehensive network traffic monitoring for future analysis.
 Option B is incorrect as it reduces the sample volume scale, potentially missing important data.
 Option C is incorrect as it only enables VPC Flow Logs in the production environment, overlooking the development environment's insights.

QUESTION 38

Answer - A) Execute the gcloud container clusters update --logging=WORKLOAD command on the GKE clusters used in the staging workflows.

Option A is the correct choice as it aligns with optimizing logging costs for staging workflows by configuring GKE clusters to capture workload-specific logs. This approach reduces unnecessary logs and minimizes costs. Option B suggests disabling the default logging sink, which may not effectively reduce costs. Option C adds an exclusion filter that might not reduce logging costs as intended for staging workflows. Option D recommends updating GKE clusters to capture system logs, which may not align with cost optimization for staging workflows.

QUESTION 39

Answer - B) Use the Dataflow template to create a log-based metric in Cloud Monitoring for the IP address. Develop a script to filter these requests from the Dataflow logs.

Option A - Incorrect: Cloud Dataflow does not natively provide IP-specific metrics.
Option B - Correct: Creating a log-based metric for the specific IP address and using a script for filtering is efficient and aligns with best practices.
Option C - Incorrect: Modifying job code is less maintenance-efficient.
Option D - Incorrect: Writing a separate script for log analysis is not the most efficient approach.

QUESTION 40

Answer - C) Utilize Metrics Explorer to analyze the container/cpu/used_cores metric for CPU usage insights at the container level.

Option A - Incorrect: Node-level CPU metrics do not provide detailed insights into individual Pod performance.
Option B - Incorrect: Without access to nodes, running htop is not possible.
Option C - Correct: Container-level CPU metrics can help in identifying specific Pods that are utilizing high CPU resources.
Option D - Incorrect: Running vmstat is not feasible without direct node access.

QUESTION 41

Answer - D) Cloud Build with Kubernetes and Helm

Option A - Incorrect: While useful for Google Cloud resources, this combination may not be as effective for a complex multi-cloud environment.
Option B - Incorrect: Jenkins is excellent for continuous integration but may not provide comprehensive deployment management for a multi-cloud setup.
Option C - Incorrect: GKE and Cloud Deploy are tailored for containerized environments and may not fully address the needs of a diverse streaming service infrastructure.
Option D - Correct: Kubernetes and Helm offer a robust platform for managing containerized applications across different clouds, and Cloud Build integrates well for continuous integration and delivery.

QUESTION 42

Answer - D) appengine/http/server/request_count

Option A - Incorrect: This metric tracks response counts, not request rates.
Option B - Incorrect: This metric measures the amount of data sent, not the request rate.
Option C - Incorrect: This metric focuses on request latencies, not the total number of requests.
Option D - Correct: This metric accurately tracks the total number of requests, which is essential for managing high traffic.

QUESTION 43

Answer - A) The incident caused a significant increase in customer support tickets. and C) A service-level objective (SLO) breach occurred for a critical customer-facing service.

Option A - Correct: A surge in support tickets often signals a severe user impact, requiring in-depth analysis.
Option B - Incorrect: While important, automated halts are part of proactive measures and might not always need in-depth reviews.
Option C - Correct: SLO breaches, especially for critical services, are key indicators for detailed reviews.
Option D - Incorrect: Educational purposes alone are not sufficient for mandatory reviews.
Option E - Incorrect: Temporary performance issues without service outage might not meet the threshold for comprehensive reviews.

QUESTION 44

Answer - A) Implement branch-level restrictions in Bitbucket for the 'prod' branch. and D) Create a Cloud Build trigger to react to 'Push to a branch' events, specifically for the 'prod' branch.

Option A - Correct: Branch restrictions in Bitbucket will ensure the 'prod' branch is updated only post-approval.
Option B - Incorrect: While 'cloudbuild.yaml' defines build steps, it is not used for branch-level policy enforcement.
Option C - Incorrect: 'Pull request' triggers are for pre-merge validations, not suitable for post-merge deployment.
Option D - Correct: A Cloud Build trigger for 'Push to a branch' on 'prod' aligns with the deployment policy.

QUESTION 45

Answer - A) Inform the incident response team, assess if other instances can handle additional load, then reroute traffic from the problematic instance and isolate it for troubleshooting.

Option A - Correct: This approach follows a structured method for incident management, ensuring minimal disruption to users while addressing the issue.
Option B - Incorrect: Immediate rerouting without assessing the capacity of other instances might lead to further issues.
Option C - Incorrect: Increasing resources first may not be necessary and could delay addressing the primary issue.
Option D - Incorrect: Adding a new instance may not be the quickest solution to an immediate

performance issue.

QUESTION 46

Answer - D) Configure the pipeline to use a dedicated Terraform state file stored in Cloud Storage, ensuring accurate tracking of deployed resources.

Option A - Incorrect: Cloud SQL is not a typical backend for Terraform state management.
Option B - Incorrect: Automatically removing all resources can lead to downtime and is not a best practice.
Option C - Incorrect: Storing state files in a version control system can cause conflicts and security issues.
Option D - Correct: Using Cloud Storage for the Terraform state file ensures accurate infrastructure tracking and prevents resource duplication.

QUESTION 47

Answer - B) Implement a policy with Binary Authorization to allow only verified container images in production deployments.

Option A - Incorrect: Private clusters improve network security but don't directly address container image control.
Option B - Correct: Binary Authorization provides a mechanism to ensure that only approved and verified images are deployed in production.
Option C - Incorrect: Cloud Security Command Center is for broader security monitoring and doesn't specifically control container image deployment.
Option D - Incorrect: Vulnerability scanning is crucial but needs to be complemented with enforcement policies for container image deployment.

QUESTION 48

Answer - B) Redirect engineering efforts to improve reliability in other areas.
E) Broaden the scope of Service Level Indicators (SLIs).

Option A suggests making the SLO more demanding, which may not be necessary if user satisfaction and reliability are already high.
Option C prioritizes new features over reliability, which goes against SRE principles.
Option D focuses on accelerating deployment frequency, which might not align with maintaining reliability.
Options B and E are recommended actions to maintain a balance between reliability and deployment frequency.

QUESTION 49

Answer - A) Use Google Cloud Cost Management tools to analyze Google Cloud resource usage.
E) Leverage Google Cloud's multi-cloud management capabilities to gain insights into resource utilization across clouds.

Option A is correct as it focuses on analyzing Google Cloud resource usage, which is essential for cost optimization within Google Cloud.

Option E is also correct as it leverages Google Cloud's multi-cloud management capabilities to gain insights into resource utilization across multiple clouds, aiding in cost optimization.
Options B and C suggest using third-party or custom solutions, which are not directly related to Google Cloud. Option D is impractical and doesn't address cost optimization across clouds.

QUESTION 50

Answer - B) Utilize GitLab CI/CD pipelines integrated with Google Cloud Data Loss Prevention (DLP) for enhanced data security and compliance.

Options A, C, D, E, and F - Incorrect. These options either introduce non-Google Cloud solutions or may not align with the security and compliance requirements for data analytics pipelines.
 Option B is the correct choice as it suggests utilizing GitLab CI/CD pipelines integrated with Google Cloud DLP for enhanced data security and compliance in CI/CD processes on Google Cloud.

PRACTICE TEST 8 - QUESTIONS ONLY

QUESTION 1

Your organization is running a critical web application on Google Kubernetes Engine (GKE). After a recent update, you encounter issues with the application's performance and stability. You need to roll back to the previous version of the container image to restore service reliability. What is the recommended approach for rolling back the deployment in GKE while minimizing impact on users and ensuring a smooth transition?

A) Reassign the 'previous' tag to the previous container image version and update the deployment.
 B) Modify the deployment to use the sha256 digest of the previous container image.
 C) Rebuild the container image with the previous version and deploy it alongside the current version.
 D) Introduce a new namespace for the previous container image version and migrate the deployment to the new namespace.

QUESTION 2

You are responsible for managing a large-scale data processing pipeline in Google Cloud. The pipeline processes sensitive financial data, and data privacy is a top priority. You want to ensure that access to this data is restricted to authorized users and applications. Which Google Cloud services and strategies should you consider to achieve this, following Google's recommended DevOps practices?

A) Implement Google Cloud Identity-Aware Proxy (IAP) for secure access to the data processing pipeline and utilize Google Cloud KMS for data encryption.
 B) Set up Google Cloud IAM roles and permissions for fine-grained access control and implement Google Cloud Pub/Sub for data streaming.
 C) Use Google Cloud Data Loss Prevention (DLP) to redact sensitive information in the data pipeline and implement Google Cloud Security Command Center for threat detection.
 D) Deploy Google Cloud Functions for serverless data processing and utilize Google Cloud AutoML for data classification and labeling.

QUESTION 3

Your organization is implementing a DevOps culture, and you are responsible for defining incident response practices. Which two practices should you prioritize for effective incident response in a DevOps environment? I. Create a blame-free culture that encourages learning from incidents. 2. Establish strict escalation procedures and assign blame to individuals for each incident. 3. Limit access to incident data to prevent information leaks. 4. Use automated incident response tools to avoid human intervention.

A) 1 and 2 B) 2 and 3 C) 3 and 4 D) 1 and 4

QUESTION 4

You're tasked with authorizing certain team members to set up dashboards for continuously streaming metrics in Cloud Monitoring. What's the recommended approach?

A) Create a Service Perimeter in Cloud IAM to control authorization.

B) Implement VPC Service Controls to manage dashboard configuration access.
C) Delegate a custom IAM role with the required permissions.
D) Assign the IAM role of monitoring.dashboardEditor to the operations team.

QUESTION 5

In your risk assessment for a new storage solution for an online gaming service, you have the following figures for the new solution: MTTD: 3 minutes, MTTR: 45 minutes, MTBF: 60 days, User Impact: 33%. What should be the risk assessment figures for the new storage solution failover?

A) MTTD: 3 MTTR: 15 MTBF: 60 Impact: 50%
B) MTTD: 3 MTTR: 15 MTBF: 60 Impact: 33%
C) MTTD: 3 MTTR: 45 MTBF: 60 Impact: 50%
D) MTTD: 3 MTTR: 45 MTBF: 60 Impact: 33%

QUESTION 6

In the context of optimizing your media processing workflow in Google Cloud's Dataflow to reduce job execution time and repetitive tasks, what steps should you consider? (Choose two.)

A) Segment the automation procedures into finer-grained components.
B) Implement automatic progression confirmations transferring from the staging area to the production zone.
C) Run a script to facilitate the setup of the media processing workflow in Google Cloud Dataflow.
D) Set up an alert to inform the designated team to proceed with the next phase when human input is needed.
E) Increase the number of personnel to execute hands-on steps.

QUESTION 7

Your company's CRM system, hosted on GKE in Google Cloud, anticipates a 15% quarterly workload increase over the next year, while the system currently uses 40% of available CPU resources. How should you manage this growth?

A) Rely on GKE's cluster autoscaler to automatically adjust resources based on demand, eliminating the need for manual intervention.
B) The current 40% CPU utilization provides enough buffer to handle workload growth without additional capacity.
C) Increase node capacity by 90% in advance to accommodate the projected quarterly workload increase and validate resource adequacy through load testing.
D) Determine node pool size limits, deploy a horizontal pod autoscaler for workloads, and perform load testing to assess the required resources for handling the expected demand increase.

QUESTION 8

Your team uses Terraform to orchestrate a network of microservices on Google Cloud, each running in its own set of Compute Engine instances. During a routine update, attempting to add more CPU resources to the instance template triggers an error due to the template being in active use. What strategy should you employ to efficiently update the instance template and maintain service continuity?

A) Adjust the Terraform configuration to exclude the instance template, update it, and then re-include it in the state.
B) Introduce a new instance template with the updated resources, reconfigure the instance group, and then retire the old template.
C) Overwrite the existing instance template via the Terraform script, ignoring the error.
D) Manually update the instance template in GCP and remove its management from Terraform.
E) Suspend the instance group operations, update the template, and then resume operations.

QUESTION 9

Your team manages a cloud-based storage service, and a recent update led to data synchronization issues across regions. The update was rolled back, resolving the problem. You are leading the analysis to prevent future occurrences, adhering to SRE principles. What should be your approach for the postmortem?

A) Identify and reprimand the team member who committed the update to prevent similar issues.
B) Focus on understanding the systemic issues that allowed the error, without assigning individual blame.
C) Emphasize accelerating new feature releases rather than dwelling on the incident.
D) Conduct individual interviews with the development team to find out who approved the update.
E) Review the incident in the context of the entire system, improving processes and safeguards.

QUESTION 10

Your company runs a global e-commerce website on GKE, with traffic from various regions. You need to optimize network costs while maintaining performance. What would be the most effective approach?

A) Deploy the application in a multi-regional GKE setup to serve users from the closest region.
B) Utilize Google Cloud's HTTP(S) Load Balancer for efficient traffic management and cost control.
C) Restructure the application to reduce the payload size of user requests and responses.
D) Enable Network Service Tiers and select the tier that aligns with your cost and performance needs.
E) Consolidate all services into a single GKE cluster to reduce inter-service data transfer costs.

QUESTION 11

Since the deployment of a new feature, your company's cloud-based image processing service has been encountering high memory usage, leading to sporadic failures. You need to identify the root cause and implement a solution. What approach should you take?

A) Utilize Cloud Logging to analyze application logs for any memory leak patterns.
B) Deploy Cloud Monitoring to observe the memory consumption patterns of your service.
C) Integrate Cloud Profiler to identify and analyze memory-intensive functions in your service.
D) Set up Cloud Trace to monitor the flow of requests and their impact on memory usage.
E) Use Google Cloud's Operations Suite to gain a comprehensive view of the service's health and performance.

QUESTION 12

Your company requires a cloud solution for processing large datasets of geographic information. These datasets are submitted intermittently by various research teams. The processing time depends on the dataset size, and expenses need to be minimized. What is the most efficient approach?

A) Set up a Cloud Storage bucket for dataset uploads with proper IAM controls. Use Cloud Functions triggered by new dataset uploads to process data, scaling the functions according to the data size.
B) Deploy a GKE cluster with autoscaling enabled. Create a service to monitor Cloud Storage for new datasets and another to process the data, scaling down when no datasets are present.
C) Implement an SFTP service on Compute Engine for secure data uploads. Trigger Cloud Functions to process datasets and automatically scale a managed instance group for processing.
D) Use Cloud Storage for dataset uploads and configure IAM appropriately. Establish a Cloud Scheduler job to periodically check for new data and initiate processing using Compute Engine VMs.
E) Create a Cloud Storage bucket for data uploads and set up a Dataflow job to automatically process new datasets, scaling the resources based on the data size.

QUESTION 13

Your company operates a cloud-based content delivery network (CDN) that serves multimedia content. You need to establish an SLO to ensure high performance and reliability. What SLI would be most relevant to measure the effectiveness of your CDN?

A) Content delivery SLI: the percentage of requests that successfully retrieve content within 200 ms.
B) System uptime SLI: the overall availability of the CDN over a given period.
C) Data throughput SLI: the average data transfer rate of the CDN.
D) Edge node performance SLI: the response time of the nearest edge node to the user.
E) Content freshness SLI: the frequency at which new content is successfully distributed to edge nodes.

QUESTION 14

Your organization is concerned about the potential for compromised containers to be deployed in your GKE clusters. You need to establish a mechanism to verify the integrity and origin of all container images before they are allowed to run. Which security measure should you implement?

A) Integrate a third-party container security solution like Aqua Security or Sysdig to scan and validate container images.
B) Use GKE's built-in vulnerability scanning to automatically scan and block images with known vulnerabilities from being deployed.
C) Implement Binary Authorization to ensure only containers with verifiable signatures are deployed in your GKE clusters.
D) Configure Cloud IAM with custom roles and conditions that permit container deployments only from approved registries.
E) Set up a policy in Cloud Security Command Center to monitor for and alert on any unverified container deployments.

QUESTION 15

Your company uses Terraform to manage infrastructure as code for deploying serverless solutions. You have modules that depend on both open-source and proprietary code. Your compliance department has raised concerns over using un-vetted open-source Terraform modules. You need to ensure consistent management of all modules, while enforcing access controls and maintaining compliance with VPC

Service Con- trols. What action should you take?

A) Manage both open-source and proprietary modules using a self-hosted GitLab server integrated with Google Workspace for identity management.

B) Set up a Terraform module registry service within a Google Kubernetes Engine (GKE) cluster, using a Cloud Storage bucket for storing the modules.

C) Store both open-source and proprietary Terraform modules in OCI format using Artifact Registry.

D) Keep both types of Terraform modules in a version—con- trolled repository, and use Cloud Build to periodically copy the modules to a Cloud Storage bucket. Use the Cloud Storage bucket as a module source, specifying the URL format https://[bucket].storage-googleapis.com/[module].

E) None of the above.

QUESTION 16

Your organization manages logs from multiple Google Cloud projects for compliance purposes. Project teams should only access logs relevant to their projects, while the compliance oversight team should have access to logs from all projects. What's the most suitable approach to ensure compliance without unnecessary expenses?

A) Create separate centralized logging projects for each team and assign project-level IAM roles for access control. Grant the compliance oversight team viewer permissions in all projects.

B) Streamline logs into individual Google Cloud Storage buckets for each project team and apply bucket-level access controls. Provide the compliance oversight team with object viewer rights in all buckets.

C) Establish BigQuery datasets for each project team within a unified logging project. Assign dataset-level IAM roles for access control, and grant the compliance oversight team BigQuery admin privileges in the central project.

D) Create custom log views for each project team and give them visibility to their respective logs. Allocate the compliance oversight team access to a custom log view containing all logs from different projects.

QUESTION 17

Your organization is developing a new service to be hosted on Google Kubernetes Engine (GKE). The primary goal is to implement a solution that consolidates various service-level metrics into a single manageable platform. You have been assigned to utilize Google Cloud solutions while minimizing the initial monitoring setup effort. What approach should you take?

A) Embed the Cloud Pub/Sub client libraries into your service, send different metrics to various topics, and aggregate the metrics in Cloud Monitoring.

B) Convert all metrics into specific log entries for your service, transfer these logs from your containers to the Cloud Logging agent, and analyze metrics in Cloud Logging.

C) Integrate the OpenTelemetry client libraries within your service, direct metrics to Cloud Monitoring as the export destination, and monitor service metrics in Cloud Monitoring.

D) Stream diverse metrics directly from your service to the Cloud Monitoring API, then access these customized metrics in Cloud Monitoring.

QUESTION 18

Your company manages a critical financial data platform on Google Cloud, and you want to evaluate its reliability from the end user's perspective without making any changes to the software. How should you proceed to accomplish this? (Select two.)

A) Inspect the existing telemetry data and introduce additional metrics as required.
 B) Modify the application's source code to collect more detailed user activity data.
 C) Analyze both historical and real-time data access logs to understand user interactions with the platform.
 D) Develop virtual user profiles capable of simulating common user actions on the platform.
 E) Concentrate exclusively on analyzing authentication logs to determine system performance.

QUESTION 19

Your automated data transformation workflows require secure access to database credentials and the ability to support credential rotation. What is the recommended approach to achieve this while following Google's best practices?

A) Instruct data engineers to manually input credentials during job setup and avoid storing them persistently.
 B) Store credentials in Secret Manager, encrypt them with a key from Cloud Key Management Service, and grant the automated workflow access through Identity and Access Management.
 C) Encrypt credentials and include them in the workflow's codebase. Store an encryption key in a separate repository and provide workflow access to this key.
 D) Store credentials in a dedicated configuration file on Cloud Source Repositories and grant specific data engineers access to this file.

QUESTION 20

Your team manages a critical web application on Google Kubernetes Engine (GKE). You want to ensure that the application can handle increased traffic without manual intervention and that costs are optimized. What should you do?

A) Manually scale up the GKE nodes during traffic spikes.
B) Use horizontal pod autoscaling in GKE to automatically adjust the number of pods based on resource utilization.
C) Implement a fixed-size cluster to ensure consistent performance.
D) Use Cloud CDN to cache dynamic content and reduce server load.
E) Upgrade all pods to the highest machine type available.

QUESTION 21

Your automated deployment pipeline, using Cloud Build, suddenly stops working after a recent update to your application's codebase. You suspect that changes in the codebase might have caused the issue. What should you do first to diagnose and resolve the problem?

A) Roll back the codebase to the previous version that was known to work with the pipeline.
B) Check the build logs and error messages in Cloud Build to identify the specific issue in the pipeline.
C) Disable the automated deployment pipeline to prevent further issues until the problem is resolved.
D) Modify the Cloud Build configuration to use a different build image.

QUESTION 22

You oversee a critical healthcare platform with a defined Service Level Objective (SLO). Frequent updates are deployed by the engineering team. To ensure that platform stability takes precedence over new feature development in case of an SLO breach, what proactive step should you take before such a scenario arises?

A) Enforce a policy that restricts any updates until the SLO breach is resolved.
B) Create a guideline that mandates an immediate halt on feature development when an SLO breach occurs.
C) Conduct regular meetings with the engineering team to stress the importance of platform stability.
D) Coordinate with product managers to delay new feature rollouts when the SLO is at risk.

QUESTION 23

You are responsible for a cloud-based database system that supports critical applications. To ensure optimal performance and resource utilization, you want to identify databases that may require tuning. What actions should you take? (Choose two.)

A) Monitor query execution times and CPU utilization of the databases. If there's a significant gap, optimize the database queries.
B) Review the network traffic and disk I/O of the databases. If there's a considerable gap, consider upgrading the database instances.
C) Analyze the query response times, memory usage, and CPU utilization of the databases. If the query response times negatively impact service objectives and the gap between memory usage and CPU utilization is small, label the databases for optimization.
D) Assess the storage consumption patterns of the databases. If consumption consistently remains high, flag the databases for optimization.
E) Check the database replication lag and network latency. If you find a large disparity, expand the network resources.

QUESTION 24

After deploying an update to your cloud-based CRM system, you notice an unexpected drop in system performance, particularly during data-intensive operations. This is causing delays in report generation and customer data processing. As a DevOps engineer, what should be your first step to mitigate the negative impact on your business operations?

A) Temporarily disable non-essential features to reduce load on the system.
B) Revert to the previous version of the CRM system until the issue is resolved.
C) Initiate a comprehensive performance analysis to identify bottlenecks.
D) Increase the frequency of automated backups to prevent data loss.
E) Collaborate with the development team to optimize query performance.

QUESTION 25

Your team is developing a cloud-native application using microservices architecture and is looking for a solution to manage configuration files across different environments (development, staging, production). Which approach is most suitable in line with Google Cloud DevOps principles?

A) Use a shared network folder with different subfolders for each environment's configuration files.
 B) Employ Google Cloud Storage with lifecycle policies to manage different versions of configuration files.
 C) Implement a Git-based version control system with branching strategies for different environments.
 D) Store configuration files in individual developer Google Drive accounts and manually merge changes for different environments.
 E) Maintain configuration files on a central database server, accessible to all team members for updates.

QUESTION 26

You manage a cloud-based application that processes large datasets. Users have reported occasional slow response times. Investigation shows these issues coincide with high CPU load on your processing servers. You decide to establish an SLI for CPU performance. Which metric should you use to define this SLI?

A) Average CPU utilization percentage across all processing servers.
 B) Ratio of data processing requests completed within a set time frame.
 C) Total number of CPU-bound tasks waiting in the queue.
 D) Frequency of auto-scaling events triggered by CPU load.
 E) Aggregate CPU idle time across the server cluster.

QUESTION 27

You are the SRE Incident Commander for a large e-commerce platform. A critical system failure has just occurred during peak shopping hours, leading to widespread checkout failures. After assigning your team roles, what should your next step be?

A) Directly engage with the engineering team to start coding a solution.
 B) Establish an internal communication channel specifically for coordinating the incident response.
 C) Immediately send a detailed technical analysis of the failure to all customers.
 D) Conduct a quick team meeting to brainstorm potential solutions.
 E) Notify senior management about the failure, detailing potential financial impacts.

QUESTION 28

After a significant data loss incident in your cloud storage service, a postmortem identifies a gap in the backup and recovery process. What steps should you take to improve resilience and data integrity?

A) Enhance backup and recovery protocols, including more frequent and comprehensive backups.
 B) Reassign team members who were responsible for the data loss to other projects.
 C) Require that all data management changes receive approval from senior IT management.
 D) Organize regular training sessions for staff on data management best practices.
 E) Limit the amount of data stored in the cloud to reduce the potential impact of similar incidents.

QUESTION 29

Your team is deploying a new application on Google Kubernetes Engine (GKE) and you want to ensure its logs are available in Cloud Logging. However, you're not seeing any logs from this application in the Cloud Logging console. What should you check first?

A) Confirm that the logging agent is correctly installed and running on each GKE node.
B) Check if the GKE cluster has network connectivity issues preventing logs from reaching Cloud Logging.
C) Verify that your user account has the necessary permissions to view logs in the Cloud Logging console.
D) Ensure that the application's containers are configured to write logs to stdout and stderr.
E) Review if the GKE cluster firewall rules are allowing traffic to Cloud Logging's endpoints.

QUESTION 30

In a DevOps process for automating infrastructure deployment with Terraform on Google Cloud, how should you manage credentials for Google service accounts used within a managed GKE cluster?

A) Create a single shared Google service account and share the JSON key among all Pods.
B) Generate separate JSON keys for each Pod and store them in a public Git repository for access.
C) Implement a dedicated Kubernetes service account for each Pod and use Workload Identity to assume the corresponding Google service account.
D) Store the JSON key for the Google service account as an environment variable within the Pods.
E) Use the GKE cluster's default service account for all Pods' IAM rights.

QUESTION 31

You are responsible for a Cloud Run service that handles incoming HTTP requests and logs events using Stackdriver Logging. After deploying a new version of the service, you notice that logs for specific HTTP requests are not showing up in the Stackdriver Logs Viewer. What should be your initial step to troubleshoot this issue while following Google Cloud best practices?

A) SSH into the Cloud Run service instance and check if the Stackdriver agent is running.
B) Check the Stackdriver agent's test log message in the Logs Viewer.
C) Upgrade the Stackdriver agent for Cloud Run services to the latest version.
D) Ensure the Cloud Run service's service account has the monitoring.write access scope enabled.

QUESTION 32

Your company manages a network of GKE clusters distributed across multiple regions. The current monitoring setup relies on Prometheus-based tools for gathering performance metrics, setting up alerts, and visualizing data. However, this setup lacks the ability to aggregate metrics effectively across all clusters globally. What approach should you take to address this issue with minimal administrative overhead?

A) Integrate individual cluster metrics with Cloud Monitoring for GKE.
B) Implement Google Cloud Managed Service for Prometheus.
C) Utilize Prometheus multi-level federation to centrally aggregate metrics.
D) Enable Prometheus cross-region federation for centralized metric collection.

QUESTION 33

You are responsible for the CI/CD pipeline of a microservices-based application deployed on Google Kubernetes Engine (GKE). The development team requests a robust rollback mechanism in case new deployments cause issues. Which approach should you recommend for implementing a reliable rollback process in this Kubernetes environment?

A) Delete the new Pods and allow GKE to automatically restart the old ones.
B) Use Kubernetes Deployment Rollback feature to roll back to the previous deployment revision.
C) Adjust the replica count of the new Pods to zero and manually start the old ones.
D) Create a new GKE cluster for every deployment and switch traffic to the old cluster in case of issues.

QUESTION 34

Your organization operates a business-critical application on Google Kubernetes Engine (GKE). The application is divided into multiple microservices, each deployed in separate Pods. Recently, you noticed that one of the microservices, named "inventory-service," is frequently experiencing Pod failures and crashes. What should you do to improve the reliability of the "inventory-service"?

A) Increase the CPU and memory resource requests in the "inventory-service" Deployment configuration.
B) Implement a liveness probe in the "inventory-service" to detect and restart unhealthy Pods.
C) Deploy a second instance of the "inventory-service" in the same cluster for redundancy.
D) Delete and recreate the "inventory-service" Deployment to start fresh.

QUESTION 35

You are part of an e-commerce company adopting Site Reliability Engineering (SRE) methodologies. Your team is about to take over a new recommendation engine from the development group. After conducting a Production Readiness Review (PRR), it's evident that the system lacks the necessary configurations to meet its Service Level Objectives (SLOs). What action should you take to ensure successful SLO attainment in the production environment?

A) Deploy the recommendation engine into production without established SLOs and develop them based on operational insights gained.
B) Inform the development group that they are responsible for supporting the system in production.
C) Adjust the SLO benchmarks to levels that the recommendation engine can meet to expedite its production deployment.
D) Identify essential service improvements for reliability that should be addressed before the transition.

QUESTION 36

You are responsible for a cloud-based video conferencing service, and the error budget for call quality has been exhausted during the current observation period. Your organization is planning a high-profile virtual event, and call quality is critical. How should you proceed while following SRE principles to ensure a successful virtual event?

A) Review additional metrics related to the video conferencing service's performance and identify SLOs with available error budget. Reallocate error budget from these SLOs to ensure a smooth virtual event.
B) Notify the event organizers about the depleted error budget and request that they conduct extensive testing to minimize call quality issues during the virtual event.
C) Initiate a formal request process to secure an increase in the error budget specifically for the virtual event to guarantee its success.
D) Inform the event organizers about the depleted error budget and discuss the option of postponing

the event or accepting potential call quality issues during the event.

QUESTION 37

You manage a video conferencing platform hosted on Google Compute Engine. You suspect unauthorized data transmissions and want to set up a monitoring solution to capture and store network traffic data for later review. What should you do?

A) Enable VPC Flow Logs on the relevant subnets within the development and production VPCs, with a sample volume scale of 1.0, starting with development and then production.
B) Enable VPC Flow Logs on the relevant subnets within the development and production VPCs, with a sample volume scale of 0.5, starting with development and then production.
C) Enable VPC Flow Logs only on the production VPC subnets with a sample volume scale of 1.0.

QUESTION 38

How can you effectively consolidate and analyze cost data from multiple cloud providers, including Google Cloud, for cost optimization?

A) Use Google Cloud's Cost Management features to track and optimize costs within Google Cloud. Implement similar cost management tools for other cloud providers to track expenses separately.
B) Leverage Google Cloud's multi-cloud management capabilities to consolidate cost data from other cloud providers and analyze it within Google Cloud's Cost Management tools.
C) Create separate budgets for each cloud provider and manually aggregate cost data from different providers for analysis.
D) Utilize third-party cost optimization tools that support multiple cloud providers and integrate them with Google Cloud's billing data.

QUESTION 39

As a cloud administrator, you're managing a Cloud Pub/Sub service and have identified a spike in messages from an unusual source. To efficiently monitor these messages, what is the recommended method to track them on Google Cloud with minimal ongoing maintenance?

A) Integrate a Cloud Pub/Sub metric in Cloud Monitoring for the abnormal source.
B) Configure Cloud Pub/Sub to create a log-based metric in Cloud Monitoring tailored to the source. Utilize a script to isolate these specific messages.
C) Modify the Pub/Sub subscriber code to report metrics of the unusual source to Cloud Monitoring.
D) Develop a script that extracts message data from Pub/Sub logs and sends metrics of the unusual source to Cloud Monitoring.

QUESTION 40

In your GKE environment, you are troubleshooting slow network performance in a cluster hosting interactive web applications. You cannot execute commands directly on the nodes or Pods. How can you determine if specific Pods are causing network congestion?

A) Use Metrics Explorer to observe the node/network/bytes_transmitted metric for network traffic analysis.

B) Investigate Pods with high network bandwidth requirements and run netstat to assess their network usage.
C) Monitor the container/network/bytes_transmitted metric in Metrics Explorer for insights into network usage at the container level.
D) Identify Pods with significant network traffic and use the ifconfig command to monitor their network activity.

QUESTION 41

After a critical system failure due to a software update in your e-commerce platform, you are conducting a post-mortem analysis. How should you proceed to prevent similar incidents in the future, adhering to SRE best practices?

A) Enhance the continuous integration pipeline to include tests that can identify such issues before deployment.
B) Identify and formally warn the development team members responsible for the update.
C) Review the approval process with the team that greenlit the update, instituting stricter control measures.
D) Set up an emergency protocol for immediate response by the incident team and senior management in case of future failures.

QUESTION 42

As a cloud engineer, you're tasked with monitoring the memory usage of an application deployed on Google App Engine to ensure optimal performance. Which Stackdriver metric should you primarily focus on for this purpose?

A) appengine/memory/usage
B) appengine/memory/total_memory
C) appengine/system/memory/usage
D) appengine/system/memory/used_bytes

QUESTION 43

In your e-commerce platform hosted on Google Cloud, an incident affected user transactions. You are updating the review policy to define when incidents require thorough investigation. Which two conditions should be included in the policy as triggers for an in-depth incident review?

A) The incident resulted in a noticeable drop in sales transactions.
B) An employee suggests the incident might be related to recent code changes.
C) The system's auto-scaling feature temporarily deployed additional resources.
D) An incident led to a violation of a critical security compliance requirement.
E) Routine maintenance was performed during the time of the incident.

QUESTION 44

You are managing an online gaming platform on Google Cloud and need to monitor the response times of game servers. You want to track the variability and distribution of these response times across your global user base. Which metric configuration and visualization method should you use in Google Cloud's

Operations Suite?

A) MetricKind: DELTA, ValueType: INT64, Visualization: Line graph
B) MetricKind: CUMULATIVE, ValueType: DOUBLE, Visualization: Stacked Bar graph
C) MetricKind: GAUGE, ValueType: DISTRIBUTION, Visualization: Heatmap graph
D) MetricKind: METRIC_KIND_UNSPECIFIED, ValueType: INT64, Visualization: Stacked Area graph

QUESTION 45

As a cloud administrator, you notice one of your NoSQL database instances in a multi-instance setup is underperforming and causing application delays. You need to mitigate this issue while keeping the application operational. What steps should you take?

A) Immediately isolate the underperforming instance, then evaluate the capacity of the remaining instances and scale if necessary.
B) Notify the incident team, reroute traffic from the troubled instance, add resources to other instances, and then isolate the problem instance.
C) Add a new instance to the database cluster, wait for it to integrate, then reroute traffic from the failing instance and start troubleshooting.
D) Conduct a real-time analysis of the failing instance while it's still in operation, then decide on rerouting traffic based on the findings.

QUESTION 46

In deploying a series of microservices on Google Cloud using Terraform, you find that your CI/CD pipeline is inconsistently managing resource creation, leading to multiple active versions of the same service. How can you modify your deployment process to rectify this issue?

A) Adjust your CI/CD pipeline to use a Terraform backend such as Cloud Storage for state management to ensure only the current version of the microservice is active.
B) Incorporate a manual approval process in the pipeline to verify and remove old service instances before deploying new ones.
C) Utilize a shared version control repository for Terraform state files, allowing the pipeline to access the most recent infrastructure configuration.
D) Implement a routine within the pipeline to query existing resources and remove them using gcloud commands before deploying updates.

QUESTION 47

You are managing a microservices-based application on Google Kubernetes Engine, and you've observed increased latency. What action should you take to pinpoint the performance bottleneck?

A) Analyze the firewall rules for your Kubernetes clusters
 B) Review the Docker container images for potential vulnerabilities
 C) Utilize Google Cloud's built-in monitoring and analysis tools
 D) Utilize a distributed tracing solution like Google Cloud Trace or Zipkin to track requests and responses between microservices

QUESTION 48

You oversee a platform that has consistently met its Service Level Objective (SLO) for the past 9 months, resulting in high user satisfaction. To adhere to Site Reliability Engineering (SRE) principles, what should you do? (Choose two.)

A) Make the SLO more stringent to increase reliability.
B) Invest engineering resources in enhancing reliability for other platforms.
C) Prioritize the introduction of new features over reliability improvements.
D) Increase deployment frequency and risk tolerance.
E) Expand the range of Service Level Indicators (SLIs).

QUESTION 49

Your organization has adopted a microservices architecture running on Google Kubernetes Engine (GKE). To enhance security, you want to implement identity and access management for the microservices. What steps should you take to achieve this? (Choose two.)

A) Configure Google Cloud Identity-Aware Proxy (IAP) to secure access to your microservices.
B) Implement Role-Based Access Control (RBAC) within your Kubernetes cluster to manage permissions.
C) Use a single service account for all microservices to simplify access management.
D) Allow anonymous access to the microservices to enhance usability.
E) Share Kubernetes credentials among the development team to expedite access provisioning.

QUESTION 50

Your team is responsible for deploying updates to a critical application on Google Cloud. How can you ensure swift issue resolution and minimize system unavailability in case of post-deployment problems?

A) Implement a continuous integration (CI) pipeline with comprehensive regression tests executed upon each code push.
B) Mandate a code evaluation by at least two colleagues before integrating new updates.
C) Insist on thorough automated performance testing by software engineers on their individual workstations prior to deployment.
D) Employ the canary release methodology for gradual updates through a continuous delivery (CD) pipeline.
E) Develop a comprehensive disaster recovery plan with data backups and redundancy.
F) Establish a dedicated incident response team with defined roles and responsibilities.

PRACTICE TEST 8 - ANSWERS ONLY

QUESTION 1

Answer - A) Reassign the 'previous' tag to the previous container image version and update the deployment.

Option A is the recommended approach. By reassigning the 'previous' tag to the previous container image version and updating the deployment, you can efficiently roll back to a known version while minimizing impact on users and ensuring a smooth transition.
 Option B suggests using a sha256 digest, which is a valid approach but may not be as straightforward.
 Option C involves deploying both versions in parallel, which may introduce complexity and resource usage.
 Option D introduces a new namespace, which is not necessary for a simple rollback scenario and may add unnecessary complexity.

QUESTION 2

Answer - A) Implement Google Cloud Identity-Aware Proxy (IAP) for secure access to the data processing pipeline and utilize Google Cloud KMS for data encryption.

Option A aligns with the data privacy and security requirements by using Google Cloud Identity-Aware Proxy (IAP) for secure access and Google Cloud KMS for data encryption. This ensures that only authorized users and applications can access the sensitive financial data.
 Options B, C, and D mention various services but do not directly address data access restrictions and encryption.

QUESTION 3

Answer - A) 1 and 4

Prioritizing a blame-free culture that encourages learning (Option 1) and using automated incident response tools to reduce human intervention (Option 4) are key practices for effective incident response in a DevOps environment. These practices foster collaboration, continuous improvement, and efficient incident resolution.
 Option 2, establishing strict escalation procedures and assigning blame, is counterproductive to a blame-free culture.
 Option 3, limiting access to incident data, may hinder effective collaboration and learning.

QUESTION 4

Answer - B) Implement VPC Service Controls to manage dashboard configuration access.

Option B is the correct choice as it efficiently restricts access to dashboard configuration using VPC Service Controls.
 Option A introduces Service Perimeter, which may not be suitable,
 Option C suggests custom roles that might not be needed,
 Option D grants a broad role without specific control.

QUESTION 5

Answer - D) MTTD: 3 MTTR: 45 MTBF: 60 Impact: 33%

Option D represents the risk assessment figures for the new storage solution failover, considering the longer MTTR, the same MTBF, and a 33% user impact.
Option A has incorrect MTTR and user impact,
Option B has incorrect MTTR and user impact,
Option C has incorrect user impact.

QUESTION 6

Answer - A and B

Options A and B are the correct choices. Segmenting automation procedures into finer-grained components (A) reduces redundancy and streamlines the workflow. Implementing automatic progression confirmations (B) helps in achieving smoother transitions between stages, reducing manual interventions.
Options C, D, and E are not directly related to optimizing the workflow.

QUESTION 7

Answer - B and D

Option B - With 40% CPU utilization, you can handle workload growth without additional capacity.
Option D - Implementing a horizontal pod autoscaler and conducting load testing is a proactive approach to manage the expected increase in demand.
Options A and C are not the optimal strategies.

QUESTION 8

Answer - B) Introduce a new instance template with the updated resources, reconfigure the instance group, and then retire the old template.

A) Incorrect - This method risks state inconsistency and potential configuration drift.
B) Correct - This approach allows for a smooth transition with the least service disruption.
C) Incorrect - Overwriting the template via script without handling the error can lead to further issues.
D) Incorrect - Manual updates outside Terraform disrupt the infrastructure as code process.
E) Incorrect - Suspending operations can lead to service downtime, which is undesirable.

QUESTION 9

Answer - B) Focus on understanding the systemic issues that allowed the error, without assigning individual blame.

A) Incorrect - SRE encourages a blameless culture to promote open investigation.
B) Correct - This approach aligns with SRE principles, focusing on systemic improvements.
C) Incorrect - Prioritizing new features over learning from incidents can lead to repeated failures.
D) Incorrect - Focusing on individual accountability can hinder open communication in postmortem analysis.

E) Incorrect - While systemic review is important, this option lacks the focus on a blameless culture.

QUESTION 10

Answer - A) Deploy the application in a multi-regional GKE setup to serve users from the closest region.

A) Correct - A multi-regional setup can reduce data transfer costs by serving users from geographically closer regions.
B) Incorrect - While HTTP(S) Load Balancer is effective for traffic management, it doesn't directly reduce data transfer costs.
C) Incorrect - Reducing payload size may help but is not as effective as geographical optimization.
D) Incorrect - Network Service Tiers provide cost flexibility but are not the most effective for a global e-commerce site.
E) Incorrect - Consolidation may reduce inter-service costs but doesn't address the global nature of the traffic.

QUESTION 11

Answer - C) Integrate Cloud Profiler to identify and analyze memory-intensive functions in your service.

A) Incorrect - Cloud Logging can help with logs, but it's not specifically designed to analyze memory usage.
B) Incorrect - While Cloud Monitoring observes memory patterns, it doesn't pinpoint specific memory-intensive functions.
C) Correct - Cloud Profiler is ideal for identifying memory-intensive functions and analyzing their impact on service performance.
D) Incorrect - Cloud Trace focuses on request flows, which might not directly help in identifying memory usage issues.
E) Incorrect - The Operations Suite provides an overall view but may not offer the specific analysis needed for memory issues.

QUESTION 12

Answer - B) Deploy a GKE cluster with autoscaling enabled. Create a service to monitor Cloud Storage for new datasets and another to process the data, scaling down when no datasets are present.

A) Incorrect - Cloud Functions might not be suitable for intensive data processing tasks.
B) Correct - GKE with autoscaling efficiently manages resource allocation and can handle varying dataset sizes.
C) Incorrect - SFTP on Compute Engine adds complexity and may not be the most cost-effective solution.
D) Incorrect - Cloud Scheduler is less dynamic and might lead to delays in processing.
E) Incorrect - Dataflow is a good option for data processing but may not be the most cost-effective for intermittent datasets.

QUESTION 13

Answer - A) Content delivery SLI: the percentage of requests that successfully retrieve content within 200 ms.

A) Correct - This SLI directly measures the performance and effectiveness of the CDN in delivering content quickly to users.
B) Incorrect - While overall uptime is important, it does not specifically measure content delivery performance.
C) Incorrect - Data throughput is an important aspect but does not directly reflect user experience in content retrieval.
D) Incorrect - Edge node performance is a component of CDN performance but does not encompass the entire delivery process.
E) Incorrect - Content freshness is important but does not directly measure the effectiveness of content delivery to end users.

QUESTION 14

Answer - C) Implement Binary Authorization to ensure only containers with verifiable signatures are deployed in your GKE clusters.

A) Incorrect - While third-party tools are valuable, they do not directly enforce deployment policies based on image integrity and origin.
B) Incorrect - Vulnerability scanning identifies known vulnerabilities but does not verify the integrity and origin of container images.
C) Correct - Binary Authorization provides a mechanism to enforce that only verified and trusted containers are deployed, based on their signatures.
D) Incorrect - Cloud IAM manages access but is not designed to enforce container image integrity and origin policies.
E) Incorrect - Cloud Security Command Center is for monitoring and alerting, not for pre-deployment verification of container images.

QUESTION 15

Answer - C) Store both open-source and proprietary Terraform modules in OCI format using Artifact Registry.

Option C is incorrect because it suggests using Artifact Registry for storage, but it doesn't provide a clear solution for addressing the specific concerns raised by the compliance department regarding open-source modules and access control.
 Option D - Option D is incorrect because it lacks a clear solution for access control and compliance with VPC Service Controls, which are crucial in this scenario.
 Option E - Option E is incorrect because there is a suitable solution among the provided options (Option A) that addresses the compliance and access control concerns.

QUESTION 16

Answer - A) Create separate centralized logging projects for each team and assign project-level IAM roles for access control. Grant the compliance oversight team viewer permissions in all projects.

Option A is the correct choice because it aligns with the compliance team's policy by creating separate centralized logging projects for each team, ensuring access control. The compliance oversight team has viewer permissions in all projects for centralized access.
 Option B - Option B is incorrect because using Google Cloud Storage buckets may not provide the

necessary granularity for log access control within a project.
 Option C - Option C is incorrect because while BigQuery datasets offer control, they may introduce unnecessary complexity, and granting BigQuery admin privileges in the central project may not align with best practices.
 Option D - Option D is incorrect because creating custom log views may not provide the necessary granularity for access control, and managing custom views for multiple projects may be less efficient.

QUESTION 17

Answer - C) Integrate the OpenTelemetry client libraries within your service, direct metrics to Cloud Monitoring as the export destination, and monitor service metrics in Cloud Monitoring.

Option C is the correct choice because it allows you to incorporate OpenTelemetry client libraries within your service and direct metrics to Cloud Monitoring, minimizing initial configuration effort for monitoring and providing a single manageable platform for service-level metrics.
 Option A - Option A suggests using Cloud Pub/Sub, which may not be the most direct approach for monitoring service-level metrics.
 Option B - Option B involves transferring metrics as logs, which may not be as efficient for monitoring service-level metrics.
 Option D - Option D mentions streaming metrics directly to the Cloud Monitoring API, which may require more configuration effort.

QUESTION 18

Answer - A) Inspect the existing telemetry data and introduce additional metrics as required.
 Answer - C) Analyze both historical and real-time data access logs to understand user interactions with the platform.

Option A and Option C are the correct choices.
 Option A - Reviewing existing telemetry data and adding more metrics, if needed, helps assess reliability without software modifications.
 Option B - Modifying the application's source code contradicts the requirement to avoid software changes.
 Option D - Developing virtual user profiles for simulation is not aligned with evaluating reliability from the user's perspective.
 Option E - Focusing only on authentication logs may not provide a complete user perspective.

QUESTION 19

Answer - B) Store credentials in Secret Manager, encrypt them with a key from Cloud Key Management Service, and grant the automated workflow access through Identity and Access Management.

Option B is the correct choice.
 Option B - Storing credentials in Secret Manager, encrypting them with a key from Cloud Key Management Service, and granting workflow access through Identity and Access Management aligns with Google's best practices for secure credential management and rotation.
 Option A - Instructing manual input of credentials is less secure and prone to errors.
 Option C - Embedding credentials in the workflow's codebase is not recommended for security reasons.
 Option D - Storing credentials in a dedicated configuration file may not provide adequate access control

and security.

QUESTION 20

Answer - B) Use horizontal pod autoscaling in GKE to automatically adjust the number of pods based on resource utilization.

Explanation for Option B - Using horizontal pod autoscaling in GKE allows the cluster to automatically adjust the number of pods based on resource utilization, ensuring the application can handle increased traffic without manual intervention. This approach optimizes costs and performance.
Explanation for Option A - Manually scaling up GKE nodes during traffic spikes is not as efficient as using autoscaling and may result in unnecessary resource provisioning and costs.
Explanation for Option C - Implementing a fixed-size cluster may not be cost-effective and may limit the ability to handle increased traffic efficiently.
Explanation for Option D - While using Cloud CDN is beneficial for content caching, it primarily addresses static content and may not fully optimize the application's performance and cost.
Explanation for Option E - Upgrading all pods to the highest machine type may significantly increase costs without a guaranteed performance improvement and may not efficiently handle traffic spikes.

QUESTION 21

Answer - B) Check the build logs and error messages in Cloud Build to identify the specific issue in the pipeline.

Explanation for Option B - Checking the build logs and error messages in Cloud Build is the first step to identify the specific issue that caused the pipeline to fail. It provides valuable information for debugging and resolving the problem.
Explanation for Option A - Rolling back the codebase to a previous version is a drastic step and should be considered after identifying the cause of the failure. It may not be necessary if the issue can be resolved in the current codebase.
Explanation for Option C - Disabling the automated pipeline prevents further deployments but doesn't address the root cause of the issue. It should be considered only after identifying and resolving the problem.
Explanation for Option D - Modifying the Cloud Build configuration to use a different build image is a significant change and should be considered after identifying the cause of the issue. It may not address the root cause of the failure.

QUESTION 22

Answer - B) Create a guideline that mandates an immediate halt on feature development when an SLO breach occurs.

Explanation for Option B - Creating a guideline that enforces a halt on feature development immediately upon an SLO breach is a proactive measure with clear instructions for prioritizing stability.
Explanation for Option A - Enforcing a policy that restricts updates until an SLO breach is resolved may lead to delays without immediate action.
Explanation for Option C - Conducting regular meetings emphasizes stability but may not ensure immediate action during critical incidents.
Explanation for Option D - Coordinating with product managers is important, but it may not guarantee

an immediate response without a predefined guideline.

QUESTION 23

A) Monitor query execution times and CPU utilization of the databases. If there's a significant gap, optimize the database queries.
C) Analyze the query response times, memory usage, and CPU utilization of the databases. If the query response times negatively impact service objectives and the gap between memory usage and CPU utilization is small, label the databases for optimization.

Option A focuses on monitoring query execution times and CPU utilization, which are essential for database performance. If a significant gap exists, optimizing queries can enhance performance.
Option B suggests looking at network traffic and disk I/O, which may not directly address database tuning.
Option C considers query response times, memory usage, and CPU utilization, making it suitable for identifying databases that impact service objectives negatively.
Option D only assesses storage consumption patterns and does not address other critical metrics.
Option E recommends expanding network resources, which may not directly relate to query execution and CPU utilization.

QUESTION 24

Answer - C) Initiate a comprehensive performance analysis to identify bottlenecks.

A) Disabling features might alleviate the load but doesn't solve the underlying performance issue.
B) Reverting the update is a potential solution, but it's more beneficial to understand the cause first.
C) This action is critical as it will help in pinpointing the exact cause of the performance degradation, allowing for a more informed decision on the next steps.
D) While ensuring data safety is important, it does not address the immediate performance issue.
E) Optimization is necessary, but first, the specific performance issue needs to be identified through analysis.

QUESTION 25

Answer - C) Implement a Git-based version control system with branching strategies for different environments.

Option A - Shared network folders can be chaotic and do not offer efficient version control for different environments.
Option B - While Google Cloud Storage is effective for storing files, it lacks the granular control offered by version control systems.
Option C - This approach allows for organized, version-controlled management of configurations across different environments, facilitating continuous integration and delivery.
Option D - Google Drive does not offer the necessary tools for efficient version control and environment-specific management.
Option E - A central database server for configuration files does not provide the version control or branching capabilities required for managing different environments.

QUESTION 26

Answer - B) Ratio of data processing requests completed within a set time frame.

Option A - While CPU utilization is important, it does not directly reflect user experience or request handling efficiency.

Option B - This metric directly correlates with the application's performance from the user's perspective, making it an appropriate SLI.

Option C - Queue length is an indirect measure and may not accurately reflect processing efficiency.

Option D - Auto-scaling frequency indicates system load but not processing efficiency or user experience.

Option E - CPU idle time is a useful metric for resource optimization but doesn't directly relate to user-perceived performance.

QUESTION 27

Answer - B) Establish an internal communication channel specifically for coordinating the incident response.

Option A - Direct engagement in solution development is secondary to establishing effective communication and coordination.

Option B - Setting up a dedicated channel ensures efficient and focused communication among responders.

Option C - Customer communication is vital, but it should be well-informed and follow internal coordination.

Option D - Brainstorming is an essential step but follows the establishment of communication protocols.

Option E - Informing management is important, but the immediate priority is to manage the incident effectively.

QUESTION 28

Answer - A) Enhance backup and recovery protocols, including more frequent and comprehensive backups.

Option A - Strengthening backup and recovery protocols directly addresses the identified gap and improves data resilience.

Option B - Reassigning team members does not solve the underlying process issues.

Option C - While oversight is important, it should not create unnecessary bottlenecks in the workflow.

Option D - Training is beneficial but should be complemented by improved protocols and systems.

Option E - Limiting data storage in the cloud is not practical for a cloud storage service and doesn't address the core issue.

QUESTION 29

Answer - D) Ensure that the application's containers are configured to write logs to stdout and stderr.

Option A - GKE clusters typically have a default logging agent, but it's worth confirming.

Option B - Network connectivity issues could affect logging, but it's a less common issue.

Option C - User permissions are important but typically not the cause of missing application logs.

Option D - Ensuring that containers write logs to stdout and stderr is crucial for Cloud Logging to capture them.

Option E - While firewall rules are important, they rarely need to be configured specifically for Cloud Logging in GKE.

QUESTION 30

Answer - C) Implement a dedicated Kubernetes service account for each Pod and use Workload Identity to assume the corresponding Google service account.

The recommended approach is to implement a dedicated Kubernetes service account for each Pod and utilize Workload Identity for secure access to the corresponding Google service account. Other options introduce security risks or lack proper isolation.

Option A - Sharing a single service account and key among all Pods is not aligned with best practices and lacks isolation. Option B - Storing separate JSON keys in a public Git repository is a security risk. Option D - Storing the JSON key as an environment variable within the Pods lacks security and proper access control. Option E - Using the GKE cluster's default service account lacks the necessary granularity and control.

QUESTION 31

Answer - A) SSH into the Cloud Run service instance and check if the Stackdriver agent is running.

Option B, checking the Stackdriver agent's test log message, may not directly address the issue of missing logs for specific HTTP requests.

Option C, upgrading the Stackdriver agent, is a valid action but not necessarily the first step to investigate.

Option D, ensuring the service account access scope, may not be the initial step in diagnosing the problem.

QUESTION 32

Answer - C) Utilize Prometheus multi-level federation to centrally aggregate metrics.

Option A, integrating with Cloud Monitoring, may not provide the comprehensive global aggregation required.

Option B, Google Cloud Managed Service for Prometheus, may not be aligned with the existing Prometheus-based setup.

Option D, enabling cross-region federation, is not a standard Prometheus feature.

QUESTION 33

Answer - B) Use Kubernetes Deployment Rollback feature to roll back to the previous deployment revision.

- Option A relies on automatic restarts and may not be as controlled as a deliberate rollback.
- Option C involves manual intervention and can be error-prone.
- Option D is resource-intensive and not a recommended approach for rollbacks.

Using the Kubernetes Deployment Rollback feature (Option B) allows you to easily and reliably roll back to a previous deployment revision, ensuring a robust rollback mechanism for your microservices-based application on GKE.

QUESTION 34

Answer - B) Implement a liveness probe in the "inventory-service" to detect and restart unhealthy Pods.

Explanation:
Option B is the correct choice because implementing a liveness probe in the "inventory-service" allows GKE to detect and automatically restart unhealthy Pods, improving the service's reliability.
Option A, increasing resource requests, may not address the root cause of Pod failures and is not as effective as a liveness probe.
Option C suggests deploying a second instance, which adds complexity and may not be necessary initially.
Option D, deleting and recreating the Deployment, may result in downtime and does not address the underlying issue of Pod failures.

QUESTION 35

Answer - D) Identify essential service improvements for reliability that should be addressed before the transition.

Option D is the correct choice as it follows SRE principles by prioritizing reliability enhancements before deployment. It ensures that the system meets its SLOs in production.
Option A is incorrect as deploying without established SLOs may lead to operational issues. Option B is incorrect because it shifts the responsibility without addressing the problem. Option C is incorrect as modifying SLO benchmarks may compromise the desired reliability.

QUESTION 36

Answer - A) Review additional metrics related to the video conferencing service's performance and identify SLOs with available error budget. Reallocate error budget from these SLOs to ensure a smooth virtual event.

Option A is the correct choice as it aligns with SRE principles by reallocating error budget from other SLOs to ensure a successful virtual event.
Option B is incorrect as it focuses on testing but does not directly address the error budget issue.
Option C is incorrect as increasing the error budget may not be the most effective way to manage errors.
Option D is incorrect as it suggests delaying the event or accepting potential call quality issues without exploring other solutions.

QUESTION 37

Answer - A) Enable VPC Flow Logs on the relevant subnets within the development and production VPCs, with a sample volume scale of 1.0, starting with development and then production.

Option A is the correct choice as it enables VPC Flow Logs with a sample volume scale of 1.0 in both development and production environments, allowing comprehensive network traffic monitoring for later review.

Option B is incorrect as it reduces the sample volume scale, potentially missing important data.
Option C is incorrect as it only enables VPC Flow Logs in the production environment, overlooking the development environment's insights.

QUESTION 38

B) Leverage Google Cloud's multi-cloud management capabilities to consolidate cost data from other cloud providers and analyze it within Google Cloud's Cost Management tools.

Option B is the correct choice. Google Cloud provides multi-cloud management capabilities that allow you to consolidate cost data from other cloud providers and analyze it within Google Cloud's Cost Management tools. This approach offers a unified view of costs and simplifies optimization efforts. Option A suggests tracking expenses separately for each cloud provider, which can be cumbersome. Option C involves manual aggregation, which is time-consuming and prone to errors. Option D proposes third-party tools, which may require additional integration and cost.

QUESTION 39

Answer - B) Configure Cloud Pub/Sub to create a log-based metric in Cloud Monitoring tailored to the source. Utilize a script to isolate these specific messages.

Option A - Incorrect: Pub/Sub does not provide direct metrics for specific message sources.
Option B - Correct: Setting up a log-based metric and using a script for specific message isolation is the most effective and maintenance-efficient method.
Option C - Incorrect: Altering subscriber code is more maintenance-intensive.
Option D - Incorrect: Creating an independent script for data extraction is less efficient.

QUESTION 40

Answer - C) Monitor the container/network/bytes_transmitted metric in Metrics Explorer for insights into network usage at the container level.

Option A - Incorrect: While useful, node-level network metrics lack the granularity needed for pinpointing specific Pods.
Option B - Incorrect: Running netstat is not an option without direct node access.
Option C - Correct: Container-level network metrics provide a more accurate view of individual Pod network usage.
Option D - Incorrect: ifconfig cannot be utilized without command execution access on nodes.

QUESTION 41

Answer - A) Enhance the continuous integration pipeline to include tests that can identify such issues before deployment.

Option A - Correct: Implementing more rigorous testing in the CI pipeline is in line with proactive SRE principles.
Option B - Incorrect: Blaming individuals goes against the SRE culture of learning and improvement.
Option C - Incorrect: While review is important, focusing on punitive measures is not constructive.
Option D - Incorrect: While emergency protocols are vital, they do not address the root cause or

prevention.

QUESTION 42

Answer - D) appengine/system/memory/used_bytes

Option A - Incorrect: This metric does not specifically relate to memory usage.
Option B - Incorrect: Total memory metric doesn't reflect the actual usage.
Option C - Incorrect: This metric is not specific to memory usage monitoring.
Option D - Correct: The used_bytes metric provides an accurate measurement of memory usage, which is crucial for performance monitoring.

QUESTION 43

Answer - A) The incident resulted in a noticeable drop in sales transactions. and D) An incident led to a violation of a critical security compliance requirement.

Option A - Correct: Significant impacts on core business functions like sales warrant thorough investigations.
Option B - Incorrect: Employee suggestions are valuable but should not be the sole criteria for in-depth reviews.
Option C - Incorrect: Auto-scaling response is part of normal operations and doesn't always indicate a need for a review.
Option D - Correct: Violations of critical compliance requirements are serious and require detailed analysis.
Option E - Incorrect: Routine maintenance, unless directly linked to the incident, is not a primary trigger for an in-depth review.

QUESTION 44

Answer - C) MetricKind: GAUGE, ValueType: DISTRIBUTION, Visualization: Heatmap graph

Option A - Incorrect: DELTA and INT64 are not ideal for capturing response time variability.
Option B - Incorrect: CUMULATIVE and DOUBLE don't suit the need to visualize response time distribution.
Option C - Correct: GAUGE with DISTRIBUTION and a Heatmap visualization is best suited for tracking and visualizing variability in server response times.
Option D - Incorrect: METRIC_KIND_UNSPECIFIED is not a specific metric type and may not effectively capture the desired data.

QUESTION 45

Answer - B) Notify the incident team, reroute traffic from the troubled instance, add resources to other instances, and then isolate the problem instance.

Option A - Incorrect: Immediate isolation without assessing the impact on the overall service can cause further issues.
Option B - Correct: Notifying the incident team and carefully managing traffic and resources ensures service continuity while addressing the problem.

Option C - Incorrect: Waiting for a new instance to integrate might cause extended service disruption.
Option D - Incorrect: Real-time analysis of a failing instance can be risky and may not offer immediate relief to the issue.

QUESTION 46

Answer - A) Adjust your CI/CD pipeline to use a Terraform backend such as Cloud Storage for state management to ensure only the current version of the microservice is active.

Option A - Correct: A Terraform backend like Cloud Storage provides reliable state management, preventing duplication of resources.
Option B - Incorrect: Manual processes are less efficient and can lead to human error.
Option C - Incorrect: Version control systems are not ideal for managing Terraform state due to potential conflicts.
Option D - Incorrect: Using gcloud commands for routine deletions is inefficient and may lead to accidental data loss.

QUESTION 47

Answer - D) Utilize a distributed tracing solution like Google Cloud Trace or Zipkin to track requests and responses between microservices

Option D is the correct choice as it recommends utilizing a distributed tracing solution to track requests and responses between microservices. This approach is effective for pinpointing performance bottlenecks in a microservices-based application.
 Option A - Analyzing firewall rules is less relevant to latency.
 Option B - Reviewing Docker images is important but not the primary focus.
 Option C - Built-in tools are useful but may not provide detailed tracing.

QUESTION 48

Answer - B) Invest engineering resources in enhancing reliability for other platforms.
E) Expand the range of Service Level Indicators (SLIs).

Option A suggests making the SLO more stringent, which may not be necessary if user satisfaction and reliability are consistently high.
Option C prioritizes new features over reliability, which goes against SRE principles.
Option D focuses on increasing deployment frequency, which might not align with maintaining reliability.
Options B and E are recommended actions to maintain a balance between reliability and deployment frequency.

QUESTION 49

Answer - A) Configure Google Cloud Identity-Aware Proxy (IAP) to secure access to your microservices.
B) Implement Role-Based Access Control (RBAC) within your Kubernetes cluster to manage permissions.

Option A is correct because it suggests using Google Cloud Identity-Aware Proxy (IAP) to enhance security by securing access to microservices.
Option B is also correct as it recommends implementing Role-Based Access Control (RBAC) within the

Kubernetes cluster, which helps manage permissions effectively.
Options C, D, and E are incorrect as they either simplify access management at the cost of security or compromise security practices.

QUESTION 50

Answer - A) Implement a continuous integration (CI) pipeline with comprehensive regression tests executed upon each code push.

Options B, C, D, E, and F - While these options may contribute to issue resolution and system reliability, they do not directly address minimizing disruptions and expediting issue resolution post-deployment. Option A is the correct choice as it focuses on automated testing and code validation to detect and address issues promptly, reducing system unavailability.

PRACTICE TEST 9 - QUESTIONS ONLY

QUESTION 1

Your organization is managing a large-scale application on Google Cloud. You want to improve security by ensuring that all Compute Engine instances use authorized and verified container images. Which approach should you take to achieve this goal while minimizing manual efforts and ensuring compliance with company policies?

A) Manually inspect and validate each container image before deployment, and update instances accordingly.
 B) Use Google Cloud IAM to restrict access to container images and enforce strict permissions.
 C) Implement Google Cloud Security Command Center to scan and verify container images, then use deployment manager to update instances.
 D) Configure a Binary Authorization policy that enforces image verification for Compute Engine instances.

QUESTION 2

Your team is responsible for managing a microservices architecture on Google Cloud. Recently, you observed that one of the microservices experiences periodic performance degradation during high load, affecting user experience. The service runs on Google Kubernetes Engine (GKE). You notice the following metrics deviations: - Average CPU utilization: Typical state: 30% Current state: 80% - Memory usage: Typical state: 40% Current state: 70% - Response time: Typical state: 50 milliseconds Current state: 300 milliseconds To address the performance issue, what action should you take while following Google's recommended DevOps practices?

A) Increase the CPU and memory limits for the Pods running the affected microservice.
 B) Implement autoscaling for the GKE cluster to dynamically adjust resources based on demand.
 C) Optimize the microservice code to reduce CPU and memory consumption.
 D) Deploy a load balancer in front of the microservice to distribute incoming traffic evenly.

QUESTION 3

You are managing a complex microservices architecture on Google Kubernetes Engine (GKE). You need to ensure high availability and reliability for your application. Which two Kubernetes concepts or techniques should you consider for achieving this goal? I. Implement PodDisruptionBudgets to control disruptions during maintenance. 2. Use Horizontal Pod Autoscaling (HPA) to adjust resources dynamically. 3. Deploy multi-cluster clusters across different regions for redundancy. 4. Set up Network Policies for fine-grained network control between microservices.

A) 1 and 2 B) 2 and 3 C) 3 and 4 D) 1 and 4

QUESTION 4

As the manager overseeing a web service streaming metrics into Cloud Monitoring, what's the recommended authorization approach for the operations team to configure dashboards?

A) Establish a Service Perimeter in Cloud IAM to regulate access.
B) Leverage VPC Service Controls to restrict dashboard configuration.
C) Delegate a custom IAM role with the necessary permissions.
D) Grant the IAM role of monitoring.dashboardEditor to the operations team.

QUESTION 5

You're in charge of a video streaming platform on GKE with varying viewer traffic. To optimize resource usage, how should you approach auto-adjusting Pods and nodes based on demand?

A) Configure the Horizontal Pod Autoscaler and enable the cluster autoscaler.
B) Configure the Horizontal Pod Autoscaler but fix the size of the node pool.
C) Configure the Vertical Pod Autoscaler and enable the cluster autoscaler.
D) Configure the Vertical Pod Autoscaler but fix the size of the node pool.

QUESTION 6

You are tasked with improving your media processing workflow in Google Cloud's Dataflow to minimize repetitive tasks and decrease job execution time. What steps should you take? (Choose two.)

A) Segment the automation procedures into finer-grained components.
B) Implement automatic progression confirmations transferring from the staging area to the production zone.
C) Run a script to facilitate the setup of the media processing workflow in Google Cloud Dataflow.
D) Set up an alert to inform the designated team to proceed with the next phase when human input is needed.
E) Increase the number of personnel to execute hands-on steps.

QUESTION 7

Your organization's CRM system, hosted on Google Cloud's GKE, expects a 15% quarterly increase in workloads for the next year, while currently utilizing 40% of available CPU resources. How should you address this workload growth effectively?

A) Rely on GKE's cluster autoscaler to automatically adjust resources as needed, eliminating the need for manual intervention.
B) The existing 40% CPU utilization provides sufficient headroom to accommodate workload growth without additional capacity.
C) Proactively increase node capacity by 90% to handle the anticipated quarterly workload increase, and validate resource sufficiency through load testing.
D) Assess the upper limits of node pool sizes, implement a horizontal pod autoscaler for workloads, and conduct load testing to determine the necessary resources for managing the expected demand increase.

QUESTION 8

Your company is exploring cost-efficient cloud solutions for batch processing tasks in Google Cloud. Which of the following scenarios would be most suitable for utilizing preemptible VM instances?

A) A continuous integration system for software development that requires consistent uptime.

B) Batch processing of satellite imagery for a mapping service, where tasks can be interrupted and resumed.
C) Hosting a primary database for a critical business application with high availability requirements.
D) Running a 24/7 online news portal with steady traffic.
E) A live streaming service for broadcasting events in real-time.

QUESTION 9

After deploying a major update to your cloud-based analytics platform, you notice an unexpected increase in API errors. The issue was promptly resolved by rolling back the update. As part of the retrospective, your goal is to apply SRE best practices. How should you proceed with the post-incident analysis?

A) Assign a team to specifically investigate and penalize the individual responsible for the error.
B) Review the deployment process to identify any gaps in testing and monitoring that led to the incident.
C) Focus on deploying the next set of features to keep up with the product roadmap.
D) Arrange meetings with each engineer involved in the update to determine who is at fault.
E) Analyze the incident holistically, looking at both technical and process improvements.

QUESTION 10

As the lead engineer for a multi-region cloud gaming service on GKE, you are exploring ways to reduce the network costs associated with high user traffic. What strategy should you adopt to achieve this?

A) Integrate a global CDN to efficiently distribute gaming content to players.
B) Shift to using smaller, more cost-effective machine types for your GKE nodes.
C) Deploy dedicated game servers in each region where you have a significant player base.
D) Implement aggressive caching mechanisms within the game to reduce data transfer.
E) Reconfigure your application to use HTTP instead of HTTPS to minimize data transfer overhead.

QUESTION 11

You have deployed a microservices architecture on GKE, which includes a critical service that interfaces with an external API. You want to optimize the scaling of this service based on its performance. What SLI would be most appropriate for scaling decisions?

A) Use the average response time of the external API calls as reported by the application logs.
B) Monitor the CPU and memory usage of the pods running the service and scale based on these metrics.
C) Implement a horizontal pod autoscaler targeting the rate of successful responses from the external API.
D) Establish a custom metric for the number of concurrent requests to the service and use it for autoscaling.
E) Scale based on the latency of network ingress to the pods servicing the external API calls.

QUESTION 12

Your organization needs a solution to handle sporadic computational jobs for financial modeling. These jobs require significant computing resources for short periods. The solution should be cost-effective and scalable. What approach would you recommend?

A) Configure a Cloud Storage bucket for job submissions, employing Cloud Functions to trigger processing jobs in a GKE cluster with autoscaling configured.

B) Develop a system using Compute Engine with preemptible VMs that automatically starts processing jobs when new data is uploaded to Cloud Storage.

C) Utilize App Engine to host the financial modeling application, setting up automatic scaling to manage computing resources based on job submissions.

D) Establish a Cloud Storage bucket for job submissions and use a Cloud Function with a google.storage.object.finalize trigger to initiate processing in an autoscaled Compute Engine managed instance group.

E) Set up a Cloud Scheduler job to regularly check a Cloud Storage bucket for new jobs and activate processing using a set of dedicated Compute Engine VMs.

QUESTION 13

Managing a cloud-based video conferencing service, you aim to establish an SLO that ensures a high-quality user experience. The service relies on a distributed microservices architecture. What SLI is most critical to monitor for maintaining user satisfaction?

A) Call setup SLI: the percentage of calls successfully set up within 10 seconds of initiation.

B) Video quality SLI: the proportion of calls with HD video quality without interruptions.

C) Audio clarity SLI: the ratio of calls with clear, uninterrupted audio throughout the duration.

D) Service availability SLI: the overall uptime of the video conferencing service.

E) Network latency SLI: the average latency experienced by users during video calls.

QUESTION 14

Your team plans to run a large-scale data processing task on Google Cloud for a three-month project. The task will require a steady amount of computing power and cannot be interrupted. You aim to manage the project cost-effectively. What approach should you take?

A) Utilize preemptible VMs for the data processing task to benefit from lower costs.

B) Purchase Committed Use Discounts for the Compute Engine instances needed for the task.

C) Set up a Managed Instance Group with autoscaling to adjust resources based on workload.

D) Deploy the task on regular Compute Engine instances and monitor usage to manually scale as needed.

E) Use Cloud Functions to handle the data processing, optimizing costs through its pay-per-use model.

QUESTION 15

Your company uses Terraform to manage infrastructure as code for deploying serverless solutions. You have modules that depend on both open-source and proprietary code. Your compliance department has raised concerns over using un-vetted open-source Terraform modules. You need to ensure consistent management of all modules, while enforcing access controls and maintaining compliance with VPC Service Con- trols. What action should you take?

A) Manage both open-source and proprietary modules using a self-hosted GitLab server integrated with Google Workspace for identity management.

B) Set up a Terraform module registry service within a Google Kubernetes Engine (GKE) cluster, using a Cloud Storage bucket for storing the modules.

C) Store both open-source and proprietary Terraform modules in OCI format using Artifact Registry.

D) Keep both types of Terraform modules in a version—con- trolled repository, and use Cloud Build to periodically copy the modules to a Cloud Storage bucket. Use the Cloud Storage bucket as a module source, specifying the URL format https://[bucket].storage-googleapis.com/[module].
E) None of the above.

QUESTION 16

Your organization follows DevOps principles, and you're the Incident Coordinator for a critical issue affecting clients. To ensure effective incident resolution, which two roles would you assign promptly?

A) Technical Lead
B) Third-party Vendor Liaison
C) Communications Coordinator
D) Operations Coordinator
E) Client Impact Analyst.

QUESTION 17

Your company is in the process of developing a new service to be hosted on Google Kubernetes Engine (GKE). The primary objective is to implement a solution that consolidates a wide range of service-level metrics into a single manageable platform. Your task is to use Google Cloud solutions while minimizing the initial monitoring setup effort. What should you do?

A) Embed the Cloud Pub/Sub client libraries into your service, send various metrics to different topics, and aggregate the metrics in Cloud Monitoring.
B) Convert all metrics into specific log entries for your service, transfer these logs from your containers to the Cloud Logging agent, and analyze metrics in Cloud Logging.
C) Integrate the OpenTelemetry client libraries within your service, direct metrics to Cloud Monitoring as the export target, and monitor service metrics in Cloud Monitoring.
D) Stream various metrics directly from your service to the Cloud Monitoring API, then access these customized metrics in Cloud Monitoring.

QUESTION 18

Your organization operates a widely-used project management platform on Google Cloud, and you need to evaluate its dependability from the user's perspective without making any software changes. What actions should you take to achieve this effectively? (Select two.)

A) Review the existing platform's telemetry data and introduce additional metrics if necessary.
B) Modify the application's source code to collect more detailed user activity data.
C) Analyze both historical and real-time project activity logs to understand user interactions with the platform.
D) Develop virtual user accounts capable of simulating typical user actions on the platform.
E) Focus exclusively on analyzing server resource logs to determine system performance.

QUESTION 19

Your Python web service on Google Kubernetes Engine (GKE) interacts extensively with external APIs, and you want to pinpoint potential performance degradation due to these integrations. What should you do to achieve this goal effectively?

A) Implement Cloud Profiler for all services.
 B) Modify the Python service to track API call durations and log this data. Utilize Cloud Logging to identify slow-response external APIs.
 C) Instrument all services with Cloud Trace and analyze span timings for external API calls.
 D) Deploy Cloud Debugger to inspect runtime state and execution flow across services.

QUESTION 20

Your company's e-commerce platform on Google Cloud experiences occasional latency issues during high-traffic periods. You want to optimize performance without incurring substantial additional costs. What should you do?

A) Upgrade all virtual machine instances to the highest CPU and memory configurations.
B) Implement autoscaling for the virtual machine instances to automatically adjust capacity based on demand.
C) Add more load balancers to distribute traffic evenly.
D) Increase the allocated bandwidth for the virtual machines.
E) Implement Google Cloud CDN to cache product images and reduce server load.

QUESTION 21

Your CI/CD pipeline, powered by Cloud Build, is failing to deploy a new version of your application to Google App Engine. The failure occurred after making changes to the deployment configuration. What should you do first to troubleshoot and resolve the issue?

A) Revert to the previous deployment configuration that was known to work.
B) Examine the build logs and error messages in Cloud Build to pinpoint the specific problem in the pipeline.
C) Pause the CI/CD pipeline to prevent further deployment failures.
D) Switch to a different App Engine environment to deploy the application.

QUESTION 22

Your team is responsible for a microservices-based application deployed on Google Kubernetes Engine (GKE). You want to ensure high availability and fault tolerance for the application. What action should you prioritize?

A) Use a single-node GKE cluster to reduce management overhead.
B) Deploy all microservices in the same availability zone for low latency.
C) Implement multi-zone GKE clusters and distribute microservices across zones.
D) Enable preemptible VMs for cost savings.

QUESTION 23

You are overseeing a Kubernetes cluster in Google Cloud for a microservices-based application. To ensure optimal resource allocation and performance, you want to identify pods that may need adjustment. What steps should you take? (Choose two.)

A) Monitor pod CPU usage and memory usage. If there's a significant gap between the two, adjust the resource requests and limits for the pods.
B) Review network traffic and storage I/O of the pods. If there's a considerable gap, consider resizing the underlying nodes.
C) Analyze pod response times, CPU utilization, and memory usage. If the response times negatively impact service objectives and the gap between CPU utilization and memory usage is small, label the pods for optimization.
D) Assess the persistent volume claims (PVC) usage patterns of the pods. If usage consistently remains high, flag the pods for optimization.
E) Check the pod restart rate and network latency. If you find a large disparity, expand the cluster capacity.

QUESTION 24

Following the launch of an image processing service on Google Cloud, you observe a rise in service latency and sporadic downtime, especially during peak usage hours. This has resulted in user complaints and potential revenue loss. To maintain service quality and customer satisfaction, what should be your initial response?

A) Adjust the auto-scaling settings of your cloud resources to handle peak loads better.
B) Immediately downgrade the service to its previous version.
C) Conduct a thorough investigation into resource utilization and traffic patterns.
D) Engage with customers directly to explain the situation and offer temporary workarounds.
E) Redistribute the workload across additional geographic regions to balance the load.

QUESTION 25

You are overseeing a cloud-based e-commerce application and want to monitor the rate of abandoned shopping carts. Events for cart abandonment are logged in Google Cloud Logging. How would you create a visual representation to track these events over time?

A) Set up a direct feed from Google Cloud Logging to Google Cloud Monitoring and create a dashboard for these specific events.
B) Configure a connection between Google Cloud Logging and Google Sheets, using scripts to analyze and visualize the data.
C) Implement a connection to BigQuery from Google Cloud Logging for detailed analysis and use Data Studio for visualization.
D) Use Google Cloud Profiler to analyze the abandonment events and display them on a custom dashboard.
E) Integrate Google Cloud Logging with a third-party visualization tool via API to chart the abandonment events.

QUESTION 26

Your company's cloud-hosted web application has seen increased traffic and occasional downtimes. You wish to implement an SLI to measure the availability of the web service. What metric should be used for this SLI?

A) The response time of the web server to HTTP requests.

B) The percentage of uptime of the web server against total time.
C) Number of user sessions that experience timeouts.
D) Bandwidth usage of the web server during peak hours.
E) The rate of new connections established with the web server.

QUESTION 27

As the Incident Commander for a cloud-based content delivery network experiencing a severe service disruption, your primary focus is to restore service. After assigning team roles, what should be your immediate next action?

A) Begin drafting an apology email to be sent to all users affected by the disruption.
B) Create a virtual war room for the incident response team to centralize communication and collaboration.
C) Start a thorough investigation into the underlying causes of the disruption.
D) Update the company website and social media channels with information about the outage.
E) Direct the team to bypass standard protocols to expedite service restoration.

QUESTION 28

You are integrating a third-party application into your GKE environment, which generates critical operational logs in a custom file path. Your task is to ensure these logs are collected in Stackdriver for analysis. The application is containerized but cannot be altered. How do you proceed?

A) Use a sidecar container with a shared volume to tail the log file and send logs to Stackdriver.
B) Modify the application's Dockerfile to change its logging path to a Stackdriver-compatible format.
C) Configure a Fluentd daemonset specifically to monitor and forward logs from the custom file path to Stackdriver.
D) Rely solely on GKE's default logging mechanisms without additional configurations.
E) Manually extract logs periodically and upload them to Stackdriver using a custom script.

QUESTION 29

You are managing a set of Virtual Machines (VMs) on Google Compute Engine (GCE) and need to monitor their system metrics in Cloud Monitoring. After setting up, you notice that metrics from some VMs are not appearing in Cloud Monitoring. What steps should you take to address this issue?

A) Verify that the Cloud Monitoring agent is installed and correctly configured on the VMs.
B) Check if the VMs' network configurations allow outbound connections to Cloud Monitoring endpoints.
C) Ensure that the service account associated with the VMs has the necessary permissions to write metrics to Cloud Monitoring.
D) Confirm that your user account has permissions to view Cloud Monitoring data for these VMs.
E) Investigate if the VMs are configured to use a custom metric namespace that is different from the default.

QUESTION 30

When configuring Terraform to authenticate with Google Cloud within a DevOps process, what is the most secure and recommended method for managing authentication credentials?

A) Share a single JSON key for a Google service account among all components of the CI/CD platform.
B) Embed the JSON key for a Google service account directly within the Terraform configuration files.
C) Utilize a separate JSON key for each infrastructure component and store them in a publicly accessible Git repository.
D) Secure the JSON key for a Google service account within your CI/CD platform's secrets management and configure Terraform to use it for authentication.
E) Leverage the GKE cluster's default service account for Terraform authentication.

QUESTION 31

You are responsible for deploying a critical backend service on Google Cloud. Load testing in the staging environment was limited, and you need to ensure a seamless and automated production deployment while monitoring performance. What should be your approach?

A) Deploy the service using a continuous delivery pipeline with canary releases. Monitor performance with Cloud Monitoring and incrementally increase traffic based on observed metrics.
B) Use kubectl to roll out the service and employ Config Connector to incrementally shift traffic between versions. Monitor performance with Cloud Monitoring and detect anomalies.
C) Implement the deployment with kubectl and configure the spec.updateStrategy.type to RollingUpdate. Use Cloud Monitoring to watch for performance issues, and if necessary, perform a rollback using kubectl.
D) Deploy the service through a continuous delivery pipeline using blue/green deployment patterns. Shift all traffic to the new version and monitor performance with Cloud Monitoring.

QUESTION 32

Your organization operates globally distributed GKE clusters managing various services. The current observability setup relies on Prometheus-based tools for collecting performance metrics, defining alerts, and visualizing data. However, this setup lacks the capability to effectively aggregate metrics across all clusters worldwide. What action should you take to achieve seamless global Prometheus queries and reduce administrative efforts?

A) Integrate individual cluster metrics with Cloud Monitoring for GKE.
B) Utilize Prometheus multi-level federation to centrally aggregate metrics.
C) Implement Google Cloud Managed Service for Prometheus.
D) Enable Prometheus cross-region federation to enable centralized metric collection.

QUESTION 33

You are managing the deployment of a web service on Google Kubernetes Engine (GKE) and need to ensure a reliable rollback mechanism. The development team follows blue/green deployment practices. What should you implement to achieve a seamless rollback capability?

A) Redirect traffic manually to the previous service version.
B) Execute a custom rollback script that reverts the changes made during deployment.
C) Adjust the replica count of the new deployment to zero to stop new Pods and restart the old ones.
D) Delete the new container image and let GKE replace it with the previous one.

QUESTION 34

Your organization operates a web application on Google Compute Engine instances. You want to monitor and analyze incoming and outgoing traffic at the network level to detect potential security threats. What should you do to achieve this goal with minimal complexity?

A) Enable VPC Flow Logs for the network subnet.
B) Implement a third-party network monitoring solution on the instances.
C) Activate firewall rules to log traffic information.
D) Deploy a dedicated network packet capture tool on each instance.

QUESTION 35

You are a member of a cloud infrastructure team implementing Site Reliability Engineering (SRE) principles. Your team is taking ownership of a new authentication service from the development group. After conducting a Production Readiness Review (PRR), it's evident that the system is not configured to meet its Service Level Objectives (SLOs). What should be your next step to ensure successful SLO attainment in the production environment?

A) Deploy the authentication service into production without established SLOs and develop them based on operational insights gained.
B) Notify the development group that they are responsible for supporting the system in production.
C) Adjust the SLO benchmarks to levels that the authentication service can meet to expedite its production deployment.
D) Identify necessary service enhancements for reliability that should be addressed before transitioning to production.

QUESTION 36

You are managing a cloud-based document collaboration platform, and the error budget for document synchronization has been fully depleted during the current observation period. The platform's users are planning a critical document collaboration session. How can you ensure a successful collaboration session while adhering to SRE principles?

A) Analyze additional performance metrics related to the document collaboration platform's operation and identify SLOs with available error budget. Reallocate error budget from these SLOs to support the collaboration session.
B) Notify the users about the exhausted error budget and request them to thoroughly test their collaboration materials to minimize synchronization issues during the session.
C) Initiate a formal process to obtain an increase in the error budget specifically for the collaboration session to ensure its success.
D) Inform the users about the depleted error budget and discuss the possibility of postponing the collaboration session or accepting potential synchronization problems during the session.

QUESTION 37

You are responsible for a Cloud Run service that generates semi-structured plain text logs. The requirement is to transition to structured logging in JSON format. What action should you take?

A) Develop a custom logging library for your service, ensuring that log records are created in JSON format with appropriate attributes.

B) Incorporate a third-party log processing tool with your Cloud Run service, configuring it to convert plain text logs into structured JSON.

C) Adjust the Cloud Run service settings to automatically convert plain text logs into structured JSON format.

D) Implement a log transformation script that runs alongside your Cloud Run service, converting logs to JSON and forwarding them to Cloud Logging.

QUESTION 38

How can you allocate costs for running cloud resources to different departments efficiently?

A) Assign a separate billing account to each department's project, enabling them to manage their own costs independently.

B) Use Google Cloud's Organization Policy to automatically allocate costs based on project usage and department affiliation.

C) Implement Google Cloud's Billing Groups to group projects by department and allocate costs accordingly.

D) Create custom scripts to extract cost data for each department and manually allocate expenses to their respective projects.

QUESTION 39

In your role as a cloud engineer, you are monitoring a Google Kubernetes Engine (GKE) cluster and notice an atypical number of requests originating from a certain IP. What is the best practice to track these requests in Cloud Monitoring with minimal upkeep?

A) Directly integrate a GKE-specific metric in Cloud Monitoring for the IP address.

B) Set up a log-based metric in Cloud Monitoring using GKE logs, and write a script to filter out requests from the unusual IP.

C) Alter the GKE application code to push metrics related to the IP directly to Cloud Monitoring.

D) Craft a script to parse GKE logs and forward metrics concerning the specific IP to Cloud Monitoring.

QUESTION 40

You are setting up an operational oversight system for a cloud-based healthcare data analysis platform using Google Cloud Operations Suite. The priority is to quickly identify issues in the patient data processing system while filtering out non-essential alerts from other projects. How do you structure access to maintain compliance with the least privilege principle?

A) Create a central Google Cloud monitoring project, initiate a Google Cloud Operations Workspace, and link only the patient data processing projects. Grant read access to relevant team members.

B) Provide Project Viewer IAM role to team members for all healthcare data analysis projects and set up separate Cloud Operations workspaces within each project.

C) Grant read access to team members on all patient data processing projects and configure individual Cloud Operations workspaces in each project.

D) Select an existing patient data processing project as the primary project for the Cloud Operations monitoring workspace.

QUESTION 41

In the wake of a network outage at your cloud service provider, which impacted your cloud-based application, you are tasked with enhancing operational resilience. What SRE principles should guide your actions to mitigate future occurrences?

A) Implement a robust monitoring system to detect and alert on similar network issues immediately.
B) Conduct a disciplinary review with the network team responsible for managing cloud resources.
C) Restructure the cloud resource management team to ensure more experienced oversight.
D) Develop and integrate automated failover mechanisms and redundancy for critical network components.

QUESTION 42

To ensure the scalability of your large-scale web application on Google App Engine, you need to monitor the instance count to manage auto-scaling effectively. What is the appropriate Stackdriver metric to track the number of App Engine instances?

A) appengine/system/instances/active
B) appengine/system/instances/total
C) appengine/flex/instances/count
D) appengine/system/auto_scaler/instance_count

QUESTION 43

Your e-commerce platform hosted on Google Cloud Platform is recording transaction logs with sensitive payment information. You need to ensure this data is filtered out promptly before reaching Cloud Logging. What is the most effective immediate action?

A) Request the development team to update the application code to prevent logging sensitive data.
B) Configure a Cloud Function to intercept and sanitize logs before they are stored in Cloud Logging.
C) Use the Fluentd filter plugin filter-record-modifier to remove sensitive information from logs in real-time.
D) Create a Data Loss Prevention (DLP) job in Google Cloud to automatically redact sensitive data from logs.

QUESTION 44

As a cloud administrator for a large e-commerce site, you want to monitor the average load time of your main page. The goal is to understand load time trends over time for optimization purposes. What type of metric and graph should you use in Google Cloud's Operations Suite to effectively track and visualize this data?

A) MetricKind: GAUGE, ValueType: DOUBLE, Visualization: Line graph
B) MetricKind: DELTA, ValueType: INT64, Visualization: Stacked Bar graph
C) MetricKind: CUMULATIVE, ValueType: DISTRIBUTION, Visualization: Heatmap graph
D) MetricKind: METRIC_KIND_UNSPECIFIED, ValueType: DOUBLE, Visualization: Stacked Area graph

QUESTION 45

In your multi-instance cloud database environment, one instance starts showing frequent timeouts, impacting user queries. What should be your approach to resolve this issue effectively while maintaining service availability?

A) Assess the load capacity of the remaining instances, inform the incident response team, reroute the traffic from the failing instance, and isolate it for analysis.
B) Immediately reroute all traffic from the failing instance to other instances, then report the incident for further investigation.
C) Enhance the processing power of the remaining instances first, then isolate the problematic instance and analyze the cause.
D) Create and integrate a new database instance into the cluster, reroute traffic to this new instance, then troubleshoot the problematic instance.

QUESTION 46

You're managing a multi-VPC setup in Google Cloud with services communicating across VPC boundaries. Recently, you observed that a service in VPC-A is unable to connect to a resource in VPC-B. You need to diagnose the network issue without direct access to the instances. What steps should you take?

A) Examine the VPC Flow Logs for both VPCs to identify any dropped packets or failed connections.
B) Conduct a Connectivity Test using the Network Intelligence Center to trace the path and identify any blockages between VPC-A and VPC-B.
C) Set up a temporary VM in VPC-A to run network diagnostics and check connectivity to VPC-B.
D) Use the gcloud command-line tool to perform a network analysis from VPC-A to VPC-B.

QUESTION 47

You're managing a complex application on Google Kubernetes Engine, and you want to ensure high availability and fault tolerance. Which Kubernetes feature should you utilize to achieve this?

A) Horizontal Pod Autoscaling
B) Pod Disruption Budgets
C) Node Affinity
D) DaemonSets
E) StatefulSets

QUESTION 48

You manage a platform that has consistently met its Service Level Objective (SLO) for the past 9 months, resulting in high user satisfaction. To align with Site Reliability Engineering (SRE) principles, what actions should you take? (Choose two.)

A) Tighten the SLO to set higher reliability standards.
B) Reallocate engineering resources to enhance reliability in other areas.
C) Prioritize the introduction of new features over reliability improvements.
D) Accelerate the platform's deployment frequency and risk tolerance.
E) Extend the scope of Service Level Indicators (SLIs).

QUESTION 49

Your organization is facing a critical security incident, and your team is responsible for managing communications. You receive messages from internal team members seeking updates and inquiries from external stakeholders concerned about the incident's impact. What is the most appropriate communication strategy to follow in this situation?

A) Forward all internal team member messages to the Communication Lead, allowing them to handle internal communications, and prioritize direct communications with external stakeholders.
B) Respond to internal team members promptly, aiming for updates every 20 minutes. Commit to 'next update' times.
C) Delegate the task of replying to internal team member messages to a trusted team member while focusing on direct communications with external stakeholders.
D) Provide regular updates to all parties involved, maintaining a 'next update' time commitment in all communications.

QUESTION 50

Your organization is planning a major update for a critical application on Google Cloud. How can you minimize system unavailability and expedite issue resolution after the update is deployed?

A) Set up a continuous integration (CI) pipeline with comprehensive regression tests executed upon each code push.
B) Employ the canary release methodology for gradual updates through a continuous delivery (CD) pipeline.
C) Develop a comprehensive disaster recovery plan with data backups and redundancy.
D) Mandate a code evaluation by at least two colleagues before integrating new updates.
E) Establish a dedicated incident response team with defined roles and responsibilities.
F) Insist on thorough automated performance testing by software engineers on their individual workstations before deployment.

PRACTICE TEST 9 - ANSWERS ONLY

QUESTION 1

Answer - D) Configure a Binary Authorization policy that enforces image verification for Compute Engine instances.

Option D is the recommended approach. Binary Authorization allows you to enforce policies on container images, ensuring that only authorized and verified images can be used for Compute Engine instances, thus improving security and compliance while minimizing manual efforts.
 Option A involves manual inspection, which can be time-consuming and error-prone.
 Option B focuses on access control but does not enforce image verification.
 Option C includes security scanning but lacks the direct enforcement of image policies during instance updates.

QUESTION 2

Answer - B) Implement autoscaling for the GKE cluster to dynamically adjust resources based on demand.

Option B is the recommended action to address periodic performance degradation during high load in a microservices architecture. Implementing autoscaling for the GKE cluster allows the system to dynamically adjust resources based on demand, ensuring optimal performance and user experience. This aligns with DevOps principles of scalability and resource efficiency.
 Option A suggests increasing resource limits, which may not be a sustainable solution and can lead to resource contention.
 Option C mentions optimizing code, which is important but may not fully address performance under high load.
 Option D proposes a load balancer, which helps with traffic distribution but does not address resource scaling.

QUESTION 3

Answer - A) 1 and 2

Implementing PodDisruptionBudgets to control disruptions during maintenance (Option 1) and using Horizontal Pod Autoscaling (HPA) to adjust resources dynamically (Option 2) are recommended Kubernetes concepts or techniques for ensuring high availability and reliability in a complex microservices architecture. These practices help maintain service availability and efficient resource utilization.
 Option 3, deploying multi-cluster clusters, may provide redundancy but adds complexity and may not directly address day-to-day high availability concerns.
 Option 4, setting up Network Policies, is important for network security but not the primary focus of availability and reliability.

QUESTION 4

Answer - B) Leverage VPC Service Controls to restrict dashboard configuration.

Option B is the correct choice as it efficiently restricts access to dashboard configuration using VPC Service Controls.
 Option A introduces Service Perimeter, which may not be necessary,
 Option C suggests custom roles that might not be needed,
 Option D grants a broad role without specific control.

QUESTION 5

Answer - A) Configure the Horizontal Pod Autoscaler and enable the cluster autoscaler.

Option A is the correct choice as it recommends configuring the Horizontal Pod Autoscaler and enabling the cluster autoscaler to dynamically adjust the number of Pods and nodes based on demand, optimizing resource usage.
 Option B fixes the node pool size, limiting scalability,
 Option C introduces the Vertical Pod Autoscaler, which is not necessary for this scenario,
 Option D also fixes the node pool size, limiting scalability.

QUESTION 6

Answer - A and B

Options A and B are the correct choices. Segmenting automation procedures into finer-grained components (A) reduces redundancy and streamlines the workflow. Implementing automatic progression confirmations (B) helps in achieving smoother transitions between stages, reducing manual interventions.
 Options C, D, and E are not directly related to optimizing the workflow.

QUESTION 7

Answer - B and D

Option B - The current 40% CPU utilization allows for workload growth without additional capacity.
 Option D - Implementing a horizontal pod autoscaler and conducting load testing is a proactive approach to manage the expected increase in demand.
 Options A and C are not the most suitable actions.

QUESTION 8

Answer - B) Batch processing of satellite imagery for a mapping service, where tasks can be interrupted and resumed.

A) Incorrect - Continuous integration systems require consistent uptime, which preemptible VMs cannot guarantee.
B) Correct - Preemptible VMs are ideal for interruptible tasks like batch processing, offering cost savings.
C) Incorrect - Critical databases need high availability, unsuitable for preemptible VMs.
D) Incorrect - A steady-traffic online portal requires consistent availability, not suited for preemptible

VMs.

E) Incorrect - Real-time broadcasting demands uninterrupted service, which preemptible VMs cannot ensure.

QUESTION 9

Answer - B) Review the deployment process to identify any gaps in testing and monitoring that led to the incident.

A) Incorrect - Punishing individuals is counterproductive to the principles of SRE.
B) Correct - This approach is in line with SRE practices, focusing on process improvement rather than blame.
C) Incorrect - Ignoring the incident to focus on new features can lead to repeated mistakes.
D) Incorrect - Individual fault-finding does not align with the blameless culture of SRE.
E) Incorrect - While a holistic analysis is good, this option does not emphasize the non-blame aspect of SRE.

QUESTION 10

Answer - A) Integrate a global CDN to efficiently distribute gaming content to players.

A) Correct - Using a CDN can effectively reduce network costs by distributing content closer to the users.
B) Incorrect - Smaller machine types reduce compute costs but do not directly impact network costs.
C) Incorrect - While regional servers provide performance benefits, they may not significantly reduce network costs.
D) Incorrect - Caching can help but may not be sufficient for a cloud gaming service with high data transfer needs.
E) Incorrect - Switching to HTTP compromises security and does not significantly reduce data transfer costs.

QUESTION 11

Answer - C) Implement a horizontal pod autoscaler targeting the rate of successful responses from the external API.

A) Incorrect - While response time is important, it might not directly reflect the service's scaling needs.
B) Incorrect - CPU and memory usage are general metrics and may not accurately represent the performance of API interactions.
C) Correct - Scaling based on the rate of successful API responses ensures the service scales in response to its actual workload.
D) Incorrect - Concurrent requests are a useful metric but do not directly indicate the success or performance of the service.
E) Incorrect - Network latency is more of a network performance metric and may not reflect the specific needs of the service.

QUESTION 12

Answer - B) Develop a system using Compute Engine with preemptible VMs that automatically starts processing jobs when new data is uploaded to Cloud Storage.

A) Incorrect - Cloud Functions and GKE might not provide the required computational power for intensive financial modeling jobs.
B) Correct - Preemptible VMs in Compute Engine offer a cost-effective solution for sporadic, resource-intensive tasks.
C) Incorrect - App Engine is more suited for web applications and might not handle the computational intensity required.
D) Incorrect - Cloud Functions may not have the necessary capacity for intensive computational jobs.
E) Incorrect - Using Cloud Scheduler and dedicated VMs might not be the most efficient or cost-effective method.

QUESTION 13

Answer - B) Video quality SLI: the proportion of calls with HD video quality without interruptions.

A) Incorrect - Call setup is important but does not encompass the ongoing quality of the call.
B) Correct - Video quality is a key aspect of user satisfaction in a video conferencing service.
C) Incorrect - While audio clarity is important, video quality typically has a higher impact on user perception of the service.
D) Incorrect - Service availability is a broader metric and does not directly measure call quality.
E) Incorrect - Network latency is a factor but does not directly address the end-to-end quality of the video calls.

QUESTION 14

Answer - B) Purchase Committed Use Discounts for the Compute Engine instances needed for the task.

A) Incorrect - Preemptible VMs are not suitable for tasks that cannot be interrupted.
B) Correct - Committed Use Discounts offer cost savings for consistent, long-term use of Compute Engine instances.
C) Incorrect - Autoscaling is not necessary for a task with steady computing needs and may lead to increased costs.
D) Incorrect - Manual scaling could be less efficient and might not optimize costs as effectively as Committed Use Discounts.
E) Incorrect - Cloud Functions are designed for short-lived, event-driven tasks, not steady, long-term processing tasks.

QUESTION 15

Answer - D) Keep both types of Terraform modules in a version—con- trolled repository, and use Cloud Build to periodically copy the modules to a Cloud Storage bucket. Use the Cloud Storage bucket as a module source, specifying the URL format https://[bucket].storage-googleapis.com/[module].

Option D is incorrect because it suggests using version control and Cloud Storage but doesn't provide a clear solution for access control and compliance with VPC Service Controls, which are essential in this scenario.
 Option E - Option E is incorrect because there is a suitable solution among the provided options (Option A) that addresses the compliance and access control concerns.

QUESTION 16

Answer - A) Technical Lead, C) Communications Coordinator

The Technical Lead (Option A) is essential for providing technical expertise and guidance during incident resolution. The Communications Coordinator (Option C) is crucial for managing communications, ensuring stakeholders are informed and updated during the incident.
 Option B - Third-party Vendor Liaison is not typically a core role during internal incident resolution.
 Option D - Operations Coordinator is important but may not be as pivotal as the Technical Lead and Communications Coordinator in the initial phase of incident resolution.
 Option E - Client Impact Analyst, while valuable, may not be among the two most pivotal roles during the initial incident response.

QUESTION 17

Answer - C) Integrate the OpenTelemetry client libraries within your service, direct metrics to Cloud Monitoring as the export target, and monitor service metrics in Cloud Monitoring.

Option C is the correct choice because it allows you to incorporate OpenTelemetry client libraries within your service and direct metrics to Cloud Monitoring, minimizing initial configuration effort for monitoring and providing a single manageable platform for service-level metrics.
 Option A - Option A suggests using Cloud Pub/Sub, which may not be the most direct approach for monitoring service-level metrics.
 Option B - Option B involves transferring metrics as logs, which may not be as efficient for monitoring service-level metrics.
 Option D - Option D mentions streaming metrics directly to the Cloud Monitoring API, which may require more configuration effort.

QUESTION 18

Answer - A) Review the existing platform's telemetry data and introduce additional metrics if necessary.
 Answer - C) Analyze both historical and real-time project activity logs to understand user interactions with the platform.

Option A and Option C are the correct choices.
 Option A - Examining existing telemetry data and adding more metrics, if needed, helps assess dependability without software modifications.
 Option B - Modifying the application's source code contradicts the requirement to avoid software changes.
 Option D - Developing virtual user accounts for simulation is not aligned with assessing dependability from the user's perspective.
 Option E - Focusing solely on server resource logs may not provide a complete user viewpoint.

QUESTION 19

Answer - B) Modify the Python service to track API call durations and log this data. Utilize Cloud Logging to identify slow-response external APIs.

Option B is the correct choice.
 Option B - Modifying the Python service to track API call durations and using Cloud Logging to identify

slow-response external APIs is an effective approach for identifying performance degradation due to API integrations.

Option A - Implementing Cloud Profiler may not provide detailed insights into external API performance.

Option C - Instrumenting services with Cloud Trace focuses on tracing but may not capture API performance nuances.

Option D - Deploying Cloud Debugger is more for debugging code and may not specifically address API integration performance.

QUESTION 20

Answer - B) Implement autoscaling for the virtual machine instances to automatically adjust capacity based on demand.

Explanation for Option B - Implementing autoscaling for virtual machine instances allows the platform to automatically adjust capacity based on demand, optimizing performance without significant additional costs. It ensures that the right amount of resources is allocated during high-traffic periods. This aligns with the goal of optimizing performance efficiently.

Explanation for Option A - Upgrading all virtual machine instances to the highest configurations may increase costs significantly without a guaranteed reduction in latency. It may not be the most cost-effective solution.

Explanation for Option C - Adding more load balancers may help distribute traffic but does not directly address the performance optimization issue and may incur unnecessary costs.

Explanation for Option D - Increasing the allocated bandwidth for virtual machines may not be sufficient to optimize performance during high-traffic periods and may not be cost-effective.

Explanation for Option E - While implementing Google Cloud CDN is beneficial for caching content, it primarily addresses static content like images and may not fully optimize the platform's performance and cost during high-traffic periods.

QUESTION 21

Answer - B) Examine the build logs and error messages in Cloud Build to pinpoint the specific problem in the pipeline.

Explanation for Option B - Examining the build logs and error messages in Cloud Build is the initial step to pinpoint the specific problem in the pipeline that caused the deployment failure. It provides crucial information for troubleshooting.

Explanation for Option A - Reverting to the previous deployment configuration should be considered after identifying and resolving the cause of the failure. It may not be necessary if the issue can be fixed in the current configuration.

Explanation for Option C - Pausing the CI/CD pipeline is a preventive measure and doesn't address the root cause of the failure. It should be done only after troubleshooting and resolving the issue.

Explanation for Option D - Switching to a different App Engine environment is a significant change and should be considered after identifying and addressing the cause of the deployment failure. It may not solve the issue.

QUESTION 22

Answer - C) Implement multi-zone GKE clusters and distribute microservices across zones.

Explanation for Option C - Implementing multi-zone GKE clusters and distributing microservices across zones enhances high availability and fault tolerance by minimizing the impact of zone failures.
Explanation for Option A - Using a single-node GKE cluster increases the risk of downtime and is not recommended for high availability.
Explanation for Option B - Deploying all microservices in the same availability zone may result in a single point of failure and is not a best practice for fault tolerance.
Explanation for Option D - Enabling preemptible VMs can provide cost savings but may not contribute directly to high availability and fault tolerance.

QUESTION 23

A) Monitor pod CPU usage and memory usage. If there's a significant gap between the two, adjust the resource requests and limits for the pods.
C) Analyze pod response times, CPU utilization, and memory usage. If the response times negatively impact service objectives and the gap between CPU utilization and memory usage is small, label the pods for optimization.

Option A involves monitoring pod CPU and memory usage, which are crucial for performance optimization. Adjusting resource requests and limits based on the gap between them can enhance resource allocation.
Option B focuses on network traffic and storage I/O, which may not directly address pod performance.
Option C considers response times, CPU utilization, and memory usage, making it suitable for identifying pods impacting service objectives negatively.
Option D assesses PVC usage patterns, but it does not cover other essential metrics.
Option E suggests expanding cluster capacity based on pod restart rate and network latency, which may not directly relate to CPU and memory utilization.

QUESTION 24

Answer - C) Conduct a thorough investigation into resource utilization and traffic patterns.

A) Adjusting auto-scaling might be beneficial but should follow an understanding of the specific cause of latency and downtime.
 B) Downgrading the service is a reactive measure that might not be necessary if the issue can be resolved with minor adjustments.
 C) This is the most logical first step, as it provides insights into why the service is experiencing increased latency and downtime, especially during peak hours.
 D) Customer engagement is important, but it should follow after identifying and starting to address the technical issues.
 E) Redistributing workload could help, but without understanding the root cause, this might not effectively resolve the issue.

QUESTION 25

Answer - A) Set up a direct feed from Google Cloud Logging to Google Cloud Monitoring and create a dashboard for these specific events.

Option A - This is the most direct and efficient way to visualize logged events within Google Cloud's native tools.

Option B - While Google Sheets can be used for data analysis, it is not as seamless or scalable as using Cloud Monitoring.
Option C - BigQuery and Data Studio are powerful tools but might be overkill for simple event tracking.
Option D - Cloud Profiler is more suited for performance profiling, not for event monitoring.
Option E - Using a third-party tool could work but is not as integrated or straightforward as using Google Cloud's native services.

QUESTION 26

Answer - B) The percentage of uptime of the web server against total time.

Option A - Response time is more about performance than availability.
Option B - Uptime percentage is a direct indicator of availability, making it a suitable SLI for this scenario.
Option C - While informative, session timeouts do not provide a complete picture of availability.
Option D - Bandwidth usage relates to capacity but not directly to availability.
Option E - Connection rates are more about demand and capacity than direct service availability.

QUESTION 27

Answer - B) Create a virtual war room for the incident response team to centralize communication and collaboration.

Option A - While communication with users is important, it's not the first action before internal coordination.
Option B - A virtual war room is crucial for effective and efficient coordination and communication during an incident.
Option C - Investigating causes is important but should come after establishing effective incident management processes.
Option D - Public updates are necessary but should be informed by the ongoing internal response efforts.
Option E - Bypassing protocols can lead to further issues; effective coordination should be the priority.

QUESTION 28

Answer - C) Configure a Fluentd daemonset specifically to monitor and forward logs from the custom file path to Stackdriver.

Option A - A sidecar container is a viable solution, but it may be less efficient than using a Fluentd daemonset.
Option B - Modifying the Dockerfile isn't possible as the application cannot be altered.
Option C - Configuring Fluentd to target specific log files and forward them to Stackdriver is the most efficient and scalable solution.
Option D - Default logging mechanisms may not capture logs from custom file paths.
Option E - Manual extraction is not scalable or reliable for continuous monitoring.

QUESTION 29

Answer - A) Verify that the Cloud Monitoring agent is installed and correctly configured on the VMs.

Option A - The Cloud Monitoring agent is essential for forwarding system metrics from VMs to Cloud Monitoring.
Option B - Network configurations could block data flow, but it's less likely if other VMs are reporting correctly.
Option C - The service account permissions are crucial for allowing the agent to send metrics.
Option D - User permissions impact data visibility but not data collection.
Option E - Custom metric namespaces could lead to metrics being stored in an unexpected location.

QUESTION 30

Answer - D) Secure the JSON key for a Google service account within your CI/CD platform's secrets management and configure Terraform to use it for authentication.

The most secure and recommended method is to store the JSON key within the CI/CD platform's secrets management and configure Terraform to use it. Other options introduce security risks or poor credential management practices.
Option A - Sharing a single JSON key among all components lacks security and isolation. Option B - Embedding the JSON key directly in Terraform files is insecure. Option C - Storing separate JSON keys in a public Git repository is a security risk. Option E - Leveraging the GKE cluster's default service account lacks control and security.

QUESTION 31

Answer - A) Deploy the service using a continuous delivery pipeline with canary releases. Monitor performance with Cloud Monitoring and incrementally increase traffic based on observed metrics.

Option B, using Config Connector, doesn't align with the concept of canary releases and gradual traffic increase.
Option C, using RollingUpdate, is a valid approach but doesn't leverage canary releases for gradual traffic increase and monitoring.
Option D, blue/green deployment, switches all traffic immediately and doesn't allow for gradual monitoring.

QUESTION 32

Answer - B) Utilize Prometheus multi-level federation to centrally aggregate metrics.

Option A, integrating with Cloud Monitoring, may not provide the comprehensive global aggregation required.
Option C, Google Cloud Managed Service for Prometheus, may not align with the existing Prometheus-based setup.
Option D, enabling cross-region federation, is not a standard Prometheus feature.

QUESTION 33

Answer - A) Redirect traffic manually to the previous service version.

- Option B involves a custom script, which may introduce complexity and potential issues.
- Option C stops all new Pods and restarts the old ones but lacks precision in the rollback process.

- Option D is not the recommended way to perform rollbacks on GKE.
Manually redirecting traffic to the previous service version (Option A) allows for a controlled and reliable rollback, ensuring a seamless transition in a blue/green deployment scenario on GKE.

QUESTION 34

Answer - A) Enable VPC Flow Logs for the network subnet.

Explanation:
Option A is the correct choice because enabling VPC Flow Logs for the network subnet provides network-level traffic monitoring and analysis without the need for complex third-party solutions or individual packet capture tools on instances.
Option B suggests implementing third-party solutions, which may introduce complexity and require additional configuration.
Option C, activating firewall rules to log traffic, may capture specific firewall-related information but is not as comprehensive as VPC Flow Logs.
Option D, deploying dedicated packet capture tools on instances, can be resource-intensive and challenging to manage at scale.

QUESTION 35

Answer - D) Identify necessary service enhancements for reliability that should be addressed before transitioning to production.

Option D is the correct choice as it aligns with SRE principles by prioritizing reliability improvements before deployment. It ensures that the system meets its SLOs in production.
Option A is incorrect as deploying without established SLOs may lead to operational issues. Option B is incorrect because it shifts the responsibility without addressing the problem. Option C is incorrect as modifying SLO benchmarks may compromise the desired reliability.

QUESTION 36

Answer - A) Analyze additional performance metrics related to the document collaboration platform's operation and identify SLOs with available error budget. Reallocate error budget from these SLOs to support the collaboration session.

Option A is the correct choice as it aligns with SRE principles by reallocating error budget from other SLOs to ensure a successful collaboration session.
Option B is incorrect as it focuses on testing but does not address the error budget issue directly.
Option C is incorrect as increasing the error budget may not be the best approach for managing errors.
Option D is incorrect as it suggests delaying the collaboration session or accepting potential synchronization problems without exploring other solutions.

QUESTION 37

Answer - A) Develop a custom logging library for your service, ensuring that log records are created in JSON format with appropriate attributes.

Option A is the correct choice as it involves developing a custom logging library within the Cloud Run

service to create log records in JSON format with the necessary attributes, meeting the requirement for structured logging.
Option B, C, and D suggest external solutions or configurations that may not be needed for achieving structured logging within Cloud Run.

QUESTION 38

C) Implement Google Cloud's Billing Groups to group projects by department and allocate costs accordingly.

Option C is the correct choice. Google Cloud's Billing Groups allow you to group projects by department and allocate costs automatically based on these groupings. This approach is efficient and aligns costs with departments accurately. Option A involves separate billing accounts, which can be complex to manage. Option B mentions Organization Policy but doesn't directly address cost allocation. Option D proposes manual scripts, which can be error-prone and time-consuming.

QUESTION 39

Answer - B) Set up a log-based metric in Cloud Monitoring using GKE logs, and write a script to filter out requests from the unusual IP.

Option A - Incorrect: GKE does not directly provide IP-specific metrics within Cloud Monitoring.
Option B - Correct: Utilizing log-based metrics and a script for IP-specific request filtering is the most effective and maintenance-efficient approach.
Option C - Incorrect: Modifying application code is more complex and less maintenance-efficient.
Option D - Incorrect: Manually scripting log parsing and metric forwarding is less efficient in terms of maintenance.

QUESTION 40

Answer - A) Create a central Google Cloud monitoring project, initiate a Google Cloud Operations Workspace, and link only the patient data processing projects. Grant read access to relevant team members.

Option A - Correct: This approach focuses on centralizing monitoring while adhering to the least privilege principle by restricting access to relevant projects.
Option B - Incorrect: Providing broad Project Viewer access contradicts the least privilege principle.
Option C - Incorrect: Individual workspaces for each project could lead to fragmented monitoring and excess privileges.
Option D - Incorrect: Using an existing project may not align with the centralized and focused monitoring required.

QUESTION 41

Answer - D) Develop and integrate automated failover mechanisms and redundancy for critical network components.

Option A - Incorrect: While monitoring is essential, it's reactive rather than preventive.
Option B - Incorrect: Focusing on punitive actions is not in line with constructive SRE practices.

Option C - Incorrect: Restructuring teams does not directly address technical or process improvements.
Option D - Correct: Enhancing system resilience with automated failover and redundancy aligns with SRE principles.

QUESTION 42

Answer - A) appengine/system/instances/active

Option A - Correct: This metric provides the current count of active instances, essential for evaluating auto-scaling.
Option B - Incorrect: Total instances may include inactive instances, which doesn't accurately reflect scaling.
Option C - Incorrect: This metric is specific to App Engine Flexible Environment and may not apply to all App Engine deployments.
Option D - Incorrect: This metric does not exist in Stackdriver for monitoring instance counts.

QUESTION 43

Answer - C) Use the Fluentd filter plugin filter-record-modifier to remove sensitive information from logs in real-time.

Option A - Incorrect: While important, code changes may not provide an immediate solution.
Option B - Incorrect: This approach can introduce delays and complexity.
Option C - Correct: Fluentd plugins like filter-record-modifier offer a real-time solution to modify logs before they reach Cloud Logging.
Option D - Incorrect: DLP jobs are effective but might not be the quickest solution for real-time log sanitization.

QUESTION 44

Answer - A) MetricKind: GAUGE, ValueType: DOUBLE, Visualization: Line graph

Option A - Correct: GAUGE with DOUBLE and a Line graph is appropriate for monitoring and visualizing average load times and trends.
Option B - Incorrect: DELTA and INT64 with a Stacked Bar graph are not the best choices for average load time trends.
Option C - Incorrect: CUMULATIVE and DISTRIBUTION are not ideal for average load time tracking.
Option D - Incorrect: METRIC_KIND_UNSPECIFIED does not provide a clear metric type for average load time analysis.

QUESTION 45

Answer - A) Assess the load capacity of the remaining instances, inform the incident response team, reroute the traffic from the failing instance, and isolate it for analysis.

Option A - Correct: This step-by-step approach ensures that service availability is maintained while addressing the issue efficiently.
Option B - Incorrect: Immediate rerouting without assessing other instances' capacity might overload them.

Option C - Incorrect: Preemptively enhancing processing power may not be necessary and could delay resolving the issue.
Option D - Incorrect: Adding a new instance could be more time-consuming than addressing the current issue.

QUESTION 46

Answer - B) Conduct a Connectivity Test using the Network Intelligence Center to trace the path and identify any blockages between VPC-A and VPC-B.

Option A - Incorrect: While VPC Flow Logs can provide insights, they may not pinpoint the exact issue in connectivity.
Option B - Correct: Network Intelligence Center's Connectivity Test can precisely diagnose network issues between VPCs.
Option C - Incorrect: Setting up a VM requires permissions and may not provide comprehensive diagnostics.
Option D - Incorrect: The gcloud tool requires instance access and might not offer detailed network path insights.

QUESTION 47

Answer - B) Pod Disruption Budgets

Option B, "Pod Disruption Budgets," is the correct choice to ensure high availability and fault tolerance by defining the allowed disruptions during maintenance. While other Kubernetes features (A, C, D, E) are important for various purposes, they do not directly address fault tolerance in the same way as Pod Disruption Budgets.

QUESTION 48

Answer - B) Reallocate engineering resources to enhance reliability in other areas.
E) Extend the scope of Service Level Indicators (SLIs).

Option A suggests making the SLO more stringent, which may not be necessary if user satisfaction and reliability are already high.
Option C prioritizes new features over reliability, which goes against SRE principles.
Option D focuses on accelerating deployment frequency, which might not align with maintaining reliability.
Options B and E are recommended actions to maintain a balance between reliability and deployment frequency.

QUESTION 49

Answer - D) Provide regular updates to all parties involved, maintaining a 'next update' time commitment in all communications.

Option D is the most appropriate strategy as it emphasizes providing regular updates to all parties involved and commits to 'next update' times during a critical security incident, ensuring effective communication.

Options A, B, and C prioritize direct communications with external stakeholders but do not address the need for regular updates and commitment to update times, which are crucial during such incidents.
Explanation:
Option A: Forwarding messages to the Communication Lead may lead to delays in communication with internal team members. Option B: While responding to internal team members promptly is important, it doesn't emphasize regular updates to all parties. Option C: Delegating tasks may not guarantee timely updates to internal team members. Option D: Provides a balanced approach with regular updates and a commitment to update times for effective communication with all parties involved.

QUESTION 50

Answer - B) Employ the canary release methodology for gradual updates through a continuous delivery (CD) pipeline.

Options A, C, D, E, and F - While these options may contribute to issue resolution and system reliability, they do not directly address minimizing disruptions and expediting issue resolution post-deployment.
 Option B is the correct choice as it focuses on gradual deployment and monitoring of updates, reducing the impact of potential issues and enabling faster issue resolution.

PRACTICE TEST 10 - QUESTIONS ONLY

QUESTION 1

Your company is managing a complex multi-cloud environment with resources spread across Google Cloud, AWS, and Azure. You need to implement a unified monitoring and alerting solution for all these environments. What approach should you take to achieve this, considering the Google Cloud DevOps best practices?

A) Use Google Cloud Operations for monitoring Google Cloud resources, set up AWS CloudWatch for AWS resource monitoring, and implement Azure Monitor for Azure resource monitoring

B) Leverage Google Cloud Monitoring for AWS and Azure resources, utilize Google Cloud Pub/Sub for cross-cloud event streaming, and implement Google Cloud Security Command Center for cross-cloud security

C) Implement Google Cloud VPN for secure cross-cloud communication, configure Google Cloud Identity and Access Management (IAM) for access control, and use Google Cloud Armor for DDoS protection

D) Set up Google Cloud Spanner for distributed database management, utilize Google Cloud CDN for content delivery, and deploy Google Cloud Load Balancing for traffic distribution

E) Use Google Cloud Deployment Manager for multi-cloud resource provisioning, implement Google Cloud Dataprep for data transformation, and configure Google Cloud Functions for serverless computing

F) Implement Google Cloud Cost Management tools for cost optimization, set up Google Cloud Storage for cross-cloud data backup, and deploy Google Cloud Memorystore for caching across clouds.

QUESTION 2

Your company's e-commerce platform experiences occasional spikes in traffic during special promotions. The platform is hosted on Google Kubernetes Engine (GKE), and you want to ensure it can handle these traffic spikes without performance degradation. You observe the following deviations in metrics during traffic spikes: - Average CPU usage: Typical state: 30% Current state during spikes: 80% - Memory consumption: Typical state: 40% Current state during spikes: 70% - Response time: Typical state: 50 milliseconds Current state during spikes: 500 milliseconds What action should you take to optimize performance during traffic spikes while adhering to Google's recommended DevOps practices?

A) Increase the CPU and memory limits for the Pods in the GKE cluster.

B) Implement manual scaling to add more Pods to the GKE cluster during traffic spikes.

C) Set up horizontal pod autoscaling (HPA) for the GKE cluster to automatically adjust the number of Pods based on resource utilization.

D) Optimize the microservices code to reduce CPU and memory consumption.

QUESTION 3

You are responsible for securing the CI/CD pipeline for your organization's critical applications on Google Cloud. Which two security best practices should you prioritize for your CI/CD pipeline? I. Implement automated vulnerability scanning for container images. 2. Store sensitive credentials and keys in plaintext within the CI/CD configuration files. 3. Use a shared Google Cloud Storage bucket for storing all build artifacts. 4. Enable multi-factor authentication (MFA) for CI/CD pipeline access.

A) 1 and 2
B) 2 and 3
C) 3 and 4
D) 1 and 4

QUESTION 4

In managing a high-traffic media streaming service on GKE with various microservices, how can you identify containers demanding the most system resources, particularly CPU and memory?

A) Deploy Prometheus to collect and aggregate container logs, then analyze data in Grafana.
B) Implement Cloud Logging to funnel application logs into BigQuery, cluster logs by container, and analyze resource usage for CPU and memory.
C) Leverage the Cloud Monitoring API to create custom metrics and categorize containers into clusters.
D) Utilize Cloud Monitoring with GKE support.

QUESTION 5

Your enterprise manages a video streaming platform on GKE with variable viewer traffic patterns. What's the best approach to optimize resource usage by auto-adjusting Pods and nodes based on demand?

A) Configure the Horizontal Pod Autoscaler and enable the cluster autoscaler.
B) Configure the Horizontal Pod Autoscaler but fix the size of the node pool.
C) Configure the Vertical Pod Autoscaler and enable the cluster autoscaler.
D) Configure the Vertical Pod Autoscaler but fix the size of the node pool.

QUESTION 6

You're examining your media processing workflow in Google Cloud's Dataflow with the goal of reducing repetitive tasks and shortening job execution times. What actions should you consider? (Choose two.)

A) Segment the automation procedures into finer-grained components.
B) Implement automatic progression confirmations transferring from the staging area to the production zone.
C) Run a script to facilitate the setup of the media processing workflow in Google Cloud Dataflow.
D) Set up an alert to inform the designated team to proceed with the next phase when human input is needed.
E) Increase the number of personnel to execute hands-on steps.

QUESTION 7

As a DevOps engineer, you're tasked with optimizing a multi-tier web application hosted on Google Cloud. The application experiences heavy traffic on weekends and moderate usage on weekdays. It's hosted on a GKE regional cluster with nodes in three zones. Your goal is to maintain high availability and optimize for cost. What would be your strategy to handle the varying traffic?

A) Implement a horizontal pod autoscaler and enable cluster autoscaler based on CPU and memory metrics.

B) Deploy additional nodes in each zone to cater to the maximum expected traffic.
C) Use a vertical pod autoscaler to automatically adjust pod sizes based on usage.
D) Manually scale up the resources every Friday and scale down on Mondays.
E) Set up a custom metric for autoscaling based on the number of user requests.

QUESTION 8

As a cloud architect, you are tasked with reducing operational costs for non-critical computational workloads in Google Cloud. Which of these tasks would be best suited to leverage the cost benefits of preemptible VM instances?

A) Running a customer support chatbot that provides real-time assistance.
B) A non-urgent data analytics job that aggregates monthly sales data.
C) Operating the primary web server for a high-traffic news website.
D) A machine learning model training task that can be paused and resumed without data loss.
E) Hosting an online multiplayer game server with continuous player interaction.

QUESTION 9

Your cloud service experienced a significant slowdown following a database schema update. The issue was mitigated by reverting to the previous schema. As the leader of the retrospective, you are committed to following SRE best practices. What is the best approach for conducting this analysis?

A) Trace the update's approval process to hold accountable the person who signed off on it.
B) Understand the sequence of events leading to the slowdown, focusing on systemic improvements.
C) Shift the team's focus to upcoming projects, avoiding dwelling on past errors.
D) Organize a review meeting to pinpoint which team member made the critical mistake.
E) Investigate the incident from a system-wide perspective, enhancing communication and review processes.

QUESTION 10

Your organization's cloud-based application is experiencing frequent outages due to developers testing in the production environment. You need to restructure the development workflow to enhance stability. What is the best approach?

A) Set up a continuous integration/continuous deployment (CI/CD) pipeline with automated testing in a separate staging environment before production deployment.
B) Restrict all testing to local development machines before pushing changes directly to the production environment.
C) Implement a strict policy where developers can only test during off-peak hours to minimize the impact on the production environment.
D) Create a clone of the production environment with limited resources for all testing and development activities.
E) Conduct all development and testing in the production environment but with enhanced real-time monitoring.

QUESTION 11

Your team is running a stateful database service in GKE, which experiences varying loads throughout the day. You want to optimize the scaling of the database pods based on operational efficiency. Which SLI would be most effective for this purpose?

A) Scale the pods based on the number of active connections to the database service.
B) Utilize the disk I/O operations per second (IOPS) of the database pods for autoscaling.
C) Implement horizontal pod autoscaling based on the average query response time.
D) Monitor the network throughput of the pods and scale based on the data transfer rates.
E) Set up a vertical pod autoscaler to adjust the resources of each pod based on CPU utilization.

QUESTION 12

You are designing a cloud-based system for processing and analyzing high-volume social media data. The data arrives in unpredictable bursts and requires immediate processing. The solution should optimize for cost and processing efficiency. What is the best setup for this scenario?

A) Utilize Cloud Storage for data uploads and set up a Pub/Sub system to trigger Dataflow jobs for processing and analysis, scaling resources based on data volume.
B) Deploy a GKE cluster with a continuous listening service for new data in Cloud Storage, using autoscaling to adjust resources for data processing.
C) Configure a Cloud Storage bucket to receive data and use Cloud Functions triggered by data uploads to process and analyze the data.
D) Create a set of Compute Engine VMs that constantly check Cloud Storage for new data and start processing upon detection.
E) Implement a Cloud Storage bucket for data collection and trigger BigQuery jobs for immediate analysis, using a custom script to manage resource scaling.

QUESTION 13

Your company uses Google Cloud for deploying a range of services and aims to maintain infrastructure consistency with an IaC approach. You're responsible for ensuring that the cloud infrastructure stays aligned with the defined configurations in your version control system. What strategy should you implement?

A) Configure a Cloud Build trigger to automatically execute Terraform scripts upon every commit to the version control repository.
B) Use a scheduled Cloud Function to run Terraform commands periodically to ensure infrastructure alignment.
C) Develop a custom script that regularly checks the state of resources in Google Cloud and manually aligns them with the Terraform configurations.
D) Implement a continuous deployment pipeline using Jenkins to apply Terraform configurations on a daily schedule.
E) Set up a Google Cloud Pub/Sub service to trigger Terraform scripts based on specific events in the cloud environment.

QUESTION 14

Your organization is deploying a year-long research project requiring significant computational resources on Google Cloud. The project will use a fixed number of Compute Engine instances continuously. Cost optimization is a priority, but the instances need to be available at all times. What is the best cost management strategy?

A) Implement a Managed Instance Group with autoscaling to efficiently manage the number of instances based on the project's needs.
B) Opt for preemptible VMs to take advantage of lower pricing, despite the possibility of occasional interruptions.
C) Purchase Committed Use Discounts for a set number of Compute Engine instances to be used for the project duration.
D) Regularly review and adjust the machine types of the instances to ensure cost-effective resource utilization.
E) Use Spot VMs for the project, balancing cost savings with the risk of occasional instance preemptions.

QUESTION 15

You're responsible for managing a Google Cloud Operations Suite custom dashboard that contains critical monitoring data. A colleague from a partner organization needs temporary access to the dashboard. What's the most secure way to provide access?

A) Share your Google account credentials with your colleague.
B) Create a new user account within your organization's Google Cloud project for your colleague.
C) Export the dashboard as a JSON file and send it to your colleague.
D) Share the dashboard via a generated link with limited access duration.

QUESTION 16

Your organization is committed to DevOps principles, and you're the Incident Coordinator for a critical issue impacting clients. To swiftly and effectively address the incident, which two roles would you assign?

A) Technical Lead
B) Third-party Compliance Officer
C) Communications Coordinator
D) Operations Coordinator
E) Client Impact Analyst.

QUESTION 17

Your organization is developing a new service to be hosted on Google Kubernetes Engine (GKE). The top priority is to implement a solution that aggregates and organizes various service-level metrics into a single manageable platform. Your responsibility is to leverage Google Cloud solutions while minimizing the initial monitoring setup effort. What steps should you take?

A) Embed the Cloud Pub/Sub client libraries into your service, send different metrics to various topics, and aggregate the metrics in Cloud Monitoring.
B) Convert all metrics into specific log entries for your service, transfer these logs from your containers

to the Cloud Logging agent, and analyze metrics in Cloud Logging.
 C) Integrate the OpenTelemetry client libraries within your service, direct metrics to Cloud Monitoring as the export target, and monitor service metrics in Cloud Monitoring.
 D) Stream various metrics directly from your service to the Cloud Monitoring API, then access these customized metrics in Cloud Monitoring.

QUESTION 18

Your healthcare technology firm is launching a patient management system for a nationwide health awareness week, expecting a significant increase in user traffic. To prepare for potential outages due to high demand, what steps should you take? (Choose two.)

A) Set up continuous monitoring using Cloud Monitoring to track vital system metrics and establish alerts for critical thresholds.
 B) Configure Cloud Monitoring to generate notifications for each common failure observed in your system's operations.
 C) Monitor disk space utilization and network bandwidth consistently.
 D) Implement a serverless architecture to handle the surge in traffic efficiently.
 E) Assess the anticipated traffic increase and request the necessary quota adjustments in advance.

QUESTION 19

Your Python web service hosted on Google Kubernetes Engine (GKE) interacts extensively with external APIs, and you need to identify potential performance issues caused by these integrations. What is the recommended course of action to achieve this goal?

A) Apply Cloud Profiler to all services.
 B) Modify the Python service to record API call durations and log this data. Use Cloud Logging to analyze slow-response external APIs.
 C) Instrument all services with Cloud Trace and analyze span timings for external API calls.
 D) Deploy Cloud Debugger to inspect the runtime state and execution flow across services.

QUESTION 20

Your organization is experiencing increased build times in Google Cloud Build due to resource contention. You want to improve build efficiency while keeping costs in check. What should you do?

A) Increase the number of available build triggers to accommodate concurrent builds.
B) Implement a build queue system to prioritize and manage build requests.
C) Upgrade all build instances to higher machine types with more CPU and memory.
D) Manually trigger builds during off-peak hours to avoid contention.
E) Use Cloud Run for specific build tasks to reduce load on Cloud Build.

QUESTION 21

You are responsible for deploying a highly scalable web application on Google Cloud that needs to handle fluctuating traffic efficiently. The application must be available across multiple regions. What should you do to ensure high availability and scalability?

A) Deploy the application in a single region and use a global HTTP(S) load balancer to distribute traffic.
B) Utilize a small instance type to keep costs low while ensuring scalability.
C) Check the resource utilization of the application in real-time to adjust the instance count as needed.
D) Implement the application in multiple regions and configure a global HTTP(S) load balancer to distribute traffic among them.

QUESTION 22

You are managing a critical financial application that requires constant monitoring and alerting to ensure reliability and security. What should be your approach to meet these requirements?

A) Use manual log analysis to detect issues and incidents.
B) Implement automated monitoring and alerting using Google Cloud Monitoring and Google Cloud Logging.
C) Rely on periodic manual checks of the application's performance.
D) Utilize third-party monitoring tools for real-time insights.

QUESTION 23

You are managing a serverless computing environment in Google Cloud. To optimize the cost and performance of functions, you want to identify functions that may require adjustments. What actions should you take? (Choose two.)

A) Monitor function execution times and memory usage. If there's a significant gap between the two, adjust the allocated memory for the functions.
B) Review the network requests and storage operations of the functions. If there's a considerable gap, consider changing the function triggers.
C) Analyze function response times, CPU utilization, and memory usage. If the response times negatively impact service objectives and the gap between CPU utilization and memory usage is small, label the functions for optimization.
D) Assess the function concurrency patterns. If concurrency consistently remains high, flag the functions for optimization.
E) Check the invocation rate and network latency of the functions. If you find a large disparity, expand the function memory allocation.

QUESTION 24

You are managing a multi-regional e-commerce application on Google Cloud and need to set up a monitoring system for your globally distributed team. The goal is to enable region-specific teams to view performance metrics of their respective regions without accessing other regions' data. How do you configure access to uphold the principle of least privilege?

A) Share a global monitoring dashboard URL with each regional team. Assign the Viewer role to all team members.
 B) Create region-specific monitoring dashboards and share them via URL. Assign the Monitoring Viewer role for respective regions.
 C) Provide each regional team with Viewer access to the entire project.
 D) Generate individual monitoring dashboards for each region and assign the Project Viewer role to each regional team.

E) Create a centralized monitoring dashboard and assign the Monitoring Editor role to regional team leads only.

QUESTION 25

As a cloud administrator, you need to track the occurrence of server errors (HTTP 500) in a web application hosted on Google Cloud. You want to visualize the frequency of these errors for analysis. What is the best approach to achieve this?

A) Create a logs-based metric in Google Cloud Logging and use Google Cloud Monitoring to visualize the data.
B) Directly export the logs to a Google Cloud SQL instance and use SQL queries for visualization.
C) Set up a routine to export logs to an external database and use a BI tool for error analysis and visualization.
D) Use Google Cloud Profiler to analyze server errors and display the results on a custom monitoring dashboard.
E) Configure Google Cloud Logging to send notifications for each server error event to a monitoring dashboard.

QUESTION 26

You oversee a cloud-based image rendering service that occasionally fails to process requests during peak usage. To address this, you plan to establish a reliability SLI. What is the most appropriate way to define this SLI?

A) The number of rendering tasks completed without errors.
B) The average time taken to render an image.
C) The ratio of successfully processed requests to total requests.
D) GPU utilization rates on the rendering servers.
E) The size of the request queue for image rendering tasks.

QUESTION 27

Your team is developing a cloud-native application using Kubernetes and Terraform. You need to ensure that infrastructure changes are automatically tested for compliance before being merged. Which approach would you take?

A) Set up GitHub Actions to run compliance tests on every pull request to the main branch.
B) Use Jenkins to execute compliance tests nightly on all development branches.
C) Require developers to manually run compliance tests before submitting pull requests.
D) Configure GitLab CI/CD pipelines to automatically execute compliance tests upon any commit to a development branch.
E) Implement Cloud Build to run tests only post-merge into the main branch.

QUESTION 28

Your team is deploying a non-modifiable, external API service on Google Cloud Run. The service writes important logs to a specific file. You need these logs to be available in Stackdriver for compliance. What approach should you adopt?

A) Configure the Cloud Run service to automatically redirect all file-based logs to Stackdriver.
B) Implement a log-forwarding agent within the service's container to send file logs to Stackdriver.
C) Utilize Cloud Run's default logging capabilities without additional configuration.
D) Schedule a Cloud Function to periodically read the log file and write entries to Stackdriver.
E) Instruct the team to manually monitor and report on the log file as part of their daily duties.

QUESTION 29

You have configured Cloud Logging for a set of Cloud Functions but are not seeing any logs in the Cloud Logging console. What are the first steps you should take to diagnose and resolve the logging issue?

A) Ensure that the Cloud Functions are writing logs to stdout or stderr.
B) Check if the Cloud Functions have the necessary IAM roles to write logs to Cloud Logging.
C) Verify that your user account has the appropriate permissions to access logs in Cloud Logging.
D) Confirm that the Cloud Functions are triggering correctly and executing their intended operations.
E) Review the network settings to ensure that Cloud Functions can communicate with Cloud Logging endpoints.

QUESTION 30

You are overseeing a large-scale IT project that involves deploying microservices on Google Cloud. To optimize service performance, what should you prioritize?

A) Reducing the number of microservices to simplify the architecture.
B) Implementing caching mechanisms at the service level.
C) Increasing the size of the microservices to handle more requests.
D) Minimizing the use of load balancing for microservices.

QUESTION 31

You are managing a complex application running on Google Kubernetes Engine (GKE). Due to limited load testing in the staging environment, you need to ensure a smooth and automated production deployment while keeping an eye on performance. What should you prioritize?

A) Use kubectl to roll out the application and employ Config Connector to incrementally shift traffic between versions. Leverage Cloud Monitoring to detect any performance anomalies.
B) Implement the deployment with kubectl and configure the spec.updateStrategy.type to RollingUpdate. Watch for performance issues via Cloud Monitoring, and if problems occur, utilize the kubectl rollback command to revert.
C) Deploy the application through a continuous delivery pipeline using blue/green deployment patterns. Switch all traffic to the new version and monitor performance with Cloud Monitoring.
D) Deploy the application using a continuous delivery pipeline with canary releases. Monitor the application performance using Cloud Monitoring, and gradually increase traffic based on the observed metrics.

QUESTION 32

Your company operates an online gaming platform with globally distributed game servers managed by Google Kubernetes Engine (GKE) clusters. Your engineering team has implemented observability using

Prometheus-based tools for collecting performance metrics, setting alerts, and visualizing data. However, this setup lacks the capability to aggregate metrics comprehensively across all clusters. You are tasked with introducing a scalable solution that facilitates seamless global Prometheus queries and reduces administrative tasks. What action should you take?

A) Integrate individual game server metrics with Cloud Monitoring for GKE.
B) Utilize Prometheus multi-level federation to centrally aggregate metrics.
C) Set up Google Cloud Managed Service for Prometheus.
D) Implement Prometheus cross-region federation to enable centralized metric collection.

QUESTION 33

Your organization is managing a large-scale containerized application on Google Kubernetes Engine (GKE). You want to ensure that in the event of a node failure, your application remains available. What strategy should you implement to achieve this high availability?

A) Use Kubernetes DaemonSets to ensure that each node runs a specific container, reducing the impact of node failures on the application.
B) Deploy your application across multiple regions to minimize the risk of regional outages affecting availability.
C) Utilize PodDisruptionBudgets to control the eviction of pods during maintenance or node failures, ensuring that a minimum number of pods remain running.
D) Implement Horizontal Pod Autoscaling to automatically adjust the number of replicas to compensate for node failures, maintaining application availability.

QUESTION 34

Your company's web application is hosted on Google Compute Engine instances. To improve security, you want to track all incoming SSH connections and capture their source IP addresses for analysis. What should you do to achieve this with minimal administrative overhead?

A) Enable VPC Flow Logs for the network subnet.
B) Set up custom logging in the SSH service configuration.
C) Deploy a dedicated SSH monitoring tool on each instance.
D) Create a central log aggregation system to collect SSH logs from all instances.

QUESTION 35

Your team is implementing Site Reliability Engineering (SRE) methodologies at a cloud-based streaming service provider. You are taking ownership of a new content delivery system from the development group. After conducting a Production Readiness Review (PRR), it becomes evident that the system is not currently configured to meet its Service Level Objectives (SLOs). What should you do to ensure successful SLO attainment in the production environment?

A) Deploy the content delivery system into production without established SLOs and develop them based on operational insights gained.
 B) Inform the development group that they will be responsible for supporting the system in production.
 C) Adjust the SLO benchmarks to levels that the content delivery system can meet to expedite its production deployment.

D) Identify necessary service enhancements for reliability that should be addressed before the transition.

QUESTION 36

You are managing a cloud-based data analytics platform, and a recent service outage prompted a postmortem analysis. Now, to prevent future issues, how should you allocate responsibility for postmortem resolution tasks?

A) Designate a responsible owner for each resolution task and involve collaborators as necessary.
 B) Nominate collaborators without explicitly assigning ownership to foster a non-punitive postmortem environment.
 C) Assign multiple task owners for each issue to ensure speedy problem resolution.
 D) Appoint the platform's lead engineer as the main owner of all resolution tasks due to their overall responsibility for system stability.

QUESTION 37

You manage a Cloud Run service that currently generates semi-structured logs in plain text. The requirement is to switch to structured logging using JSON format. What should you do?

A) Develop a custom logging library for your Cloud Run service, ensuring that log records are created in JSON format with the required attributes.
 B) Incorporate a third-party log processing tool with your Cloud Run service, configuring it to parse plain text logs into structured JSON.
 C) Adjust the Cloud Run service's log settings to automatically convert plain text logs into structured JSON format.
 D) Implement a log transformation script that runs alongside your Cloud Run service, converting logs to JSON and sending them to Cloud Logging.

QUESTION 38

You are managing a video processing service on Cloud Run, and you need to transition from plain text logs to structured JSON logs. How can you achieve this efficiently?

A) Adapt the service to employ the Cloud Logging library, ensuring that log records are created with a jsonPayload attribute.
 B) Attach a Fluentd sidecar to your Cloud Run service, configuring it to parse logs into JSON format.
 C) Adjust the settings of the logging agent to transform plain text log messages into JSON structured data.
 D) Embed the logging agent within the Cloud Run service's container image, then utilize this agent to relay log data to Cloud Logging.

QUESTION 39

As an SRE, you are involved in optimizing a new cloud-based analytics platform on Google Cloud. Your input is requested to enhance the operational efficiency of the system. At what stage should you contribute your expertise for maximum impact?

A) Initiate a pilot test of the platform in a controlled environment, evaluate scalability and reliability, and provide feedback to the developers.
B) Engage after the system passes basic quality assurance tests, deploy it in a staging environment, and report any performance or reliability issues.
C) Work closely with the development team from the outset, focusing on the system's architectural design to ensure operational viability.
D) Wait until the system is deployed in a production environment by a department, then analyze error logs and performance metrics to give feedback.

QUESTION 40

In managing a multi-tier e-commerce platform on Google Cloud, you need to efficiently monitor critical payment gateway operations while minimizing distractions from alerts in non-production environments. What strategy should you employ to align with best practices in access control and operational efficiency?

A) Establish a dedicated Google Cloud monitoring project with a Cloud Operations Workspace linked to payment gateway projects, giving necessary team members read-only access.
B) Allocate the Project Viewer IAM role to key team members across all e-commerce platform projects, with individual Cloud Operations workspaces in each.
C) Provide necessary team members with read permissions for all e-commerce platform projects, setting up Cloud Operations workspaces in each one.
D) Use a primary e-commerce platform project as the anchor for the Cloud Operations monitoring workspace.

QUESTION 41

Following an incident where a database misconfiguration led to data inconsistencies in your real-time analytics platform, you are developing a strategy to prevent future occurrences. What SRE guidelines should you follow to enhance system reliability?

A) Introduce a more rigorous code review and approval process for all database configuration changes.
B) Identify the team members involved in the misconfiguration and take necessary disciplinary actions.
C) Mandate additional training for all staff involved in database management and configuration.
D) Incorporate automated checks in the deployment process to validate database configurations against predefined standards.

QUESTION 42

As a cloud infrastructure lead in a financial services firm, you need to manage Terraform configurations for a growing team. It's essential to prevent conflicting changes and ensure comprehensive documentation of updates. How should you organize and manage your Terraform configurations?

A) Utilize a cloud-based file storage service for Terraform files, with a structured directory and manual versioning system. Regularly upload updated files to a versioned bucket.
B) Store Terraform files in a centralized file system, with a manual check-in/check-out process for team members. Use a dated naming convention for version tracking.
C) Implement a Git-based version control system for Terraform files, using branches and pull requests to manage changes and ensure code reviews before merging.

D) Save Terraform files in a distributed file system, allowing team members to independently update and merge changes. Periodically, sync these files to a versioned cloud storage.

QUESTION 43

In a cloud-based healthcare application, logs are being generated with patient data, which needs immediate redaction from the logs. What approach should you take to ensure compliance and prevent sensitive data from being logged in Cloud Logging?

A) Adjust the application's logging configuration to exclude sensitive data from logs.
B) Use a Google Cloud Dataflow job to process and redact sensitive information from logs before they are stored.
C) Implement the Fluentd fluent-plugin-sanitizer to filter and sanitize logs as they are collected.
D) Configure a Cloud Pub/Sub topic to process logs and remove sensitive data using a Cloud Function before logging.

QUESTION 44

You are tasked with monitoring the number of active users on a video conferencing service hosted on Google Cloud. You need to visualize the data to see the peaks and troughs in user activity throughout the day. What metric configuration and graph type should you select in Google Cloud's Operations Suite?

A) MetricKind: GAUGE, ValueType: INT64, Visualization: Line graph
B) MetricKind: DELTA, ValueType: DOUBLE, Visualization: Stacked Bar graph
C) MetricKind: CUMULATIVE, ValueType: DISTRIBUTION, Visualization: Heatmap graph
D) MetricKind: METRIC_KIND_UNSPECIFIED, ValueType: INT64, Visualization: Stacked Area graph

QUESTION 45

You manage a cloud-based application on Google Cloud and need to set up email alerts for your team in case of critical system errors detected by Cloud Monitoring. What steps should you take to ensure prompt and effective notification to your team?

A) Directly configure email alerts in Cloud Monitoring for each monitoring policy and ensure team members have their email addresses set up in their Cloud Monitoring profiles.
B) Use the Cloud Monitoring Webhook alert feature to integrate with an external email notification service, where team members register their email addresses.
C) Set up alerts in Cloud Monitoring to send notifications to a dedicated Slack channel, then configure Slack to forward these alerts to team emails.
D) Implement a third-party email notification service that integrates with Cloud Monitoring and have team members input their email details in this system.

QUESTION 46

In your Google Cloud environment, two applications in different VPCs (VPC-X and VPC-Y) are experiencing intermittent connectivity issues. As a network administrator, you are tasked with identifying the cause of these issues. What approach should you take, given limited instance access?

A) Enable VPC Flow Logs in both VPC-X and VPC-Y and analyze the traffic patterns for anomalies.

B) Utilize the Network Intelligence Center's Connectivity Test to assess the network path between the two VPCs.
C) Deploy network diagnostic VMs in both VPCs to perform traceroute tests between the applications.
D) Configure a third-party network monitoring tool to observe traffic between VPC-X and VPC-Y.

QUESTION 47

You are tasked with optimizing the cost of running containerized workloads on Google Kubernetes Engine. What approach should you consider to achieve cost-efficiency while maintaining performance?

A) Use preemptible VMs for all nodes
B) Implement Horizontal Pod Autoscaling
C) Utilize the GKE Autopilot mode
D) Opt for the GKE Standard mode

QUESTION 48

In a DevOps-oriented transition, your application faced sporadic performance issues recently. A leader from a different department asks for a formal rundown of the incident to facilitate preventive measures. What action should you take?

A) Create a detailed incident report highlighting the issues and insights gained, and distribute it exclusively to the department leader who requested it.
B) Generate an incident report outlining the problems, insights, and individual accountability, then share it across the company's technical documentation repository for reference.
C) Formulate an incident report summarizing the issues, insights, and a structured set of corrective actions. Share it solely with the inquiring department leader.
D) Develop an incident report detailing the problems, insights, and a structured set of corrective actions. Disseminate it across the company's technical documentation platform for broader access.

QUESTION 49

Your organization is experiencing a major outage impacting critical services. As the communication lead, you are receiving messages from your internal team members seeking updates and inquiries from customers demanding information on the status of their services. What approach should you adopt to handle this situation and ensure effective communication?

A) Forward all internal team member messages to the Communication Manager, letting them handle internal communications, and prioritize direct communications with customers.
B) Respond promptly to internal team members, aiming for updates every 15 minutes. Commit to 'next update' times.
C) Assign the task of replying to internal team member messages to another trusted team member, while you focus on direct communications with customers.
D) Provide regular updates to all parties involved, maintaining a 'next update' time commitment in all communications.

QUESTION 50

Your team launches a major update for a customer-facing e-commerce platform on Google Cloud during a planned maintenance window. How can you reduce system unavailability and expedite issue resolution in case of post-update problems?

A) Insist on thorough automated performance testing by software engineers on their individual workstations before deployment.

B) Implement a real-time monitoring system and automated alerting for critical performance metrics.

C) Set up a continuous integration (CI) pipeline with comprehensive regression tests executed upon each code push.

D) Develop a comprehensive disaster recovery plan with data backups and redundancy.

E) Employ the canary release methodology for gradual updates through a continuous delivery (CD) pipeline.

F) Establish a dedicated incident response team with defined roles and responsibilities.

PRACTICE TEST 10 - ANSWERS ONLY

QUESTION 1

Answer - B) Leverage Google Cloud Monitoring for AWS and Azure resources, utilize Google Cloud Pub/Sub for cross-cloud event streaming, and implement Google Cloud Security Command Center for cross-cloud security.

Option B aligns with best practices for implementing a unified monitoring and alerting solution across multi-cloud environments, including the use of Google Cloud services and cross-cloud event streaming. Option A suggests using different monitoring solutions for each cloud provider, which does not provide a unified approach.
Options C, D, E, and F mention various services but do not directly address the unified monitoring requirements.

QUESTION 2

Answer - C) Set up horizontal pod autoscaling (HPA) for the GKE cluster to automatically adjust the number of Pods based on resource utilization.

Option C is the recommended action to optimize performance during traffic spikes in a Google Kubernetes Engine (GKE) cluster. Setting up horizontal pod autoscaling (HPA) allows the cluster to automatically adjust the number of Pods based on resource utilization, ensuring that the platform can handle traffic spikes without manual intervention. This aligns with DevOps principles of automation and scalability.
Option A suggests increasing resource limits, which may not efficiently handle dynamic traffic changes.
Option B proposes manual scaling, which is not as efficient or automated as HPA.
Option D mentions code optimization, which is important but may not address resource scaling.

QUESTION 3

Answer - D) 1 and 4

Implementing automated vulnerability scanning for container images (Option 1) and enabling multi-factor authentication (MFA) for CI/CD pipeline access (Option 4) are critical security best practices for a CI/CD pipeline. These practices help detect and mitigate security vulnerabilities in container images and ensure secure access to the pipeline.
Option 2, storing sensitive credentials in plaintext, is a security risk and should be avoided.
Option 3, using a shared storage bucket, may not directly relate to pipeline security and may introduce access control challenges.

QUESTION 4

Answer - B) Implement Cloud Logging to funnel application logs into BigQuery, cluster logs by container, and analyze resource usage for CPU and memory.

Option B is the correct choice as it efficiently allows you to analyze resource usage by aggregating application logs using Cloud Logging.

Option A introduces Prometheus and Grafana, which are not the most suitable for this scenario,
Option C suggests creating custom metrics, which may not be necessary,
Option D is too vague and doesn't provide a clear solution.

QUESTION 5

Answer - A) Configure the Horizontal Pod Autoscaler and enable the cluster autoscaler.

Option A is the correct choice as it suggests configuring the Horizontal Pod Autoscaler and enabling the cluster autoscaler to dynamically adjust the number of Pods and nodes based on demand, optimizing resource usage.
Option B fixes the node pool size, limiting scalability,
Option C introduces the Vertical Pod Autoscaler, which is not necessary for this scenario,
Option D also fixes the node pool size, limiting scalability.

QUESTION 6

Answer - A and B

Options A and B are the correct choices. Segmenting automation procedures into finer-grained components (A) reduces redundancy and streamlines the workflow. Implementing automatic progression confirmations (B) helps in achieving smoother transitions between stages, reducing manual interventions.
Options C, D, and E are not directly related to optimizing the workflow.

QUESTION 7

Answer - A) Implement a horizontal pod autoscaler and enable cluster autoscaler based on CPU and memory metrics.

A) Correct - This approach dynamically adjusts resources based on traffic, ensuring availability and cost optimization.
B) Incorrect - Constantly having additional nodes for peak traffic is not cost-effective.
C) Incorrect - Vertical scaling might not be sufficient for handling large, sudden increases in traffic.
D) Incorrect - Manual scaling is inefficient and may not react quickly to traffic changes.
E) Incorrect - Custom metrics are useful, but not as efficient as standard CPU and memory metrics for this scenario.

QUESTION 8

Answer - D) A machine learning model training task that can be paused and resumed without data loss.

A) Incorrect - Real-time customer support requires consistent uptime, unsuitable for preemptible VMs.
B) Incorrect - While non-urgent, analytics jobs may suffer from frequent interruptions on preemptible VMs.
C) Incorrect - High-traffic web servers need reliable, uninterrupted service.
D) Correct - Machine learning tasks, which are pause-resumable, benefit from the cost efficiency of preemptible VMs.
E) Incorrect - Online gaming servers demand constant availability, not ideal for preemptible VMs.

QUESTION 9

Answer - B) Understand the sequence of events leading to the slowdown, focusing on systemic improvements.

A) Incorrect - Focusing on individual accountability goes against the SRE principle of blameless postmortems.
B) Correct - This aligns with SRE best practices, aiming to improve the system without assigning blame.
C) Incorrect - Moving on without learning from the incident can lead to future failures.
D) Incorrect - Identifying individual mistakes is not the goal of an SRE-led analysis.
E) Incorrect - While systemic investigation is key, this choice does not explicitly emphasize the blameless approach.

QUESTION 10

Answer - A) Set up a continuous integration/continuous deployment (CI/CD) pipeline with automated testing in a separate staging environment before production deployment.

A) Correct - A CI/CD pipeline with a separate staging environment ensures that testing does not impact the production environment.
B) Incorrect - Testing on local machines does not replicate the production environment accurately and can miss critical issues.
C) Incorrect - Testing during off-peak hours still risks potential production issues.
D) Incorrect - While creating a clone is a step in the right direction, it lacks the structured process of a CI/CD pipeline.
E) Incorrect - Testing in the production environment, even with monitoring, is risky and can lead to disruptions.

QUESTION 11

Answer - B) Utilize the disk I/O operations per second (IOPS) of the database pods for autoscaling.

A) Incorrect - Active connections are important but may not fully represent the load or efficiency of a database service.
B) Correct - Disk IOPS is a crucial metric for databases, reflecting the actual operational load and performance.
C) Incorrect - Query response time is significant but doesn't always correlate directly with the need for scaling.
D) Incorrect - Network throughput is more related to network performance than database operational efficiency.
E) Incorrect - CPU utilization alone may not be the best indicator for scaling a stateful database service.

QUESTION 12

Answer - A) Utilize Cloud Storage for data uploads and set up a Pub/Sub system to trigger Dataflow jobs for processing and analysis, scaling resources based on data volume.

A) Correct - Dataflow, combined with Pub/Sub and Cloud Storage, provides a scalable and efficient solution for processing high-volume, bursty data.
B) Incorrect - GKE is powerful but may not offer the most cost-effective solution for bursty data

processing.
C) Incorrect - Cloud Functions are suitable for lighter tasks and might not handle high-volume data efficiently.
D) Incorrect - Constantly running VMs checking for new data can be resource-intensive and less efficient.
E) Incorrect - BigQuery is excellent for analysis but might not be the best option for the initial processing of high-volume data.

QUESTION 13

Answer - A) Configure a Cloud Build trigger to automatically execute Terraform scripts upon every commit to the version control repository.

A) Correct - This approach ensures that changes in the infrastructure code are automatically applied, maintaining consistency and alignment with the defined configurations.
B) Incorrect - Cloud Functions are not typically used for infrastructure management tasks like running Terraform commands.
C) Incorrect - A custom script requires manual intervention and does not fully embrace the IaC approach.
D) Incorrect - While Jenkins can be used, Cloud Build is more integrated with Google Cloud for IaC practices.
E) Incorrect - Pub/Sub is more suited for event-driven applications, not for managing infrastructure consistency.

QUESTION 14

Answer - C) Purchase Committed Use Discounts for a set number of Compute Engine instances to be used for the project duration.

A) Incorrect - Autoscaling is not ideal for projects with consistent computational needs throughout their duration.
B) Incorrect - Preemptible VMs are not suitable for projects that require uninterrupted availability.
C) Correct - Committed Use Discounts provide significant cost savings for consistent and uninterrupted usage over a long period.
D) Incorrect - Regularly adjusting machine types can be resource-intensive and may not lead to significant cost savings.
E) Incorrect - Spot VMs, like preemptible VMs, are not ideal for uninterrupted usage required by the project.

QUESTION 15

Answer - D) Share the dashboard via a generated link with limited access duration.

Option D is the correct choice because it allows you to share the dashboard securely with your colleague without compromising your account credentials or creating additional accounts. The limited access duration ensures temporary access.
 Option A - Option A is incorrect because sharing account credentials is a security risk and not recommended.
 Option B - Option B is incorrect because creating a new user account for temporary access might be overly complex and not necessary.
 Option C - Option C is incorrect because exporting the dashboard as a JSON file may not provide real-

time access and is not the most secure option.

QUESTION 16

Answer - A) Technical Lead, C) Communications Coordinator

The Technical Lead (Option A) is crucial for providing technical expertise and guidance during incident resolution. The Communications Coordinator (Option C) is essential for managing communications, ensuring stakeholders are informed during the incident.
 Option B - Third-party Compliance Officer is not typically a core role in internal incident resolution.
 Option D - Operations Coordinator is important but may not be as pivotal as the Technical Lead and Communications Coordinator during the initial phase of incident resolution.
 Option E - Client Impact Analyst, while valuable, may not be among the two most pivotal roles during the initial incident response.

QUESTION 17

Answer - C) Integrate the OpenTelemetry client libraries within your service, direct metrics to Cloud Monitoring as the export target, and monitor service metrics in Cloud Monitoring.

Option C is the correct choice because it allows you to incorporate OpenTelemetry client libraries within your service and direct metrics to Cloud Monitoring, minimizing initial configuration effort for monitoring and providing a single manageable platform for service-level metrics.
 Option A - Option A suggests using Cloud Pub/Sub, which may not be the most direct approach for monitoring service-level metrics.
 Option B - Option B involves transferring metrics as logs, which may not be as efficient for monitoring service-level metrics.
 Option D - Option D mentions streaming metrics directly to the Cloud Monitoring API, which may require more configuration effort.

QUESTION 18

Answer - A) Set up continuous monitoring using Cloud Monitoring to track vital system metrics and establish alerts for critical thresholds.
 Answer - B) Configure Cloud Monitoring to generate notifications for each common failure observed in your system's operations.

Option A and Option B are the correct choices.
 Option A - Setting up continuous monitoring with Cloud Monitoring helps track vital system metrics and set alerts for critical thresholds, ensuring robustness during high demand.
 Option C - Monitoring disk space and network bandwidth is important but not directly related to addressing potential outages.
 Option D - Implementing a serverless architecture is relevant but not specific to handling outages.
 Option E - Assessing traffic and requesting quota adjustments is a good practice but doesn't directly address ensuring system robustness during outages.

QUESTION 19

Answer - B) Modify the Python service to record API call durations and log this data. Use Cloud Logging to analyze slow-response external APIs.

Option B is the correct choice.
 Option B - Modifying the Python service to record API call durations and analyzing slow-response external APIs using Cloud Logging is a recommended approach for identifying performance issues with external API integrations.
 Option A - Applying Cloud Profiler is more focused on profiling code performance and may not capture external API issues.
 Option C - Instrumenting services with Cloud Trace focuses on tracing and may not provide the detailed API performance data needed.
 Option D - Deploying Cloud Debugger is more for debugging code and may not address API integration performance specifically.

QUESTION 20

Answer - B) Implement a build queue system to prioritize and manage build requests.

Explanation for Option B - Implementing a build queue system helps prioritize and manage build requests, improving build efficiency by reducing resource contention. This approach optimizes build processes and resource utilization.
Explanation for Option A - Increasing the number of build triggers may not effectively address resource contention and may lead to increased resource consumption and costs.
Explanation for Option C - Upgrading all build instances to higher machine types may increase costs significantly without a guaranteed reduction in build times. It may not be the most cost-effective solution.
Explanation for Option D - Manually triggering builds during off-peak hours may help reduce contention but does not address the underlying resource contention issue and is not as efficient as other options.
Explanation for Option E - Using Cloud Run for specific build tasks may introduce complexity and may not be the most suitable solution for improving build efficiency in all cases.

QUESTION 21

Answer - D) Implement the application in multiple regions and configure a global HTTP(S) load balancer to distribute traffic among them.

Explanation for Option D - Implementing the application in multiple regions and configuring a global load balancer ensures high availability and scalability, as it distributes traffic across regions. This approach aligns with the requirement for availability and efficiency.
Explanation for Option A - Deploying the application in a single region with a global load balancer may provide high availability but doesn't address the need for regional presence and efficient traffic distribution.
Explanation for Option B - Utilizing a small instance type may help control costs, but it doesn't ensure scalability or regional availability, which are key requirements.
Explanation for Option C - Monitoring resource utilization and adjusting instance counts is a good practice for optimizing performance but doesn't address the initial planning for regional availability and scalability.

QUESTION 22

Answer - B) Implement automated monitoring and alerting using Google Cloud Monitoring and Google Cloud Logging.

Explanation for Option B - Implementing automated monitoring and alerting with Google Cloud services allows for real-time detection of issues and proactive responses, ensuring reliability and security.
Explanation for Option A - Manual log analysis is time-consuming and may not provide real-time insights, making it less effective for ensuring reliability and security.
Explanation for Option C - Relying on periodic manual checks is not sufficient for meeting the constant monitoring requirements of a critical financial application.
Explanation for Option D - While third-party monitoring tools can be useful, using native Google Cloud services is a more integrated and cost-effective approach.

QUESTION 23

A) Monitor function execution times and memory usage. If there's a significant gap between the two, adjust the allocated memory for the functions.
C) Analyze function response times, CPU utilization, and memory usage. If the response times negatively impact service objectives and the gap between CPU utilization and memory usage is small, label the functions for optimization.

Option A focuses on monitoring function execution times and memory usage, which are essential for optimizing serverless functions. Adjusting memory allocation based on the gap between them can improve performance.
Option B suggests reviewing network requests and storage operations, which may not directly address function performance.
Option C considers response times, CPU utilization, and memory usage, making it suitable for identifying functions that impact service objectives negatively.
Option D assesses function concurrency patterns, but it does not cover other crucial metrics.
Option E recommends expanding memory allocation based on invocation rate and network latency, which may not directly relate to CPU and memory utilization.

QUESTION 24

Answer - B) Create region-specific monitoring dashboards and share them via URL. Assign the Monitoring Viewer role for respective regions.

A) This option doesn't restrict access to region-specific data, violating the principle of least privilege.
 B) This approach is most aligned with the least privilege principle, allowing regional teams to view only their relevant data.
 C) Providing Viewer access to the entire project exposes more data than necessary for each team.
 D) Assigning the Project Viewer role allows access beyond what is necessary for monitoring their specific region.
 E) The Monitoring Editor role grants more permissions than required for viewing dashboards, and a centralized dashboard may not restrict access to region-specific data.

QUESTION 25

Answer - A) Create a logs-based metric in Google Cloud Logging and use Google Cloud Monitoring to visualize the data.

Option A - This is a straightforward and effective method to monitor specific log events within Google's ecosystem.
 Option B - Exporting logs to Cloud SQL for visualization is less efficient and more complex than using Cloud Monitoring.
 Option C - Using an external database and BI tool can work but is not as integrated as using Google Cloud services.
 Option D - Cloud Profiler is not primarily designed for log event analysis.
 Option E - Sending individual notifications is not practical for visualization and trend analysis.

QUESTION 26

Answer - C) The ratio of successfully processed requests to total requests.

Option A - Completed tasks provide insights but don't account for the total volume of requests.
 Option B - Time taken is a performance metric, not a direct measure of reliability.
 Option C - This ratio directly reflects the service's ability to reliably handle requests, making it an appropriate SLI.
 Option D - GPU utilization is about resource usage, not directly about request handling success.
 Option E - Queue size is an indirect measure of system load, not a direct measure of reliability.

QUESTION 27

Answer - A) Set up GitHub Actions to run compliance tests on every pull request to the main branch.

Option A - This ensures that compliance tests are automatically and consistently performed before code is merged, aligning with best CI/CD practices.
 Option B - Nightly tests might delay identifying issues in real-time.
 Option C - Relying on manual execution can lead to inconsistencies.
 Option D - Testing upon every commit is thorough but may be excessive for compliance checks.
 Option E - Post-merge testing can allow non-compliant code to enter the main branch.

QUESTION 28

Answer - B) Implement a log-forwarding agent within the service's container to send file logs to Stackdriver.

Option A - Cloud Run does not automatically redirect file-based logs to Stackdriver.
 Option B - Implementing a log-forwarding agent within the container is an effective way to ensure custom log files are sent to Stackdriver.
 Option C - Cloud Run's default logging might not capture logs from specific files.
 Option D - Using Cloud Functions for this task could be complex and may not provide real-time logging.
 Option E - Manual monitoring is inefficient and not feasible for continuous operations.

QUESTION 29

Answer - A) Ensure that the Cloud Functions are writing logs to stdout or stderr.

Option A - Cloud Functions automatically send logs written to stdout or stderr to Cloud Logging.
 Option B - Cloud Functions generally have the necessary roles by default for logging.

Option C - User permissions are important for accessing logs but don't affect log collection.
Option D - Ensuring that the functions are triggering and executing as expected is a fundamental step.
Option E - Network settings typically don't need to be configured for Cloud Functions to communicate with Cloud Logging.

QUESTION 30

Answer - B) Implementing caching mechanisms at the service level.

Option A, reducing the number of microservices, may not be feasible or practical in a large-scale IT project.
Option C, increasing the size of microservices, might not necessarily improve performance and can lead to resource inefficiency.
Option D, minimizing the use of load balancing, is not advisable as load balancing is essential for distributing traffic and ensuring high availability.

QUESTION 31

Answer - D) Deploy the application using a continuous delivery pipeline with canary releases. Monitor the application performance using Cloud Monitoring, and gradually increase traffic based on the observed metrics.

Option A, using Config Connector, doesn't align with the concept of canary releases and gradual traffic increase.
Option B, using RollingUpdate, is a valid approach but doesn't leverage canary releases for gradual traffic increase and monitoring.
Option C, blue/green deployment, switches all traffic immediately and doesn't allow for gradual monitoring.

QUESTION 32

Answer - B) Utilize Prometheus multi-level federation to centrally aggregate metrics.

Option A, integrating with Cloud Monitoring, may not provide the comprehensive global aggregation required.
Option C, Google Cloud Managed Service for Prometheus, may not align with the existing Prometheus-based setup.
Option D, enabling cross-region federation, is not a standard Prometheus feature.

QUESTION 33

Answer - C) Utilize PodDisruptionBudgets to control the eviction of pods during maintenance or node failures, ensuring that a minimum number of pods remain running.

Option C is the correct choice because PodDisruptionBudgets allow you to control the eviction of pods during node failures or maintenance, ensuring that a minimum number of pods remain running and maintaining high availability. This is a best practice for GKE applications.
Option A, using Kubernetes DaemonSets, focuses on node-level redundancy but may not handle node failures gracefully.

Option B, deploying across multiple regions, is a valid strategy but may introduce complexity and cost.
Option D, Horizontal Pod Autoscaling, is more about handling increased load than node failures.

QUESTION 34

Answer - A) Enable VPC Flow Logs for the network subnet.

Explanation:
Option A is the correct choice because enabling VPC Flow Logs for the network subnet allows you to track all incoming SSH connections and capture their source IP addresses with minimal administrative overhead.
Option B, setting up custom logging, may require additional configuration and is specific to the SSH service.
Option C, deploying a dedicated SSH monitoring tool on each instance, can be resource-intensive and complex to manage.
Option D, creating a central log aggregation system, introduces additional complexity and may not be as efficient for this specific task.

QUESTION 35

Answer - D) Identify necessary service enhancements for reliability that should be addressed before the transition.

Option D is the correct choice as it adheres to SRE principles by prioritizing reliability improvements before deployment. It ensures that the system meets its SLOs in production.
Option A is incorrect as deploying without established SLOs may lead to operational issues. Option B is incorrect because it shifts the responsibility without addressing the problem. Option C is incorrect as modifying SLO benchmarks may compromise the desired reliability.

QUESTION 36

Answer - A) Designate a responsible owner for each resolution task and involve collaborators as necessary.

Option A is the correct choice as it aligns with effective postmortem practices by assigning clear ownership while allowing collaboration.
Option B is incorrect as it lacks explicit ownership, which can lead to accountability issues.
Option C is incorrect as multiple owners may create confusion and delays.
Option D is incorrect as placing sole ownership on one individual may not involve the necessary expertise for resolution.

QUESTION 37

Answer - A) Develop a custom logging library for your Cloud Run service, ensuring that log records are created in JSON format with the required attributes.

Option A is the correct choice as it involves developing a custom logging library within the Cloud Run service to create log records in JSON format with the necessary attributes, fulfilling the requirement for structured logging.

Option B, C, and D suggest external solutions or configurations that may not be necessary for achieving structured logging within Cloud Run.

QUESTION 38

B) Attach a Fluentd sidecar to your Cloud Run service, configuring it to parse logs into JSON format.

Option B is the correct choice. By attaching a Fluentd sidecar to your Cloud Run service and configuring it to parse logs into JSON format, you can efficiently transition from plain text logs to structured JSON logs. This approach maintains flexibility and ease of use. Option A mentions the Cloud Logging library but doesn't address the specific requirement of JSON logs. Option C suggests adjusting the logging agent settings, which may not be as straightforward. Option D involves embedding the logging agent within the container image, which can be complex.

QUESTION 39

Answer - C) Work closely with the development team from the outset, focusing on the system's architectural design to ensure operational viability.

Option A - Incorrect: While testing is important, early involvement is more impactful.
Option B - Incorrect: Post-QA involvement misses early design optimization opportunities.
Option C - Correct: Early collaboration in the design phase allows for incorporating operational insights effectively.
Option D - Incorrect: Waiting for production deployment limits the opportunity for preemptive improvements.

QUESTION 40

Answer - A) Establish a dedicated Google Cloud monitoring project with a Cloud Operations Workspace linked to payment gateway projects, giving necessary team members read-only access.

Option A - Correct: This setup allows for focused monitoring of critical operations while maintaining least privilege access control.
Option B - Incorrect: Broad access across all projects may lead to unnecessary alert noise and privilege issues.
Option C - Incorrect: Setting up multiple workspaces can dilute focus and may not comply with the least privilege principle.
Option D - Incorrect: Centralizing on a primary project might not effectively segregate critical monitoring needs.

QUESTION 41

Answer - D) Incorporate automated checks in the deployment process to validate database configurations against predefined standards.

Option A - Incorrect: While code reviews are important, they are not foolproof and can be subjective.
Option B - Incorrect: Punitive measures do not foster a culture of learning and improvement.
Option C - Incorrect: Training is valuable, but it does not provide an immediate solution to prevent misconfigurations.

Option D - Correct: Automated validation checks are a proactive approach to prevent configuration errors.

QUESTION 42

Answer - C) Implement a Git-based version control system for Terraform files, using branches and pull requests to manage changes and ensure code reviews before merging.

Option A - Incorrect: Cloud-based file storage lacks the necessary controls for concurrent changes and versioning.
Option B - Incorrect: A manual check-in/check-out process is prone to errors and lacks scalability.
Option C - Correct: A Git-based system with pull requests and branches is best for managing collaborative changes and maintaining a clear history of updates.
Option D - Incorrect: Independent updates in a distributed system can lead to conflicts without proper version control and code review mechanisms.

QUESTION 43

Answer - C) Implement the Fluentd fluent-plugin-sanitizer to filter and sanitize logs as they are collected.

Option A - Incorrect: Modifying the application's logging might not be immediate.
Option B - Incorrect: Dataflow processing introduces unnecessary complexity and delay.
Option C - Correct: Fluentd's fluent-plugin-sanitizer can provide immediate log sanitization, which is critical for compliance.
Option D - Incorrect: Using Cloud Pub/Sub and Cloud Functions can be effective but less immediate than Fluentd plugins.

QUESTION 44

Answer - A) MetricKind: GAUGE, ValueType: INT64, Visualization: Line graph

Option A - Correct: GAUGE with INT64 and a Line graph is suitable for real-time monitoring of active users, showing fluctuations in activity.
Option B - Incorrect: DELTA and DOUBLE are not the best fit for real-time user count visualization.
Option C - Incorrect: CUMULATIVE and DISTRIBUTION are not typically used for tracking active user counts.
Option D - Incorrect: METRIC_KIND_UNSPECIFIED does not specify the type of metric needed for this purpose.

QUESTION 45

Answer - A) Directly configure email alerts in Cloud Monitoring for each monitoring policy and ensure team members have their email addresses set up in their Cloud Monitoring profiles.

Option A - Correct: Cloud Monitoring allows direct configuration of email alerts, which is efficient and straightforward.
Option B - Incorrect: While possible, using a Webhook for email alerts adds unnecessary complexity.
Option C - Incorrect: Using Slack as an intermediary for email notifications is less direct and can be less reliable.

Option D - Incorrect: A third-party service is not required for email alerts when Cloud Monitoring supports it natively.

QUESTION 46

Answer - B) Utilize the Network Intelligence Center's Connectivity Test to assess the network path between the two VPCs.

Option A - Incorrect: Flow Logs provide traffic details but may not directly identify connectivity issues.
Option B - Correct: The Connectivity Test is a powerful tool for diagnosing network paths and can identify specific points of failure.
Option C - Incorrect: Deploying VMs for diagnostics may not be feasible without appropriate permissions.
Option D - Incorrect: Third-party tools might not integrate seamlessly with Google Cloud's network infrastructure.

QUESTION 47

Answer - C) Utilize the GKE Autopilot mode

Option C, "Utilize the GKE Autopilot mode," is the correct choice as it is designed for optimizing costs while maintaining performance automatically.
Option A and D are not as effective for cost optimization.
Option B, while useful, doesn't provide the same level of automation as Autopilot mode.

QUESTION 48

B) Generate an incident report outlining the problems, insights, and individual accountability, then share it across the company's technical documentation repository for reference.

Option B is the correct choice because it provides a detailed incident report with insights, individual accountability, and circulates it across the company's technical documentation repository for broader access and reference.
Option A lacks details on individual accountability and relies on a narrower distribution.
Option C distributes to the department leader but lacks individual accountability details.
Option D is similar to Option B but lacks individual accountability, making Option B more comprehensive.

QUESTION 49

Answer - B) Respond promptly to internal team members, aiming for updates every 15 minutes. Commit to 'next update' times.

Option B is the recommended approach as it prioritizes timely responses to internal team members with updates every 15 minutes and commits to 'next update' times, ensuring effective communication during a major outage.
Options A, C, and D prioritize direct communications with customers but do not emphasize the need for regular updates and time commitments, which are crucial during an outage.
Explanation:
Option A: Forwarding messages to the Communication Manager may lead to delays in communication

with internal team members. Option C: Assigning tasks may not guarantee timely updates to internal team members. Option D: Provides a balanced approach with regular updates and a commitment to update times for effective communication with all parties involved.

QUESTION 50

Answer - B) Implement a real-time monitoring system and automated alerting for critical performance metrics.

Options A, C, D, E, and F - While these options may contribute to issue resolution and system reliability, they do not directly address minimizing disruptions and expediting issue resolution post-update.
 Option B is the correct choice as it focuses on real-time monitoring and automated alerts to detect and address issues promptly, reducing system unavailability.

ABOUT THE AUTHOR

Step into the world of Anand, and you're in for a journey beyond just tech and algorithms. While his accolades in the tech realm are numerous, including penning various tech-centric and personal improvement ebooks, there's so much more to this multi-faceted author.

At the heart of Anand lies an AI enthusiast and investor, always on the hunt for the next big thing in artificial intelligence. But turn the page, and you might find him engrossed in a gripping cricket match or passionately cheering for his favorite football team. His weekends? They might be spent experimenting with a new recipe in the kitchen, penning down his latest musings, or crafting a unique design that blends creativity with functionality.

While his professional journey as a Solution Architect and AI Consultant, boasting over a decade of AI/ML expertise, is impressive, it's the fusion of this expertise with his diverse hobbies that makes Anand's writings truly distinctive.

So, as you navigate through his works, expect more than just information. Prepare for stories interwoven with passion, experiences peppered with life's many spices, and wisdom that transcends beyond the tech realm. Dive in and discover Anand, the author, the enthusiast, the chef, the sports lover, and above all, the storyteller.

www.ingramcontent.com/pod-product-compliance
Lightning Source LLC
LaVergne TN
LVHW081752050326
832903LV00027B/1907